SHAKESPEARIAN COMEDY

Shakespearian Comedy

———

H. B. CHARLTON

LONDON

METHUEN & CO LTD

First published 24 February 1938
Reprinted eight times

First published as a University Paperback 1966
Reprinted four times
Reprinted 1979

Printed in Great Britain at the
University Press, Cambridge

ISBN 0 416 69260 5

TO MY WIFE

TOTUM MUNERIS HOC TUI EST

Preface

CHAPTERS 2 to 9 in this volume were first published in numbers of the Bulletin of the John Rylands Library between July 1930 and October 1937. Chapter 2 was reprinted in the World's Classic's volume, *Shakespeare Criticism 1919-1935*. I wish to thank my fellow-governors of the John Rylands Library for permission to reprint these chapters. In particular, I want to make avowal of obligation to my friend Dr. Henry Guppy, Librarian of the John Rylands Library. As one of the John Rylands lecturers, it is not for me to praise him for his choice of lecturers. I can however say that his programme of lectures during the last thirty years has made scholars in Europe and America gratefully realize the wealth of the library of which he is the devoted guardian. And I am surely quite free to express my personal gratitude for the forethought with which he eases the lecturer's task and for the charm with which from the chair he adds dignity and grace to the occasion of the lecture.

H.B.C.

Contents

I

Preliminary

THE lectures which make up this book were given one by one in eight successive years. They were given extempore at the John Rylands Library, and were then, within a month or two of their delivery, written out for publication in the John Rylands Bulletin. They are now brought together without further re-writing. This may very likely be the wrong way to build a book. For one thing, the style is naturally nearer to the range of the spoken idiom than to the patterns of the written word. Moreover, over a spread of eight years, it is certain that the mood of that evening which happens to be the one appointed for the lecture, and the adventitious way in which the lecturer responds to that evening's audience will unconsciously modify the particular manner of his lecture. It has, however, seemed best not to tamper with what served its temporary purpose and answered its separate occasion; for though the individual lectures were shaped in the weeks immediately leading to their delivery, the whole scheme of them was devised before the first was given. They were meant to be consecutive steps in a continuous argument. To rewrite them now would perhaps throw the structure of their central idea into clearer relief. It would certainly permit of the excision of repetition here and there. But those paragraphs which occur in the separate sections as summaries of as much of the general argument as has gone before may possibly help to keep the main structure in mind.

As the series now appears in print, it is labelled "Shakespearian Comedy." That title has been chosen because it appears to be

9

the simplest and most objective description of the material handled and the briefest indication of the object of that handling, namely, the attempt to trace in Shakespeare's comedies the growth of his "comic idea." But the title has been adopted with misgiving; for it suggests a comparison of this book with the vastly profounder volume which Bradley devoted to Shakespearian tragedy. Deliberately to invite such a comparison is to call upon oneself the proper penalty for sheer arrogance: Bradley was one of the really great Shakespearian critics of the last half-century. There is no claim that this book means to do for comedy what he did for tragedy. But there is a hope that it may lead to wiser and more competent efforts for making up the enormous lee-way into which the consideration of comedy has fallen in comparison with the progress which has been made in exploring the grounds of criticism in tragedy. The philosophy of tragedy has drawn hosts of thinkers; for tragedy deals with issues which seem greatly to transcend those of comedy. Perhaps even more important, European thought about tragedy has started on solid foundations, for Aristotle's treatise on tragedy is extant, and his discourse on comedy is lost. Moreover, from what remains in his *Poetics* and in such attenuated survivals of its tradition as exist in the *Tractatus Coislinianus*, it would hardly seem that the body of comic material available to him would have allowed him to exploit on it the magnificent method by which he digs so deeply into the idea of tragedy. The progress of comedy from its Greek origins has been infinitely fuller, more varied and richer than has the growth of tragedy since the Greeks gave to it their characteristic stamp. But it may not be impossible to apply Aristotle's critical method to the huge and varied body of later comedy. That, at all events, is the belief on which this book rests. Even so, a long succession of far abler critics must devote themselves to the adaptation of such a method before the criticism of comedy can reach the same stage of development as the theory of tragedy had already reached in Aristotle's treatise.

It is no doubt tactless in these days to declare one's faith in Aristotle so roundly, for some of the most illuminating critics of our time have very little use for him. Indeed, the present trend of fashionable criticism appears to have little use even for drama. To our most modern coteries, drama is poetry or it is nothing; and by poetry they mean some sort of allegorical arabesque in which the images of Shakespeare's plays are far more important than their men and women. To these critics, characterisation is rather an accidental than an essential element in drama, and all that really counts is the mystically symbolic patterning of tonal and visual form. The appreciation of Donne is distorting the valuation of Shakespeare. Yet drama is a representation of action; and to our simple sense the actors in it do look more or less like human beings; wherefore, to consider them as images of men and women seems the safest way of trying to understand them.

There is much virtue in this safety for a merely academic person whose occupation is in a department of literature in a university institution. But it is a safety which must not be bought at the cost of substituting scholarship for criticism. Departments for the study of English literature are now established in universities as an accepted means for effecting that particular spiritual and intellectual discipline which is a primary object of academic study. But there is still uncertainty as to how best they may contribute to this object. The real problem is to determine the right relationship between scholarship and criticism. Our own impression, after twenty five years spent as a university teacher of literature, is that in the main we are lacking in courage. Confronted with this vast body of material which we call English literature, we find a multitude of ways of handling it which can easily be justified as proper activities in the pursuit of knowledge. Such, for instance, are all the opportunities it offers for what in the most obvious sense can be called historical research. The lives of the poets are to be traced from documents and registers in the Record Office; the social, economic, political and religious background of their time is to be similarly constructed. Then there is the history of the poet's works in their physical form—his manuscripts, his copyists, his proofs, his printer, his bookbinder, and, if he be a dramatist, his company, his censor, his prompter, and, may be, also his pirate. Without enquiries of this sort, it is clear that we can never really know just what it was which the poet wrote; and our generation in particular owes an enormous debt to the historico-bibliographers who are establishing for us a definitive text of Elizabethan drama. A further much practised method of literary study is the specifically comparative method, from mere *Quellenforschungen*, arid pursuit of sources, to the tracing of a tale or a tradition as it takes on different shapes in different ages and amongst different peoples.

Yet when all this is done, a fear remains that the main issue has been overlooked. There is no harm in a mere professor of English literature locking himself up in the Record Office or devoting his life to the tenth-rate company of authors whose writings the wiser world has willingly let die. But only two or three of our young folks in a generation need be submitted to the technical training for this sort of a career. The primary reason for admitting the study of literature into an academic organisation is the belief that literature has a contribution to make to the spiritual and intellectual growth of man and of the world. In its final resolution, the study of literature is the study of "poetry", the study of what artists have created, whether their creation is epic, lyric, drama or novel. From the infancy of the world, it has been felt that what the artist and the poet could give was a mode of experience which none but artists and poets could provide. Their worth as artists and as poets was the value to mankind of the peculiar and distinctive experience which they as poets had experienced and which they as poets had the art to communicate to men. Their merit, then, is their meaning, so long as "meaning" is taken to be their significance and not merely their lesson. They are finally therefore to be assessed philosophically rather than historically. A teacher of literature must not be satisfied to present a body of unquestionable facts: he must brace himself to measure values. He must be prepared not only to say what a poet was, but to judge what his worth is. Scholarship must lead to criticism.

But by his very scholarship an academic man knows how precarious are the judgments of the critics. Above all, he knows the properly repressive weight of knowledge. He realises that a mind naturally dedicating itself to the pursuit of truth will inevitably be chary in pronouncing judgment. He will feel that there is an inherent though not an inevitable antipathy between temperaments which most readily take to scholarship and those whose proclivity is to utter values. It is the old and lasting problem in which the scholar's subject, Shakespeare, taking sides, came down riotously and scornfully against academic and bookish students. Nothing is more vain than painfully to pore upon a book to seek the light of truth:

> "Small have continual plodders ever won
> Save base authority from others' books. . . .
> Such universal plodding prisons up
> The nimble spirits in the arteries."

There is no author in the world teaches such beauty as a woman's face. The reading of books is a slow art which entirely keeps the brain, a barren practice which scarcely shows the harvest of such heavy toil. The real ground, the book, the academes from whence doth spring the true Promethean fires are, of course, not libraries, but women's eyes.

Though a mere scholar may enter his caveats against this comprehensive rejection of academic learning, he will nevertheless recognise that the very instincts which have led him to devote himself to scholarship are probably a sign that in his own mental make-up, the gift of rapid insight and the aptitude for instantaneous and undoubting decisions are not markedly predominant amongst his endowments.

Hence his dilemma. How is he to make his scholarship serviceable to his own practice in the art of criticism? How is he to use his scholarship to atone for his relative deficiency in a natural acumen for coming to artistic judgments? It was precisely for this that Aristotle seemed extraordinarily helpful to one novice when a quarter of a century ago he began his career as a teacher of literature.

It was, however, not so much what Aristotle had to say in detail about this, that, or the other aspect of Greek tragedy. Rather, it was the method of Aristotle's enquiry, and the summary exposition of that method which has come down to us imperfectly in the first four brief chapters of the *Poetics*.

A philosopher with a bent for biological modes of thought, Aristotle found that the origin of poetry was a clue to its specific nature. It was what it was because it came into being to fulfil a particular function. Mankind was discovering the possibility of certain refinements of simple instinctive pleasures. Poetry is the outcome of the impulse to gratify a group of those conscious and relatively refined pleasures. That being the primary cause of poetry, then poetry is the specific thing which displays the characteristic activity of poetry. The nature of the mouse is to achieve the specific capacity of mouseness, and the law of its growth is its development in evolutionary progression to a more and more complete fulfilment of the inherent possibilities of mouseness. The nature of a developed horse is its capacity to realise the progressive functions of horse-ness, say, for instance, its ability to run with a rider. All its separate properties, the shape of its bones, and their articulation, the disposition and the proportion of its legs, the size and the relative positioning of its nostrils, all these are excellent only in so far as they contribute to the efficiency of the animal in its specific function of horseness. Like an animal organism, poetry is never static; it grows organically under a vital compulsion to realise its capacity and its function. It is this sense of a controlling objective as the law of poetic form which was the essential motive of Aristotle's theory of *Katharsis*, though it was his opposition to Plato which determined the particular formulation of it. The impulse for the invention, and the general acceptance when invented, of all distinct art-forms like flute-music, arousing and appealing to "enthusiasm", and like comedy, arousing and appealing to the emotions which express themselves most simply in laughter, and like tragedy, arousing and appealing to pity and fear—this itself implies that each and all of these emotions are in the majority of men most readily and most mightily excited by the casual, multitudinous and inevitable accidents of life. They are thus the emotions perpetually liable to strive for outlet; and their striving involves a continual disturbance of settled composure and of controlled personality. But by flute-music, by comedy, and by tragedy, the particular emotions which have prompted the creation of the particular artistic kinds or species secure periodic opportunity for an ordered way of exercise, discharge or purgation. This process of the exercise and the discharge of perturbing feelings is in itself a feeling of pleasure and it results in a pleasurable feeling of relief and of consequent well-being. It is *Katharsis*, then, in Aristotle's terminology, which is the function controlling the form of tragedy. His primary conception of poetry as an organic creation is patent in his insistence of function as the law of its being.

Hence, his method of criticism. Poetry meant to him a vast range of poems, the creation of the golden age in the past of his own country. Surveying his material and endeavouring to see it historically, he discovered in it an evolutionary emergence. Poetry as such had demonstrably tended to more or less clearly defined species—epic, and dramatic in particular. The emergence of these species suggested a classification on a zoological or organic basis. Their generic characteristics were the means, material object, and manner of them as modes of imitation. But the specific characteristics were the different types of means, of material objects, and of manner in which as distinctive species they exercised their imitative activity. Then, within the reorganised species, the critic found differentiating modifications of the specific means, material object and manner, so that either a recognisable sub-species emerged, or within the sub-species there was a recognisable trend to the realisation of a purer form of the species. It is a process which is a progressive movement towards the ideal type; and we need not follow Aristotle in his belief that in some species that process had already reached its goal.

Comedy may be looked at, as Aristotle looked at tragedy, without assuming that either comedy or tragedy has yet reached perfection. Comedy, like tragedy, may be taken as a species because it is commonly recognized as such. History will reveal the consolidation of its specific traits in the progress of its growth. Its means, material objects, and manner will be seen as organically distinct from those of epic and of tragedy. Moreover, more or less distinct variations of it have already been duly recognised and labelled. These can be examined as separate members of the genus comedy or as examples of a comic species, and thus it may be seen how modifications within the generic essentials coalesce to produce a new species. In that way the line of growth of each species will become clearer. Carry the process further and further—follow sub-species and sub-species, and the nature of comedy in general and of all comedies in particular will be illuminated.

The method is technically historical and comparative. Whatever may be the metaphysical justification of it as a method, in practice it does appear to help in the problem of grappling intelligently with literature. It was certainly Aristotle's method which prompted the most original and the most fruitful speculations of those critics in Italy in the sixteenth century who were laying the foundations of modern European literary criticism. The best of them were often strongly opposed to particular principles of the Aristotelian theory: but they learnt from him how to embark on the problems of critical enquiry. Castelvetro is Aristotelian in mind, and often anti-Aristotelian in detail. Cinthio, to whom as yet no one has paid proper critical tribute, was even more markedly an exponent of the Aristotelian method, and no less free from bondage to the Aristotelian edict. They were, of course, mainly concerned with tragedy. They are of enormous assistance to the modern scholar who tries to understand the complex development of tragedy in Renaissance Europe, when Italy, France and England each took from a common tradition and produced a body of drama as different in national characteristics as in permanent artistic worth:[1] the sixteenth century brought forth great tragedy in one country only, and even there, only one Shakespeare. It is doubtless easier to see the movements in the growth of European tragedy than in the development of its comedy. Comedy is much more sensitive to topical circumstance. It is therefore much more variable and apparently casual in the forms it takes on. Even so, the mass of Renaissance comedy is seen to settle itself into some sort of intelligible pattern, if the survey of it is stretched to cover English, Italian, French and Spanish variations of it. In all these countries the problem was similar: it was the attempt to gratify a world-old sense of the comic or ludicrous at the same time as a new sensibility for the romantic. It weighed less heavily in Spain and in France than in England and in Italy. In Spain, the theatre had never established itself as the provider of so much general and common fun as had the English medieval stage: Spanish drama could therefore undertake to show the high falutin' tales of sixteenth century romance without any feeling that it was thereby stifling common humanity's taste for the ludicrous. France, in its turn, had not only a racial sense for the ludicrous, it had also already in the Middle Ages anticipated the Renaissance problem up to a point in its dramatisation of realistically or poetically pastoral scenes. But when the full stress of romantic taste swayed France in the sixteenth century, it was for a romance which had been distorted into channels too exclusive, too exotic and too aristocratic to be compatible with the spirit of popular drama. Italy and England were the real battlefield of the new impulses. But Italy was side-tracked into a merely partial solution of the problem. English dramatists wrote for Court and University and Bankside. Italian

---

[1] See Introduction to the *Poetical Works of Sir W. Alexander*, Vol. I, edited Kastner and Charlton, Manchester University Press, 1921.

audiences were more select and less representative. English plays were often ludicrous in the crudity of their stagery: Italian resources were more elaborate and artistic. English audiences had a sense of humour not inconsistent with illiteracy. Italian audiences were prouder of the exquisiteness of their literary taste. Moreover, English audiences wanted fun on the stage, the boisterous horseplay of miracle and morality and interlude. But Italian audiences were Roman by blood and Boccaccian by culture: the art and the intrigue of sexual comedy was their inherited idea of theatrical entertainment. So Italy never realised the inherent possibilities of romantic comedy. They stuck in the main to a modified classical sort; and they provided a modicum of theatrical satisfaction for romantic impulse by inventing the more ornate pastoral play such as *Pastor Fido* and *Aminta*. But *Pastor Fido* is both dramatically and comically a tawdry and unworthy counterpart to *As You Like It*. England alone displayed the genius to shape a satisfying compromise between romance and comedy. But perhaps even in England, it was only Shakespeare who made the achievement more than a *tour-de-force*. And even he did not make the discovery by sudden and plenary inspiration. He grew from *Love's Labour's Lost* to *Twelfth Night* and *As You Like It*. The theme of these lectures is the course of that growth.

II

Romanticism in Shakespearian Comedy

IT is a common-place of criticism to label Shakespeare's comedies romantic comedies. What else should one call comedies which are set in Illyria or in forests of Arden, and through which Violas and Orsinos, Rosalinds and Orlandos fleet the time to such music as is the food of love? And what is a fantasia like *A Midsummer's Night's Dream* but the very ecstasy of romanticism? So the epithet goes unquestioned. It not only seems to fit the quality of Shakespeare's comedies; it catches in a word the prevailing atmosphere of Elizabethan literature at large. And for what concerns comedy in particular, it has an additional recommendation. Being named "romantic comedies," Shakespeare's can be easily and conveniently distinguished from the counterblasts with which, in the name of the classical comedians, Ben Jonson retaliated on them. Why not, therefore, let well alone, and continue to talk of Shakespeare's romantic comedies, especially as "romantic" is so variable and vague in its connotation that it can be used to mean almost anything which anybody may take Shakespeare's comedies to be.

Moreover, there can hardly be any doubt that Shakespeare's audience clamorously demanded that their comedies should include certain features which in any sense of the word must be called romantic, features which enter comedy for the first time in Shakespeare's day, features which more than any others bear the stamp of the imaginative and emotional fashion of his generation.

His *Comedy of Errors* provides an excellent clue to the taste of his times. He took the main tale of it from Latin comedy, from Plautus. But he made strange additions. His Plautine material is in the boisterous, gross, realistic pattern of Latin comedy: a virago of a wife, a thick-skinned husband, and a common courtesan deal with each other in the coarser way of earthy trafficking. But into this Hogarthian group Shakespeare slips one or two figures who belong to another world: an old man weighed down by the grief of many years' fruitless search for the wife and for the son torn from him by shipwreck, and a gentle-hearted girl whose lips speak in the sweet new style singers and sonneteers were consecrating to lovers and to love-making.

Such incongruously intrusive figures can only have gained their entry by being the sort of people Shakespeare's public wanted. They surround a Dutch interior with a tale of love and of adventure; and what is a romance but a tale of love and adventure, of prouesse and courtesie? That is the justification for calling the Elizabethan age a romantic age. Shakespeare and his fellows were romantic in the strict sense that they clamoured for fuller draughts of that spirit of romanticism which the Middle Ages had first discovered and revealed in their tales of chivalry and knight-errantry. To them, a lover and his lass or a lord and his lady were the most engrossing of God's creatures: their comedies as Jonson contemptuously said, had to be of a duke in love with a countess, the countess to be in love with the duke's son, and the son to love the lady's waiting-maid, with other such cross-wooing. For wooing was the most exciting of man's emotional experiences; and tuned to that key he eagerly responded to those other phases of existence wherein the stress of exceptional circumstances aroused stranger stirrings of the passionate life. The plot of the *Comedy of Errors* is Roman, classical, realistic; but old Ægeon and fair Luciana are the offspring of an un-Roman, unclassical and unrealistic sentiment: they are the outcome of romance. Of the two, Luciana is the more significant.

Romantic comedy is pre-eminently the comedy of love. It is its specific occupation with wooing which distinguishes it most markedly from classical or Roman comedy. And although between a fully grown romantic comedy such as *As You Like It*, and a Roman comedy such as the *Menæchmi* of Plautus, there may appear to be the widest difference in matter and in spirit, the one has in fact grown out of the other by a gradual modification of the current view of the way of a man with a maid. Classical dramatists dealt freely with amorous intrigues between young men and girls; but solicitation is a social institution, whereas wooing is a mystical experience. The Romans treated such situations as mere incidents in the casual sowing of wild oats, which was by no means a bad training for a young fellow about to enter the world at large. Their real concern was with the older men who had already taken rank in that world. When modern comedy started in Italy at the beginning of the sixteenth century, its founders eagerly imitated classical models. But in the intervening sixteen hundred years, man and his universe had moved. He had been initiated into notions of chivalry. Italian audiences in 1500 were descended from knights who had given their lives to courtesy and to high endeavour. Dante had transmuted womankind for them. He had opened their eyes to the image of woman whose coming is as from heaven to reveal a miracle, and at the sound of whose voice the heart is filled with all of sweetness and humility:—

> E par che sia una cosa venuta
> Di cielo in terra a miracol mostrare. . . .
>
> Ogni dolcezza, ogni pensiero umile
> Nasce nel core a chi parlar la sente.

Merely to see her is to add to one's spiritual stature a new susceptibility, an "intelligenza nuova." By the simple glance of her eye mankind is lifted to a finer civilisation: "empiendo il core a ciascun di virtute." Perhaps such a transcendent "intellect of love" was too ideal for the sense of the bulk of men. But Petrarch had made the miracle manifest on earth. He had clothed the new soul of woman in the human beauty of woman's body:—

> ogni virtute
> Ogni bellezza, ogni real costume
> Giunti in un corpo a mirabil tempre—

and had made her earthly existence more intimate by turning from the idea she symbolised in heaven to lament the heaviness of life when the transfiguring angel of it departs, leaving her lover a desolate and solitary voyager on the dreary waves of time.

With these new sensations pulsing in their blood, Italy's audiences in the sixteenth century were much more thrilled by youth than by age, and youth in love was its most alluring theme. Its comic writers might set themselves to imitate Roman drama as closely as possible; but without knowing it, they could not escape dallying with the young folks of the play far more than Roman precedent warranted. At the very outset of the new comedy, for his *Calandria*, Bibbiena borrows largely from the self-same play of Plautus from which Shakespeare was to borrow for his *Comedy of Errors*. But Bibbiena, taking his twins from Plautus, transforms one of them into a woman, as the later Shakespeare was to do for his *Twelfth Night*. And in Ariosto's comedies, the young gradually supersede the old, until the old man, who stood in the middle limelight of Roman comedy, is pushed into the wings of the stage to make room for the youthful lovers whose Roman prototypes were but accessory figures. The plot of his *Cassaria* is a typically classical plot, except that the old man has at the beginning embarked on a journey which keeps him out of the play until almost the end of it. There is still, of course, as there must be in any play for an audience of Boccaccio's countrymen, much of the bawdy side of love: but the object of exhibiting it is, nominally at all events, to expose it to the flick of satire, whilst in Roman comedy it enters more or less as a natural escapade of the admirable young spark. Moreover, Ariosto's last comedy, the *Scolastica*, not only ties its interest down to the love of its youths for its maidens; it even gives to that love something of the quality of romantic devotion. Without intention, and as yet, without much change in outward form, classical comedy is moving gradually to romantic comedy, and is taking to itself a situation and a temper which in due course will transform the type to the sort which characterises romantic comedy. The transition is not so clearly discernible in the work of the English comic dramatists of the sixteenth century. For one thing, classical comedy never fastened itself so securely onto our stage as it did in Italy: and when our Elizabethan comedy was being forged, our romantic temper was urgent and largely conscious of itself. Yet something of the transitional process may be seen in the plays of John Lyly: and its main stages stand out clear as signposts in the two plots which together make *The Taming of a Shrew*. But in the main, Elizabethan romantic comedy did not emerge through a process of natural evolution: it was the product of an obligation imposed ruthlessly on the dramatists by their own age. They were required to beat out a play which should be comic and romantic at once; and at first, they scarcely realised that the task involved almost insuperable difficulties. It seemed a simple matter merely to lift the romances bodily on to the comic stage: the whole history of Elizabethan comedy is a tale of the reluctance of comedy to compromise itself with romance. Not realising his difficulties, Shakespeare sat down light-heartedly to write a romantic comedy, *The Two Gentlemen of Verona*. Before he had finished, he had encountered and had blundered through unexpected obstacles.

To realise what they were and to appreciate the reluctance of romantic material to be naturalised on the comic stage will involve us in a closer examination of romantic taste and of its primary cause, the romances of the Middle Ages. Romantic taste will not tolerate any sort of love-story. Mediæval romances are love-stories, and something besides. Not only are they stories of a particular kind of love; they also incorporate a larger tradition which moulds the quality of every element in their material. The range of their incidents, the temper of their sentiments, the pattern of their heroes, the atmosphere of their scenery, and the trend of their ideas, each and all contribute to the homogeneity of the tradition. And in the making of the tradition, life and literature had played complementary parts. The romances reflect the ideal of knighthood by their imaginative idealisation of the experience of knights.

What chivalry is in morals and feudalism in politics, so are the romances in literature. They are the artistic counterpart of the moral and political society which produced them. Socially, one thinks of the Middle Ages as a feudal edifice. Feudalism built itself on an ascending scale of suzerainities. Its elaborate distinctions of precedence created colleges of heralds and a code of social etiquette, as well as a Round Table compromise. But politically and socially speaking, such a system was fragile as a castle of cards, capable of destruction by mere exposure to the winds of heaven, unless cemented by the strongest of moral and sentimental ties. And the only moral tie which could hold the fabric erect was the sense of loyalty. So, out of mere political necessity in the first place, loyalty is the virtue above all other virtues in the mediæval knight's equipment; to be false to a plighted oath is first in the catalogue of a recreant's sins. As in the life of the body politic, so in the communion of the Catholic Church. The representative of God on earth called for absolute obedience, and religion consecrated loyalty. Life's highest ideal was unswerving devotion to an all-exacting service, the quest of a holy grail. Inevitably these public ideals were closely reflected in those phases of man's life which come most intimately to his hearth. His private and domestic existence was governed by a code of conduct in the same range of values. Like his worship of God and his faith to his suzerain was the love of his lady. It called for a dedicated life.

And as it was the article of his faith which lay closest to his bosom, his love of woman tended to loom more largely in his consciousness than did the less peculiar elements of his creed. Love became the corner stone of the whole fabric of chivalry. The *chansons de gestes* passed into the romances of a Chretien de Troyes: and in them, the love of woman was the cause and not the consequence of devotion to God and to king.

> Qui fist Lancelot et Artus
> En armes si aventureux,
> Tristan, Percheval et Pontus,
> Sinon qu'ilz furent amoureux?

But, theoretically, it was love more like Dante's for Beatrice than Petrarch's for Laura. The pattern knight was he whose days were solemnly devoted to unselfish service for his church, his country, or his love. He was vowed to absolute renunciation of all merely personal desire in the pursuit of his hazardous quest. The superhuman exaltation of the ideal transfigured every circumstance connected with it. The love of woman was a state of mystic adoration removed entirely from the attractions of the flesh. The worshipper was a Sir Galahad, a maiden knight to whom is given such hope he knows not fear, whose strength is as the strength of ten because his heart is pure. A love like this has become a ritual, and expresses itself in social behaviour with an elaborate etiquette of courtesy in word and deed. Mediæval romance depicts an ideal world of which each element is occasioned by the ideal of chivalry. It is a world of prouesse and courtesie. Its heroes are without fear and without reproach. They are initiated in courtly forms of service in the lady's bower, until with manhood they lay their heart before the lady of their choice, and from thenceforward their lives are dedicated to proofs of their worthiness by facing unprecedented trials and overcoming incredible obstacles in the uttermost parts of the earth. That is why the mediæval love-story is perforce a story of adventure. Its wooing follows elaborately prescribed formalities, and its quests penetrate strange remote regions where deeds of unexampled valour are called forth by the attacks of terrifying monsters more horrible than the eye of man has seen.

Turn, for instance, to the tale of Owein and Lunet. "Having," says Cynon, "conquered in all deeds of valour those who were in the same country as myself, I equipped me and travelled through the uttermosts parts of the earth and its wildernesses." Amongst his adventures, he is told that he will meet "a large black man on the top of a tumulus, who is in no way smaller than two of the men of this world." When, in fact, he meets the man, even expectation is outdone: "I had been told he was huge; much larger was he than that; and his iron staff which it had been said to me was a burden for two men, it was clear to me was a burden for four warriors"—Falstaff's romancing about men in Lincoln green scarcely outdoes the original romances themselves. Of course there was variety in the haps of knight-errantry. Not always was it a black man who crossed one's path. Owein, at one point of his journey, finds himself in the presence of maidens sewing brocaded silk in golden chairs, and more marvellous by far was their fairness and beauty than what Owein had been told. At such a revelation, every true man "must burn with love until every part of him is filled." One is reminded of the solemn injunction laid on Peredur: "Should you see a fair woman, woo her, even if she desires you not; she will make you, for that reason, a better man and a more flourishing leader." These are examples from the *Mabinogion*, that is, from the body of romance before it had been fully romanticised. But for that very reason, they display even more clearly the elements which are indigenous to romance. In the full elaboration to which they were to grow, everything—incident, figure, atmosphere, and sentiment—shapes itself to play its part naturally in the whole substance. Comprehensively, these elements provide a universe in which the code of chivalry as a moral and as a social ideal can exemplify itself most significantly. No doubt in the historic origins of romance, the material adventures provide the main if not the entire interest: the *chansons de gestes* precede the romances. But the prevailing current of ideals infused itself slowly through the corporal matter, until the whole of it became the visible incorporation of the spirit and the temper of the mediæval world. And at the moment of its highest attainment, the soul of it was indubitably its characteristic sense of the meaning of woman and of love.

In its first intention, Elizabethan romantic comedy was an attempt to adapt the world of romance and all its implications to the service of comedy. *The Two Gentlemen of Verona* shows that intention at its crudest. In the story of it, there are all the main marks of the mediæval tradition as that tradition had been modified, elaborated and extended by the idealism of Petrarch and by the speculations of the Platonists. It is yet the same tradition in its essence, corroborated rather than altered by the modifying factors; as, for instance, at the hands of Ficino, Platonism brought a medico-metaphysical theory to explain the love-laden gleam of a beautiful eye. Shakespeare's play embodies a literary manner and a moral code; its actions are conducted according to a conventional etiquette and are determined by a particular creed; and every feature of it, in matter and in sentiment, is traceable to the romantic attitude of man to woman. It presents as its setting a world constituted in such fashion that the obligations and the sanctions of its doctrines could best be realised. The course of the whole play is determined by the values such doctrine attaches to the love of man and woman.

A note struck early in the play recalls one of the few passionate love-stories of classical legend—"how young Leander crossed the Hellespont,"—and at another moment, Ariadne is remembered "passioning for Theseus' perjury." But the real colour of the tale is given unmistakably by the presence amongst its characters of Sir Eglamour. By his name is he known and whence he springs. He points straight back to the source of the religious cult of love: "servant and friend" of Sylvia, he is ready at call to rush to any service to which she may command him. His own lady and his true love died, and on her grave he vowed pure chastity, dedicating himself to the assistance of lovers in affliction, recking nothing what danger should betide him in the venture. His home is in the land of mediæval romance; and his brethren are those consecrated warriors who will undertake all danger, though it stands next to death, for one calm look of Love's approval. He comes to life again in a play where knightly vows are spoken, where errantry is the normal mode of service, where the exercise of tilt and tournament is the traditional recreation, where lovers name themselves habitually the servants of their ladies, where such service may impose as a duty the helping of one's lady to a rival, and where the terms of infamy to which the utmost slander can give voice are "perjured, false, disloyal." And that is the world in which Shakespeare makes his Two Gentlemen live.

Throughout the play, "Love's a mighty lord,"

> There is no woe to his correction
> Nor to his service no such joy on earth.

This is the state of the lover as the old *Romaunt of the Rose* had depicted it:

> The sore of love is merveilous,
> For now is the lover joyous,
> Now can he pleyne, now can he grone,
> Now can he syngen, now maken mone;
> To day he pleyneth for hevynesse,
> To morowe he pleyeth for jolynesse.
> The lyf of love is full contrarie,
> Which stounde-mele can ofte varie.

Heavy penance is visited on unbelievers

> for contemning Love,
> Whose high imperious thoughts will punish him
> With bitter fasts, with penitential groans,
> With nightly tears and daily heart-sore sighs.

Sleep is chased from such a rebel's now enthralled eyes, to make them watchers of his own heart's sorrow. From true votaries, nothing less than absolute devotion is required. They must hold no discourse except it be of love. Absent from their lady, they must let no single hour o'erslip without its ceremonial sigh for her sake. The more such languishing fidelity appears to be spurned, the more must it grow and fawn upon its recalcitrant object. Apart from love, nothing in life has the least significance:

> banished from her,
> Is self from self, a deadly banishment.
> What light is light, if Sylvia be not seen?
> What joy is joy, if Sylvia be not by?
> Except I be by Sylvia in the night,
> There is no music in the nightingale.
> Unless I look on Sylvia in the day,
> There is no day for me to look upon.
> She is my essence, and I leave to be,
> If I am not by her fair influence
> Fostered, illumined, cherished, kept alive.

Such is the consecrated desolation of the romantic lover: the mediæval sense of a world emptied of its content persists through romantic poetry and is the undertone of the Renaissance sonneteers' woe. Bembo puts it not unlike Valentine in the play:

> Tu m'hai lasciato senza sole i giorni,
> Le notte senza stelle, e grave e egro
> Tutto questo, ond'io parlo, ond'io repiro:
> La terra scossa, e'l ciel turbato e negro;
> Et pien di mille oltraggi e mille scorni
> Me sembra ogni parte, quant'io miro.
> Valor e cortesia si dipartiro
> Nel tuo partire; e'l mondo infermo giacque;
> Et virtu spense i suoi chiari lumi;
> Et le fontane a i fiumi
> Nega la vena antica e l'usate acque:
> Et gli augelletti abandonaro il canto,
> Et l'herbe e i fior lasciar nude le piaggie,
> Ne piu di fronde il bosco si consperse.

But the lover has ample recompense for his sorrow. Setting the world at nought, he gains a heaven in its stead:

> she is mine own,
> And I as rich in having such a jewel
> As twenty seas if all their sand were pearl.
> The water nectar, and the rocks pure gold.

Inevitably, a creed of such ardent devotion has its appropriate liturgy. Stuffed with protestation, and full of new-found oaths, the lover utters his fears in wailful sonnets, whose composed rhymes are fully fraught with serviceable vows:

> . . . and on the altar of her beauty
> You sacrifice your tears, your sighs, your heart:
> Write till your ink be dry, and with your tears
> Moist it again, and frame some feeling line
> That may discover such integrity:
> For Orpheus' lute was strung with poets' sinews,
> Whose golden touch could soften steel and stones,
> Make tigers tame, and huge leviathans
> Forsake unsounded deeps to dance on sands.
> After your dire-lamenting elegies,
> Visit by night your lady's chamber window
> With some sweet concert; to their instruments
> Tune a deploring dump: the night's dead silence
> Will well become such sweet-complaining grievance.
> This, or else nothing, will inherit her.

With oceans of tears, and twenty thousand soul-confirming oaths, the lover excites himself to a fervid bacchanalian orgy, and in his braggardism proclaims his lady "sovereign to all the creatures on the earth," threatening destruction to all who will not at once subscribe, and extermination to any who but dare to breathe upon her. In the intervals of these ecstatic outbursts, the lover stands before the picture of his love, sighing and weeping, wreathing his arms like a malcontent, until at length he walks off alone like one that hath the pestilence.

When cruel circumstance separates him from his lady,

etiquette prescribes the proper behaviour and the right demeanour. He resorts to the congenial solitude of woods or wildernesses. In the earlier days of the cult, his manner on these occasions was more violent than ceremonious. Tristan, as Malory tells us, exiled and separated from his love, goes mad for grief; he would unlace his armour and go into the wilderness, where he "brast down the trees and bowes, and otherwhyle, when he found the harp that the lady sent him, then wold he harpe and playe therupon and wepe togethre." But in the course of time the manners of solitaries became more polite. Chaucer (or the author of the *Romaunt of the Rose*) advises the lover to cultivate a proper solitude:

> For ofte, whan thou bithenkist thee
> Of thy lovyng, where so thou be,
> Fro folk thou must departe in hie,
> That noon perceyve thi maladie.
> But hyde thyne harme thou must alone,
> And go forthe sole, and make thy mone.

It is only one more stage to the final artistic decorum of the habit. The lover in the French romance *Flamenca* "in the dark of night goes of custom to listen to the nightingale in the wood." Just, in fact, as does Valentine: in the intervals between inspecting the arms or allocating the booty of his bandit-band, he takes his laments for Sylvia into the woods for orchestral effects from the nightingales:

> These shadowy, desert, unfrequented woods
> I better brook than flourishing peopled towns:
> Here can I sit alone, unseen of any,
> And to the nightingale's complaining notes
> Tune my distresses and record my woes.

Such is the way of lovers in romances, and in *The Two Gentlemen of Verona*. Their state of spiritual ecstasy is revealed by the progressive ætherialisation of their sustenance. A collection of the menus of romantic feasts is more than a gastronomic document. In the beginnings of romance, eating and drinking was a major occupation. Owein ate and drank "whilst it was late in the time of the nones"; and once he was bidden to a feast which took three months to consume and had taken three years to prepare. But later, the initiate have so far purged their mortal grossness that eating and loving begin to appear incompatible. Again the *Romaunt of the Rose* brings the evidence:

> Such comyng and such goyng
> Such hevynesse and such wakyng
> Makith lovers, withouten wene,
> Under her clothes pale and lene.
> For love leveth colour ne cleernesse,
> Who loveth trewe hath no fatnesse;
> Thou shalt wel by thy-silf ysee
> That thou must nedis assaied be;
> For men that shape hem other weye
> Falsly her ladyes to bitraye,
> It is no wonder though they be fatt,
> With false othes her loves they gatt.
> For oft I see suche losengours
> Fatter than abbatis or priours.

On occasion, the true lover, like Jehan in *Jehan and Blonde*, is like to fade away, and can only eat when his lady serves the dishes to him with her own delicate hands. Our Valentine had been a good trencherman before he became a romantic lover; in those days, when he fasted, it was presently after dinner. But once he becomes a votary, not even ambrosia nor nectar is good enough for his æthereal table: "now can I break my fast, dine, sup, and sleep upon the very naked name of love." How he thrives on this diet will become a primary article of the literary and dramatic criticism of *The Two Gentlemen of Verona.*

So much for the spirit of romance in the play. Now for the world in which it is set,—since, taking its religion thence, it must also take the romantic world in which such religion may reveal itself. Not men living dully sluggardised at home, but those bred and tutored in the wider world, seeking preferment out, trying their fortunes in war or discovering islands far away,—these are they who have scope to put such religion to the proof. So in *The Two Gentlemen of Verona*, the scene is laid in Italy, the country which to Shakespeare's fellows was the hallowed land of romance. But it is an Italy of romance, not of physiographic authenticity. It has inland waterways unknown to geographers; the journey from Verona to Mantua is a sea-voyage; it is indeed a scenario in which all the material trappings of romance may be assembled. Mountain and forest are indispensable, mountains which are brigand-haunted, and forests in the gloom of which are abbeys from whose postern gates friars creep into the encircling woods, so wrapt in penitential mood that lurking lions, prowling hungrily for food, are utterly forgotten. In such a locality, the tale of true love may run its uneven course. The poetically gifted lover meets such obstacles as a rival, at whom he hurls his cartel, and a perverse father whose plans for his daughter are based on such irrelevant considerations as the rivals' bank-balances. The father's castle has its upper tower far from the ground, and built so shelving that to climb it is at apparent hazard of one's life. And here is the angelic daughter's chamber wherein she is nightly lodged, within doors securely locked, so that rescue can only be by a corded ladder to her chamber window. Then unexpected difficulties will be expected to intrude: the best-laid plot to carry her away is foiled by the machinations of a villain out of the least suspected quarter. Banishment naturally follows, and at length, with the flight of the heroine and the pursuit of her by the entire court, all will work out well by a series of surprising coincidences, to which rivals, brigands, friars, and lions are all somehow contributory. In this way, romantic love makes its romantic universe; and this in fact is the setting and the story of *The Two Gentlemen of Verona*.

This, both in matter and in spirit, is the tradition which the Elizabethan dramatists desired to lift bodily on to their comic stage. But something somehow went wrong. The spirit of mediæval romance seemed to shrivel in the presence of comedy. Something similar had in fact happened in the real world outside the theatre. The last hero of romance had lived gloriously and had died quite out of his part. Jacques de Lalaing, le bon chevalier, the mirror of knighthood who adorned the Burgundian court in the middle of the fifteenth century, had become the pattern of chivalry for all Europe. To his contemporaries, "fair was he as Paris, pious as Æneas, wise as Ulysses, and passionate as Hector": and his exploits in tournament and in knight-errantry had carried his fame through many lands. He died an early death in 1453. But he did not die of a lover's broken heart; nor was he slain in tourney by a foeman worthy of his steel and of his thirty-two emblazoned pennants. He was shot down by a cannon ball in an expedition against the merchants and shopkeepers of Ghent. The gross ponderable facts of a very material world swept the symbol of an outworn ideal from off the face of the earth. So in *The Two Gentlemen*, a sheer clod of earth, Launce by name, will, quite unwittingly, expose the unsubstantiality of the romantic hero with whom the play throws him into contact. But we are anticipating. The consequences of Shakespeare's attempt to dramatise romance must be watched in closer detail.

There is little wonder that the Elizabethan dramatists saw the dramatic possibilities of such material, and did not at first perceive its dramatic disadvantages. They felt the dramatic thrill of following these lovers and setting the world at nought. Nor is it very difficult to set the geographical world at nought, at least to the extent of making inland seas in Italy or liberating living lions in its woods. Yet sometimes the distortions of the physical universe necessarily ventured by the romanticist entail violent wrenches of our common consciousness. The dukes of Shakespeare's Italy, for instance, apparently have magic power over the flight of time; for whilst a banished man is speaking but ten lines, the proclamation of his banishment is ratified, promulgated, and has become publicly known throughout the duchy, and sentinels have already been posted along the frontiers to prevent a surreptitious return of the exile to the land which he has not yet had time to pack his suit-case for leaving. It is a land too where optical illusions, or perhaps optical delusions, are the normal way of vision. A man seeking a page-boy interviews an applicant for the post; he is just enough of a business man to know that some sort of reason must be advanced for taking on a servant who can show neither character nor reference from previous employers, and so Proteus, engaging the disguised Julia, says that the engagement is specifically on the recommendation of the applicant's face; but he does not recognise, as he gazes into this face, that it was the one he was smothering with kisses a few weeks before when its owner, in her proper dress, was his betrothed. Yet these are really only minor impediments, requiring but a little and a by no means reluctant suspension of our disbelief. They are altogether insignificant compared with the reservations involved when romance displays its peculiar propensity for setting the world of man at nought. To satisfy its own obligations, it perforce demanded super-men; at all events, the heroes it puts forward as its votaries in the play are something either more or less than men.

Romantically speaking, Valentine is the hero, and not alone in the technical sense. In classical comedy the hero is simply the protagonist, the central figure who is the biggest butt of the comic satire. But here the protagonist is the upholder of the faith on which the play is built, the man with whom the audience is called upon to rejoice admiringly, and not the fellow at whom it is derisively to laugh. He is to play the hero in every sense of the word. Yet in the event, the prevailing spirit of romance endows him with sentiments and provides him with occupations which inevitably frustrate the heroic intention. The story renders him a fool. Convention may sanctify his sudden conversion from the mocker to the votary of love, and may even excuse or palliate his fractious braggardism when he insults Proteus with ill-mannered comparisons between Silvia and Julia. But his helplessness and his impenetrable stupidity amount to more than the traditional blindness of a lover. Even the clown Speed can see through Silvia's trick, when she makes Valentine write a letter to himself. But Valentine plays out the excellent motion as an exceeding puppet, unenlightened by the faintest gleam of common insight. And despite his vaunt that he knows Proteus as well as he knows himself, he is blind to villainies so palpable, that Launce, the other clown of the piece, though he be but a fool, has the wits to recognise them for what they plainly are. The incidents are dramatically very significant, for both Launce and Speed come into the play for no reason whatever but to be unmistakable dolts. One begins to feel that it will be extremely difficult to make a hero of a man who is proved to be duller of wit than the patent idiots of the piece. Even when Valentine might have shone by resource in action, he relapses into conventional laments, and throws himself helplessly into the arms of Proteus for advice and consolation. Heroic opportunity stands begging round him when he encounters the brigands. But besides demonstrating that he can tell a lie—witness his tale of cock and bull about having killed a man—the situation only serves to discredit him still more: for the words of his lie, his crocodile tears for the fictitious man he claims to have slain, and his groundless boast that he slew him manfully in fight without false vantage or base treachery, are in fact nothing but an attempt to make moral capital by means of forgery and perjury. They have not even the recommendation of the Major-General's tears for the orphan boy. When at length Valentine is duly installed as captain of the brigands, his chief occupation is to vary highway robbery with sentimental descants on the beauty of nature in her "shadowy, desert, unfrequented woods":

> Here can I sit alone, unseen of any—

and we already know his favourite hobby on these saunterings—

> And to the nightingale's complaining notes
> Tune my distresses and recording woes.

He is own brother to Gilbert's coster, who, when he isn't jumping on his mother, loves to lie abasking in the sun, and to the cut-throat, who, when not occupied in crimes, loves to hear the little brook agurgling and listen to the merry village chimes. But Valentine's utmost reach of ineptitude comes with what, again romantically speaking, is meant to be the heroic climax of the play. When he has just learnt the full tale of the villainy of Proteus, the code permits him neither resentment nor passion. Like a cashier addressing a charwoman who has pilfered a penny stamp, he sums up his rebuke—"I am sorry I must never trust thee more." And worse follows immediately. With but five lines of formal apology from the villain, Valentine professes himself so completely satisfied that he enthusiastically resigns his darling Silvia to the traitor. Even Valentine must have seen that the gesture was a little odd, because he quotes the legal sanction. It is the code, a primary article in the romantic faith—"that my love may appear plain and free." But it makes a man a nincompoop. Nor does it help much that after this preposterous episode, Valentine is allowed to spit a little fire in an encounter with another rival, Thurio. He has already proved himself so true a son of romance that he can never again be mistaken for a creature of human nature.

Proteus is less hampered by romantic obligations; because the plot requires him to have just sufficient of salutary villainy to make him throw over their commandments for his own ends. Yet the villain of romance suffers almost as much from the pressure of romanticism as does the hero. The noble fellows whom he, as villain, is called upon to deceive are such gullible mortals that little positive skill is necessary. Proteus can fool Thurio and Valentine and the Duke without exerting himself. But on the one occasion when he might have shown his wits, he only reveals his lack of them. Making love to

Silvia, he meets her protest against his disloyalty to Julia by inventing the easy excuse that Julia is dead. Silvia replies that, even so, he should be ashamed to wrong Valentine. It is, of course, a tight corner: but the best Proteus can do is to say "I likewise hear that Valentine is dead." He might at least have displayed a little more ingenuity in invention; he fails in precisely such a situation as would have permitted the clown of classical comedy to triumph. Moreover, the main plot requires Proteus to be guilty of incredible duplicity, and of the most facile rapidity in changing morals and mistresses. But he need scarcely have made the change explicit in words so ineptly casual and banal as his remark: "*Methinks* my zeal to Valentine is cold." The phrase is accidentally in keeping with the unintended complacence he displays when, wooing the lady who will have none of him, he begins by informing her that "he has made her happy" by his coming. The trait becomes intolerably ludicrous when, all his sins forgiven him, and Julia restored to his arms, all he can utter in confession is his own fatuous self-conceit:

> O heaven, were man
> But constant, he were perfect.

It is, of course, a fine sentiment; but the audience, having seen Valentine, simply will not believe it.

Even the brigands of romance will scarcely stand the test of the stage. They enter with metaphorical daggers in mouths bristling with black mustachios and with desperate oaths. Callous and bloodthirsty ruffians, spoiling for a fight, their chief regret is that fate is sending only one defenceless traveller to be rifled instead of ten. But when the destined victim turns out to be two, courage perhaps abates a little: at all events, the travellers are warned to keep their distance, and throw over the booty or otherwise to assume a sitting posture, whilst the rifling is safely done by the desperadoes themselves. Perhaps this, and not his customary ineptitude in speech, is what makes Valentine address the villains as "My friends." But, of course, his assumption is, for the trade of brigandage, economically unsound. And so, with apologies for correcting him, Valentine is informed that he is not playing the game—"that's not so, sir; we are your enemies." But the outlaws are connoisseurs of masculine beauty, and Valentine's fine figure secures him an opportunity for a hearing: one cannot but note that this is the first time that any of his romantic attributes has made for his advantage, and that he misuses it scandalously for his lying brag. Hearing the fiction, however, the bandits feel at once that here is a fellow spirit, given, like themselves, to "so small a fault" as homicide. Straightway they implore him to show them his diploma in the modern languages, promising him the kingship of the band if it is of good honours' standard. Becoming convivial, they reveal their amiable dispositions in snatches of their life-history. One has amused himself with attempts at abduction. Another, when the whim takes him, "in his mood," has the merry trick of stabbing gentlemen unto the heart; and his gaiety makes us forget that a mood in Shakespeare's English was not quite the casual fancy it now is. Another acclaims these and other "such like petty crimes" as congenial peccadilloes in his own repertory. By this time, the brigands have become so hilarious with their reminiscences, that they are no longer minded to scrutinise Valentine's academic credentials. They will take him for a linguist merely "on his own report," and, mainly because he "is beautified with goodly shape," they offer him the leadership, pathetically promising to love him as their commander and their king. Clearly such a thoroughly unbrigandlike procedure as this election has almost put them out of their parts. They must be allowed to recover in a traditional tableau. Daggers are whipped out, threats become fierce, and Valentine, with steel points at his throat, is given the choice of being a king or a corpse. Perhaps his fear is responsible for the odd proviso that "silly women" shall be exempt from the depradations of the gang over which he is to rule; but it is of course too much to expect of better men than Valentine to require them to anticipate a variation in the meaning of a word. Neither before nor after *The Two Gentlemen of Verona* has dramatic literature known a band of outlaws like to these—except once: there are the Pirates of Penzance: but then Gilbert meant his to be funny.

One begins to suspect that everything which is hallowed by the tradition of romance is made thereby of no avail for the purposes of drama. But there are Julia and Launce to reckon with; and these are figures universally accounted the most substantial beings in the play. So indeed they are. But they owe it entirely to the fact that they are under no obligation whatever to the code of romance. The behaviour of Valentine is entirely conditioned by the doctrine of romantic love. But the code allowed to woman no duty but to excite by her beauty the devoted worship of her knight. If England instead of France had performed the final codification of chivalry, its women might have had other and less lady-like propensities, such, for instance, as King Horn's Rimenhild displayed. But when a French romance elaborates its portrait of womanhood, it gives her patience rather than character: women with the forcefulness of a distinct personality might have turned the energies of their knights away from consecrated paths of knighthood, as Chretien's Enide turned her Erec:

> Mes tant l'ama Erec d'amors
> Que d'armes mes ne li chaloit,
> Ne a tornoiemant n'aloit
> N'avoit mes soing de tornoiier.

Wherefore Chretien's romance tells of Erec's regeneration through the discipline by which he reduces his Enide to absolute submission. At the end, she has attained complete self-suppression—

> Ne je tant hardie ne sui
> Que je os regarder vers lui—

and, to the modern eye, has become the perfect pattern of an exquisitely charming nonentity.

When Shakespeare takes over a tradition whose women are like these, so long as he preserves the beauty of their faces, he can endow them with whatever character he may please. His Julia is a creation, not a convention. As she is a woman, acting on a woman's instinct—"I have no other but a woman's reason, I think him so because I think him so"—she is depicted in moods, whimsies, and vagaries which are in fact the stuff of dramatic characterisation. Like the heroine of romance, she will cover her first love-letter with kisses, and press the precious manuscript to her heart. But like the spirited independent young lady of the world, she will not expose herself to the chuckles of her maid by exhibiting the common symptoms of her affections. Hence the pretended contempt, and the struggle to keep up appearances, even at considerable risk to the sacred document. But for what seriously concerns her love, Julia is too level-headed to over-reach herself. As far as may be, she will avoid the disapproval of opinion: but where there is no remedy, she will defy a scandalised world, and undertake her pilgrimage of love. She knows the hazards of the road and the many weary steps it will involve. But she also knows her own capacities, and has duly taken note of all material things she will stand in need of. And although Proteus is a poor thing on whom to lavish so much love, Julia knows that love is indeed a blinded god; and in her capable hands even a Proteus may be moulded to something worth the having.

Launce is another who insists on remaining in the memory. He has no real right within the play, except that gentlemen must have servants, and Elizabethan audiences must have clowns. But coming in thus by a back-door, he earns an unexpected importance in the play. Seen side by side with Speed, his origin is clear. Whilst Speed belongs to the purely theatrical family of the Dromios, with their punning and logic-chopping asininities, Launce harks back to the native Costard. And as Costard shows his relationship to Bottom by his skill in village theatricals, so Launce reveals by his wooing his family connection with Touchstone, and Touchstone's Audrey,

who was a poor thing, but his own. All the kind of the Launces
are thus palpably a mighty stock. Their worth, compared
with that of the Speeds and the Dromios, is admirably indicated
by Launce's consummate use of Speed's curiosity and of his
better schooling. Launce gets his letter deciphered; he gets also
an opportunity to display his own superior breeding, and to
secure condign punishment for the ill-mannered Speed: "now
will he be swinged for reading my letter; an unmannerly slave,
that will thrust himself into secrets! I'll after, to rejoice in the
boy's correction."

Launce is happiest with his dog. Clownage can go no
farther than the pantomimic representation, with staff and shoe
and dog, of the parting from his home-folks. Laughter is
hilarious at Launce's bitter grief that his ungrateful cur declined
to shed a tear. That Launce should expect it is, of course, the
element of preposterous incongruity which makes him a
clown. But when he puts his complaint squarely, that his
"dog has no more pity in him than a dog," the thrust pierces
more than it was meant to. Romance itself has expected no
less largely of Valentine, of Proteus, and of the rest. It has
demanded that man shall be more than man, and has laid upon
him requisitions passing the ability of man to fulfil. At the
bidding of romance, Valentine and Proteus have become what
they are in the play, and the one thing they are not is men like
other men. A further incident in which Launce is concerned
takes on a similarly unexpected significance. He has made as
great a sacrifice as did Valentine himself: he has given up his
own cur in place of the one which Proteus entrusted to him to
take to Silvia. But the effect hardly suggests that self-sacrifice
is worldly-wise. And so once more it seems to bring into question the worldly worth of the code which sanctifies such deeds.
Unintentionally, Launce has become the means by which
the incompatibilities and the unrealities of romantic postulates
are laid bare. And Launce is palpably the stuff of comedy:
awakening our comic sense, he inevitably sharpens our
appreciation of the particular range of incongruities which are

the province of comedy—the incongruity between what a thing really is and what it is taken to be.

Romance, and not comedy, has called the tune of *The Two Gentlemen of Verona*, and governed the direction of the action of the play. That is why its creatures bear so little resemblance to men of flesh and blood. Lacking this, they are scarcely dramatic figures at all; for every form of drama would appear to seek at least so much of human nature in its characters. But perhaps the characters of the Two Gentlemen are comic in a sense which at first had never entered the mind of their maker. Valentine bids for the sympathy, but not for the laughter of the audience: the ideals by which he lives are assumed to have the world's approbation. But in execution they involve him in most ridiculous plight. He turns the world from its compassionate approval to a mood of sceptical questioning. The hero of romantic comedy appears no better than its clowns. And so topsy-turvy is the world of romance that apparently the one obvious way to be reputed in it for a fool, is to show at least a faint sign of discretion and of common sense. Thurio, for instance, was cast for the dotard of the play, and of course he is not without egregious folly. But what was meant in the end to annihilate him with contempt, turns out quite otherwise. Threatened by Valentine's sword, he resigns all claim to Silvia, on the ground that he holds him but a fool that will endanger his body for a girl that loves him not. The audience is invited to call Thurio a fool for thus showing himself to be the one person in the play with a modicum of worldly wisdom, a respect for the limitations of human nature, and a recognition of the conditions under which it may survive. Clearly, Shakespeare's first attempt to make romantic comedy had only succeeded so far that it had unexpectedly and inadvertently made romance comic. The real problem was still to be faced.

III

The Recoil from Romanticism

WHEN last session I was privileged to speak to a John Rylands audience, the object of my lecture was to examine an early play of Shakespeare's in order to ascertain what in general was the prevailing quality of Elizabethan romanticism, and to discover whether such quality was easily amenable to the tradition of drama. The conclusion reached was that when a story, romantic in temper, in person, and in incident, such as is that of *The Two Gentlemen of Verona*, is lifted from its *milieu* in the body of literary romance and is re-set for enactment under the conditions which constitute drama, a host of unexpected difficulties emerge in the process of an apparently simple transference. The demands imposed by drama seemed at many points inconsistent with the obligations indigenous to romance, so inconsistent, indeed, that for the moment there may have appeared to be little hope of reconciling one set of claims with the other. It may very well be that when Shakespeare finished *The Two Gentlemen*, oppressed by the devastating effect of its internecine war between the comic and the romantic, out of sheer physical disgust he turned for an antidote to an old play of shrew taming which had scarcely been contaminated at all by any romantic sentiment. If his own *Taming of the Shrew* happened so, he was certainly enjoying a boisterous retaliation on the very sanctum of romance, mocking its sacred creed and profaning its hallowed ritual. The solemn ceremonies of its most ecstatic experience, the sublime mystery of wooing, are sacrilegiously burlesqued. Courtship is transferred from moon-

44

lit pleasances to be set in lawyers' offices, where specialties and covenants suited to a merely mundane contract may be properly drawn. It speaks, not with flowers and songs and flageolets, but with strident argument, with fisticuffs, with three-legged stools for missiles, and even with harsh penal dietaries. The lover in romances nourishes his spirit on the ambrosial air of love alone: but in *The Taming of the Shrew*, from the first appearance of the reprobate old interloper Sly, there is plentiful talk of good eating and drinking, of bread, and beef, and beer.

The Taming of the Shrew is literally Shakespeare's recoil from romance. But it is not proposed in the present argument to pursue the implications peculiar to *The Taming of the Shrew*. That will provide occupation for a later occasion. For the moment, it may be better to face the general situation. It is scarcely likely that *The Taming of the Shrew* was Shakespeare's first recoil from romance, though it is certainly a rollickingly emphatic one. Moreover such recoil and recovery, further recoil and further recovery, make the natural movement of Elizabethan dramatic history: for the fundamental problem of Elizabethan comedy was to discover a mode by which the peculiar romantic temperament of the time might find adequate satisfaction without at the same time depriving itself of such pleasure as an older, a bigger, and a more permanent world had found and was to find in comedy. In so far as Shakespeare and his fellows were Elizabethans, they were romantic; in so far as they were human beings, they inherited man's instinct for the comic. Their difficulty was to know how to be both at once.

Perhaps Shakespeare's first stumblings on the problem carry us back to his earliest attempts at play-making. There is much to be said for taking *Love's Labour's Lost* as his first comedy. It is assuredly his least substantial; and the one more than any other circumscribed by the fashions of his day. It is made of such stuff as a Tatler, a Bystander, or a revue-maker would offer us in ours. But as far as there is in it a colouring sentiment, it is

the exuberant assertion of the high claims of romance, not
only of its exalted ecstasies, but of the exclusive spiritual values
of the romantic doctrine of love.

> For when would you, my lord, or you, or you,
> Have found the ground of study's excellence
> Without the beauty of a woman's face?
> From women's eyes this doctrine I derive;
> They are the ground, the books, the academes
> From whence doth spring the true Promethean fire.
> Why, universal plodding prisons up
> The nimble spirits in the arteries,
> As motion and long-during action tires
> The sinewy vigour of the traveller.
>
> .   .   .   .
>
> For when would you, my liege, or you, or you,
> In leaden contemplation have found out
> Such fiery numbers as the prompting eyes
> Of beauty's tutors have enrich'd you with?
> Other slow arts entirely keep the brain;
> And therefore, finding barren practisers,
> Scarce show a harvest of their heavy toil:
> But love, first learned in a lady's eyes,
> Lives not alone immured in the brain;
> But, with the motion of all elements,
> Courses as swift as thought in every power,
> And gives to every power a double power,
> Above their functions and their offices.
> It adds a precious seeing to the eye;
> A lover's eyes will gaze an eagle blind;
> A lover's ears will hear the lowest sound,
> When the suspicious head of theft is stopp'd:
> Love's feeling is more soft and sensible
> Than are the tender horns of cockled snails;
> Love's tongue proves dainty Bacchus gross in taste:
> For valour, is not Love a Hercules,
> Still climbing trees in the Hesperides?
> Subtle as Sphinx; as sweet and musical
> As bright Apollo's lute, strung with his hair;
> And when Love speaks, the voice of all the gods
> Make heaven drowsy with the harmony.
>   —(IV. iii. 299 ff.)

This is a novel educational curriculum; and those of us who are slavishly habituated to books and to mundane scholastic institutions, may feel a little diffident before abolishing our organisations to set up in their place these Promethean academies of women's eyes. Or at least, seeing the King, Biron, Longaville and Dumain as the disciples of the new programme, we may feel entitled to somewhat more substantial proofs of its value than they provide: for as scholars, they are but poor advertisements for a new school, and their Prometheanism seems, if anything, still further to blind them to rudimentary differences between green geese and goddesses.

But though *Love's Labour's Lost* is mere gay trifling, its peculiar gaiety almost frustrates itself by the formlessness and the spinelessness of the thing as a play. And Shakespeare's first recoil from the insouciant romantic formlessness of *Love's Labour's Lost* seems to have been a feeling that plays without backbone are hopelessly crippled. No plot, no play. And so apparently the recoil turned him to Classical comedy. Putting himself to school to Plautus for his *Comedy of Errors*, he submitted himself to a discipline which, however uncongenial to the spirit, was a salutary apprenticeship to the mechanics of play-building. But it was much more than that. When Shakespeare took the Roman comedians for his pattern, he was reverting to the practice on which his English predecessors, and French and Italian pioneers before them, had established the new comedy of modern Europe. Modern comedy begins with Plautus and Terence; and the shades of Menander need not here be invoked to measure his contribution to the endowment.

It is easy to be unjust to classical comedy, and to Plautus and Terence. A modern, or even a sixteenth-century reader of Roman comedy, may find in it nothing but a string of ludicrous intrigues. It appears to be absorbed in mere incidents, to be farce at most, and rarely to attain to comedy in our modern sense. But events and situations which strike us as only isolated examples of the ludicrous, interesting or otherwise

merely for themselves, may in the past have had a larger significance for contemporaries. When Shakespeare took the stories
of Plautus for his *Comedy of Errors*, he could only take their
material substance; their significance remained behind in the
Roman civilisation of two thousand years ago. Even a colourable English imitation can impart little of the original but its
external features. We roar hilariously at the ludicrous predicament and the crude discomfiture of bawd and pimp and procurer in play after play of Plautus and Terence. But the display
is a farce for our entertainment, lacking almost all such reper-
cussion in the circumstances of our social existence as would
raise it to the level of comedy. Yet in our own day, if a
dramatist calls any of Mrs. Warren's profession into his
dramatis personae, without further thought he is taken to be a
playwright obsessed with the notion of turning his plays to
profound problems of our social life. It is at least worth
examining Roman comedy to discover whether its vitality is
merely due to its expertness in theatrical trickery, or, on the
contrary, whether it had not a larger hold on the idea of
comedy.

All that is commonly known of the Romans would argue a
particular aptitude for the art of comedy. Their paramount
interests were social and civic; their boast was to be citizens of
no mean city. They had, of course, an urban delight in Sabine
farms; but they were emphatically men of the world. Problems of conduct were more urgent for them than were enquiries into belief. They discussed morals more eagerly than
they embarked on metaphysical speculations. They were
more at home in law courts and market-places than in temples.
On a large scale, their social interest effected the political
organisation of the empire. In a narrower circle, it made for the
establishment of institutions, conventions, and manners calculated to assure for man the advantages and the amenities of
intercourse with his fellows in ordered corporate life. Society
became for them a sort of citizen's club. From such a point of
view, virtue is largely a matter of good form. "Leniter qui

saeviunt sapiunt magis:" don't be too hard on a youth's frolics, says old Philoxenus (*Bacchides*, 408): and though his later actions show him as a poor pattern of right conduct, he has nevertheless the sympathetic worldly wisdom and the tolerant human understanding which commend him to his audience. "Paulisper, Lyde, est libido homini suo animo obsequi:" only for a time is a decent fellow eager to indulge his passions, and very soon he comes to hate himself for doing so—"iam aderit tempus, cum sese etiam ipse oderit." In the meantime, bear with offenders who keep just on the right side of the allowed margin—"praeter aequom ne quid delinquat." Morality is at best a sense of decency and a respect for property. In your escapades, avoid disgrace in the eyes of your fellows: that is the rule prescribed for the young spark:—

> ita tuom conferto amare semper, si sapis,
> ne id quod ames populus si sciat, tibi sit probro.
> —(*Curculio*, 28.)

So long as you keep off another man's preserves, the world is free for your pleasures:

> nemo ire quemquam publica prohibet via;
> dum ne per fundum saeptum facias semitam,
> dum ted abstineas nupta, vidua, virgine,
> iuventute et pueris liberis, ama quid lubet.
> —(*Curculio*, 35 ff.)

Thus propriety, wherein property and decency merge, is the standard of good form, the pledge and safeguard of common welfare. Wrong varies with person, and particularly with time and place. "Itidem ut tempus anni, aetatem aliam aliud factum condecet" (*Mercator*, 984), an old man is told when he is being reproved for acts lightly condoned in his own son's case:

> nam si istuc ius est, senecta aetate scortari senes,
> ubi locist res summa nostra publica?

The very pillars of society are shaken by such offences against decorum; youth is precluded from exercising its own prerogative, if it must compete with old men, and especially with old men who can control its material resources. Old Demipho is not only held up to scorn for his own goatishness; he is particularly reproached for filching a properly purchased mistress from his own son:

> nam te istac aetate haud aequom filio fuerat tuo
> adulescenti amanti amicam eripere emptam argento suo.
> —(*Mercator*, 972.)

That is the good form of Roman comedy, though, of course, not necessarily of Rome itself. But comedy is generally a closer historian of its society than the members of it would willingly admit, and often indeed far truer than they would trouble to realise. Evil, for Roman comedy, lies not in wickedness and in sin: its root is unclubbableness. The enemies of society are not the villains who defy it overtly; for society has prisons strong enough to exclude the villain from his evil-doing. Its most numerous enemies are those who, whilst managing a livelihood recognised and approved by society, abuse the circumstances which justify their existence. So the comic dramatist never ceases to scourge parasites, and lays the lash in all his plays on pimps and bawds and procurers, because they are prone to take unfair advantage of their allowed status, and thus vastly to diminish the resources of a youth, who after his apprenticeship in the big world of which they are a part, will succeed to full social responsibility.

But though bawds and courtesans occur in every play, they are never the main figures in Roman comedy. They come in incidentally to take their share of ignominy and contempt. Far more dangerous enemies of society are those whose formal rights to full membership of it are unquestionable, but whose personal qualities render them incapable of recognising its obligations. The man one blackballs at the club-election is not he whose discretion keeps his private immoralities under the rose, but he whose irrepressible babbling perpetually breaks into the silence of the reading-room. It is arrogances of this sort which arouse the contempt or the amusement of those whose chief care is to maintain the decencies. And Rome not only created satire; it seized on the opportunity to convert Greek comedy into a still more effective because a more social weapon than is literary satire for the preservation of the conventions which make corporate social life possible and pleasant. Comedy exposed offences against social decorum by rendering the offenders ludicrous. Its significance lay almost exclusively in its social satire. It is this which determined its range of interest, its favourite characters and its typical mechanism. Doubtless the mechanism—plottings, intrigues, tricks and deceptions—admirable as it was for its significant purpose, was just the sort to get out of hand, and to go on gyrating simply by its own momentum, thereby the more easily deluding a modern reader into taking it for a merely mechanical contrivance. But the spirit of comedy itself is the power which animates the plays of Plautus, and, though less vigorously, those also of Terence.

It is a comedy essentially realistic in temper. In matter, also, its realism is closer than a first glance reveals. Not only are its people very much the people of the earth, they are the men and women of its own day, though for the story they are not infrequently called upon to appear in conventional rather than in realistic situations. In heart and mind they are Roman contemporaries of Plautus, though their name and often, too, their dresses are Greek. Nominally, too, the scene is Greece: but on closer description, it is no other than their familiar Rome, endowed in fact with localities and institutions actually peculiar to Rome. Perhaps the Watch Committee of Rome insisted on this nomenclature: in any case, the motive of it is a strong social instinct, protecting the feelings of society even against its own protectors, the comic dramatists. Moreover, it may very well be that as its stock-types are the perpetual and timeless nuisances of social intercourse, bores, busybodies, braggarts and such like, and are therefore common to all comedy,

ancient and modern, Greek and Roman, they are often allowed
to appear in an inherited conventional form which is not completely naturalised to Roman society; superficially, the parasite
may be more of a particular parasite in Greece, and less of a
general sponger in Rome. But the plays abound in incidental
details which reveal how thoroughly steeped they are in the
circumstances of Roman life. There is Menæchmus, for
instance, tripping off to a surreptitious lunch at his mistress's
maisonette, flouting the ordinances of God, the decencies of
man, and the wrath of his wife to do so. But the tasty dishes
must be left to go cold, and the mistress to excite herself into
such a tantrum that only an expensive present will mollify
her, all through a peculiarly Roman incident which none but a
Roman could encounter, which would have kept none but a
Roman from his lust, and which perhaps was the only sanction
capable of so restraining a Roman. By mere accident, on his
way to his mistress's, Menæchmus ran into one of his depen-
dents who then and there demanded his help in the law-
courts (*Menæchmi*, 588 ff.).

The outstanding feature of the whole body of Roman
comedy is that whilst it is full of sex, it is almost entirely
devoid of love. There is nothing in it of love as modern
literature makes love. Mere names are misleading. Most of
the plots of the Roman dramatists are intrigues in pursuit of a
woman; and often, too, the plotter is a passionate youth. But
the object is almost invariably illicit: the *Captivi* stands almost
alone for its chastity, and it was so marked a departure from
custom that Plautus bragged of it—or apologised for it—in an
epilogue:

> Spectatores, ad pudicos mores facta haec fabula est,
> neque in hac subigitationes sunt neque ulla amatio.
> —(1029 ff.)

In the rest of the whole Roman repertory, there is nothing at
all rightly to be called a wooing, for wooing was fashioned by
romantic sentiment still to be learnt by man in the evolution

of his consciousness. The way of a Roman youth with the maids or the one-time maids of Roman comedy was the way of solicitation: and solicitation is a social institution. Its practice was a branch of social economics; familiarity with its ways and means was incidental to the daily routine of the proficient citizen, and was therefore a necessary discipline in the curriculum of youth. But the extent to which youth avails himself of the system has little bearing on his reputation for essential morality; and, of course, however much he sought for experience in this kind, he could not, by the nature of the case, regard it as an occasion for promoting any sort of union but mere unions of the flesh. This is Plautus's Latin *amare*, but it is not English *love*. The sensations comprised in the two terms may have a large community, but the sentiments attaching thereto have little in common. The words expressing the passion may still survive as a prevailing idiom:

> Quia si illa inventa est, quam ille amat, recte valet;
> si non inventa est, minus valet moribundusque est.
> animast amica amanti: si abest, nullus est;
> si adest, res nullast: ipsus est, nequam et miser.
> —(*Bacchides*, 191 ff.)

This is very near the text of Valentine's lament for Silvia's absence—

> banished from her
> Is self from self: a deadly banishment.
> What light is light, if Silvia be not seen?
> What joy is joy, if Silvia be not by?
> . . . .
> She is my essence, and I leave to be,
> If I be not by her fair influence
> Foster'd, illumined, cherish'd, kept alive.
> —(*Two Gentlemen of Verona*, III. i. 172 ff.)

And Leonida, witnessing the enforced parting of his young master and Philenium, saw a sight such as was seen when Proteus parted from Julia—"lacrumantem lacinia tenet lacrumans" (*Asinaria*, 587). But both these girls in Plautus were inmates of a bawdy house, and only the conventional coincidences of his plots were in the end miraculously to cleanse them from the contamination of it.

There are moreover moments when the lover in Roman comedy utters as with the tongue of an Elizabethan sonneteer the exquisite pains of love-longing, describing its bitter-sweet ravages and its all-absorbing tyranny:

> Credo ego Amorem primum apud homines carnificinam
> commentum.
> hanc ego de me coniecturam domi facio, ni foris quaeram,
> qui omnes homines supero [atque] antideo cruciabililatibus animi.
>
>> iactor [crucior] agitor stimulor, versor
>> in amoris rota, miser exanimor,
>> feror differor distrahor diripior,
>> ita nubilam mentem animi habeo.
>
> Ubi sum, ibi non sum, ubi non sum, ibist animus,
>> ita mi omnia sunt ingenia;
> quod lubet, non lubet iam id continuo,
> ita me Amor lassum animi ludificat,
> fugat, agit, appetit, raptat, retinet,
> lactat, largitur: quod dat non dat; deludit:
> modo quod suasit, id dissuadet,
>> quod dissuasit, id ostentat.
>>> maritumis moribus mecum experitur:
>> ita meum frangit amantem animum;
> neque, nisi quia miser non eo pessum,
> mihi ulla abest perdito permities.
>>>>> —(*Cistellaria*, 203 ff.)

At rarer moments, the most exquisite and exalted raptures of the romantic lover seem but echoes of a voice from a Roman play—"Bid me to cross seas for a kiss from you," says Stratophanes to Phronesium, "and I would leap at once to claim it"—

>> si hercle me ex medio mari
> savium petere tuom iubeas, petere hau pigeat [me],
>>> mel meum.
>>>> —(*Truculentus*, 527.)

But Stratophanes is a braggart mouthing it bombastically for comic effect, and the lady, to whose lips he aspires, is a whore playing with him for her own profit. Even Alcesimarchas who sang the hymn to love in phrases so romantically Elizabethan was stirred to sing it by his passion for a girl whom he had bought of a procuress, and with whom as yet he could not have dreamed of decent marriage.

It cannot then be doubted that, despite superficial similarities in phrase, for these young Romans love is other than it was for Shakespeare and his contemporaries. The points where in appearance they seem to touch, yet in reality remain completely and diametrically opposed, are nowhere better illustrated than in the long soliloquy, too long to cite, with which Charinus opens *Mercator*. Physical and nervous sensations are common to both experiences; but the accompanying sentiments are as remote from each other as earth is from Heaven. Scapha, as old and experienced in the world as Juliet's nurse, put the Roman view succinctly when she warned Philematium, still young in the arts of allurement.

> non vestem amatores amant [mulieris], sed vestis fartim.
> —(*Mostellaria*, 169.)

But Juliet and Shakespeare had left the world of her Nurse and of Scapha many centuries behind them.

It is entirely misleading to name Roman plays love-plays unless an ample gloss is appended to illustrate the peculiar and exclusive connotation of the term, a connotation characteristically exemplified by such incidents as those which fill *Casina*. Cleostrata is doing her utmost to further her son's suit for Casina: but her motive for abetting him is merely to frustrate her husband's (and, of course, her son's father's) lust for the girl. The plotters on both sides resort to the coarsest bestiality to achieve satisfaction of their appetites: Cleostrata would secure Casina for her son by marrying her to his complaisant servant; and her husband plans to reserve the girl for his own use by marrying her to his bailiff Olympio, who is quite willing to have her on those terms. The whole mentality of the lover in Roman comedy is contained in old Antipho's proposal to his son-in-law, with whom he is trying to strike a bargain to obtain a music-girl from the son-in-law for his own purposes:

> ego tibi meam filiam, bene quicum cubitares, dedi:
> nunc mihi reddi ego aequom esse abs te quicum cubitem censeo.
> —(*Stichus*, 547.)

These are words modern feeling prefers to leave in the Latin to which they belong.

> O lyric love, half-angel and half-bird,
> And all a wonder and a wild surprise.

Terence, it is generally held, shows less of the beast in these matters. But if there is a difference in degree, it is too slight to count against the immeasurable distance separating all Roman love from that of the poets of Shakespeare's day. One of Terence's heroines, for instance, a girl in his *Eunuch*, implores her lover to permit her, as a means for securing their mutual pleasures in future, to give herself to a rival so that by her service he may be made to help them:

> sola sum; habeo hic neminem,
> neque amicum neque cognatum; quamobrem, Phaedria,
> cupio aliquos parare amicos beneficio meo.
> id, amabo, adiuta me, quo id fiat facilius:
> sine illum priores partes hosce aliquot dies
> apud me habere.
> —(*Eunuchus*, 147 ff.)

And the other hero of the same play pays his devotion to his lady by intruding himself, disguised as a eunuch, into the service of her guardian, and raping her in her sleep. "Do lovers in romances sin that way?" It is a code of behaviour exclusive to classic comedy.

As Roman comedy concerns itself with sexual appetite rather than with love, it is necessarily far less limitedly occupied with young men and girls than is romantic comedy. It has its young men, of course; perhaps in mere number they preponderate, for after all they are the society of the future. They must be apprenticed to citizenship of the world, and of a very earthy and a very fleshly world. But the sowing of wild oats is an excellent discipline; and the amorous escapades of young bloods are to be condoned or even tacitly approved. Complacent indulgence could hardly exceed that of Demaenetus in the *Asinaria*. He will purchase his son's filial love by buying the son a mistress, even as he in his youth was supplied by his own father—and all of it, in the name of proper *pietas:*

praesertim quom is me dignum quoi concrederet
habuit, me habere honorem eius ingenio decet;
quom me adiit, ut pudentem gnatum aequomst patrem . . . et cetera
—(*Asinaria*, 80 ff.)

These pleasant disportings of undisciplined youth justify a mild reproach. Better still, they allow the comic dramatist to warn an inexperienced and full-blooded young fellow how properly to deal with, and not to be out-witted by, such mercenary social necessities as pimps. Terence, of course, would add that a young man is let loose amongst the bawds to learn to hate them: but that is Terence's nominal excuse for Plautus's habitual practice:

me reperisse, quo modo adolescentulus
meretricum ingenia et mores posset noscere:
mature ut quum cognorit, perpetuo oderit.
Quae dum foris sunt, nihil videtur mundius,
nec magis compositum quidquam nec magis elegans:
quae, cum amatore suo quum coenant, liguriunt.
harum videre ingluviem, sordes, inopiam.
—(*Eunuchus*, 931 ff.)

Young men, therefore, are naturally admitted to Roman comedy to exhibit their venial follies. But their right of entry differs greatly from that of the *jeune premier* into modern drama, who enters, not to be laughed at, but to be idolised as the perfect lover. Even if Plautus and Terence had known such a lover, they would have found almost insuperable material obstacles in the way of exhibiting him in his characteristic *milieu:* for social custom, and the theatrical imitation of it, rigidly prevented the free-born respectable girl from emerging openly into the normal intercourse of daily affairs. Girls who could be loved in the romantic sense were, therefore, excluded from Roman plays, and only those appear who may be solicited in the way of their trade. The real situation is not altered by the fact that, as a rule, dramatists claimed the privilege to discover at the end of the play that most of the girls they had taken from brothels had, in fact, been accidentally recruited to the profession by some mischance or other which had caused their respectable and free birth to remain hidden. Not infrequently, indeed, the dramatists asserted that they had preserved the chastity of these chosen inmates of houses of ill fame. But even the largest extension of such a purely theatrical convention hardly avails to alter the character of these young girls of Roman comedy. Here, at least, are no Silvias, no Perditas, no Mirandas. The two young girls, the Bacchides, for instance, for love of whom the gallant young heroes of the piece plan their stratagems, are doubtless charming prizes; but to win their young men, they trick these young men's fathers by an exhibition of extreme expertness in the enticing arts of professional solicitation. And Philenium, to secure whose love Argyrippus becomes the young hero of the *Asinaria*, not only plays a similar part by alluring his lascivious father into a compromising situation; she reveals her nature and her trade by the remark she jestingly throws after the old fool when his wife comes on them suddenly to drag him from her embraces—"de palla memento, amabo," "don't forget the dress you promised me, sweetheart" (*Asinaria*, 949), She is even truer to her craft in the jibe with which she follows this up; for, as the old lecher's wife orders him home, Philenium, enjoying his discomfiture, begs him to give her a kiss at least, before he goes: "da savium etiam prius quam abis," "just one kiss before we part." Most of the ladies of these plays are unashamedly bent on making the best bargains out of their casual and promiscuous lovers.

But the young men and the girls and their mutual loves were not the dramatist's main concern. They gave him a situation suited to his comic needs, but in themselves they were subsidiary, and might even be left out entirely. Casina gives her name to a play of which the nominal subject is the love of Euthynicus for her; but neither Casina nor Euthynicus appear even once in the play. Their complete exclusion is a little drastic even for classical comedy. Youth is by no means so barren a field in which to find folly. But, after all, there is no fool like an old fool. It is the old men who are prime favourites with classical dramatists. Even where the dominant interest brings the sexes together, a libidinous or merely amorous old man is richer matter for comedy than is a hot-blooded youth. Not that the world will be too hard on the occasional flings of an old man. Periplecomenus is the genial pattern of an old bachelor: but he prides himself that he retains sympathy with and capacity for these pleasures:—

> et ego amoris aliquantum habeo umorisque etiam in corpore
> neque dum exarui ex amoenis rebus et voluptariis.
> —(*Miles Gloriosus*, 639.)

Even old benedicts may be permitted casual aberrations, for such incidents are neither new nor wonderful nor uncommon nor unintelligible:—

> Hic senex si quid clam uxorem suo animo fecit volup,
> neque novom neque mirum fecit nec secus quam alii solent;
> nec quisquam est tam ingenio duro nec tam firmo pectore,
> quin ubi quicque occasionis sit sibi faciat bene.
> —(*Asinaria*, 942 ff.)

But the very tolerance made the dramatists more alert to pour contempt on excesses. The epilogue to the *Bacchides* preaches its moral. These old men have disgraced humanity, not because they have planned illicit loves, but because, instead of demeaning themselves decorously in licentiousness by taking mistresses in the open market, they have tried to commandeer their sons' light o' loves.

> Hi senes nisi fuissent nihili iam inde ab adulescentia,
> non hodie hoc tantum flagitium facerent canis capitibus;
> neque adeo haec faceremus, ni antehac vidissemus fieri,
> ut apud lenones rivales filiis fierent patres.
> —(*Bacchides*, 1207 ff.)

The general object of the dramatist's satire in these cases, and its particular point, are declared at the end of the *Mercator*:—

> Immo dicamus senibus legem censeo,
> prius quam abeamus, qua se lege teneant contentique sint.
> annos gnatus sexaginta qui erit, si quem scibimus
> si maritum sive hercle adeo caelibem scortarier,
> cum eo nos hac lege agemus: inscitum arbitrabimur,
> et per nos quidem hercle egebit qui suom prodegerit
> neu quisquam posthac prohibeto adulescentem filium
> quin amet et scortum ducat, quod bono fiat modo;
> siquis prohibuerit, plus perdet clam quasi praehibuerit palam.
> haec adeo ut ex hac nocte primum lex teneat senes.
> —(*Mercator*, 1015 ff.)

But the folly of an old fool not only emerges through his libidinousness. The very crabbedness of crabbed age is its passport into universal comedy; for such is its conventional characteristic, and it is a property alien by its very nature from the ends and the uses of society. Grumpiness, tyrannising, niggardliness, joy-killing—these are ills to which old age is particularly liable, and these are patently hostile to any and every notion of sociability. Wherefore old men are doubly qualified for the protagonist's rôle in Roman comedy.

The real significance of old men in classical comedy has been obscured by the gallivantings of its youngsters and by our habit of reading wrong values into these revelries. Their part would appear in truer light if they themselves could be extricated from the sensuality which spreads itself over all Roman comedy like a fog and distorts our view of it. But as no Roman dramatist has written for us a play in which such separation is consistent, it may not be amiss to construct a Roman comedy for ourselves.

Its main figure will be an old man, some old fool afflicted with a disease fatal to the health and vigour of social life. With the help of Molière, it is easy to diagnose, in the many unsocial symptoms of Plautus's and Terence's patients, one particularly virulent malady the effects of which, whilst not in themselves exhibiting lustfulness, are yet no less malignant to the well-being of society. Let our hero be a miser: for miserliness dams up the circulation of the material resources of life. As our protagonist, the miser is to be the man whose follies will move us to hilarious contempt. At the outset, there he sits on his money-bags, and our comedy, if it does not cure this covetous man of his covetousness, must at least make it plain to the audience that miserliness is a profitless occupation. The comedy must wrest the money-bags from the miser. An obvious device therefore would be to introduce a burglar as a character in the play. Bare theft is indeed not rare in Roman comedy; but it is not an ideal instrument; for the burglar is in fact as unsocial an institution as the miser. Something less anarchic than sheer robbery is desirable. What is needed is a figure, who, taking the money bags, will carry also the partial sympathy of the audience; some one who is merely anticipating a claim sanctioned by social custom. Give the old miser a son. So the young man enters the story. He does so, however, not in virtue of the general attractiveness of youth. His primary qualification for admission to the play is that, if he should need money, our audience will tacitly recognise in him some sort of right to his father's hoard. He must at all costs, therefore, be in need of money. Our plot may almost write itself for the next act. Young men are most in need of money when they are thinking of marrying and setting up house. Wherefore, let the miser's son find himself in that happy plight, and let him convince us of his passion for the lady by displaying the usual symptoms in manner and in word. But here is an unexpected quandary. He wants money to provide himself with a wife. He seeks our permission to help himself from the family chest; but, obviously, to secure our consent, he must produce the lady and assure us of her worthiness to be the occasion of a slightly irregular financial transaction. He cannot, however, present her to us: for any lady such as he might marry is strictly forbidden to make such a public appearance. Hence our plot cannot avail itself of any proposals for a genuine marriage. But our young man must need money; betrothals barred, he must be involved in a less proper situation, caught in the toils of the sort of woman he could not marry. Let him be mixed up in a liaison with some mistress or other. It may appear a much less reputable predicament: but it will at least extend the reach of our comic lash. Procurers and all who trade in sex will be additional material; and there will also be the advantage, that whilst furthering our young hero's schemes, we shall have occasion for administering suitable admonishment. Maybe, too, the predicament will more effectively serve our primary comic purpose: for the miser will endure a more bitter torment in seeing his wealth converted into necklets for a whore than in merely having to accept an anticipation of the post-mortem change of ownership from father to son.

So our scenario is complete. All now needed is a plot by which the old man's money may be transferred to assist the young man in his dilemma. A modern may find difficulty in contriving a suitable machinery for an operation of this sort. But at this point a Roman had no difficulty: he had a perfect mechanism ready-made for him. A distinctive feature of his social institutions provided him with an ideal instrument for the purpose, the particular domestic slave who acted as man-servant in the household. This person's office provided him with ample opportunity for attempts of the requisite kind, and his mode of life had produced in him the qualities of character, mind, and aptitude fitting him to execute the attempt expertly.

> Saepe ego res multas tibi mandavi, Milphio,
> dubias, egenas, inopiosas consili,
> quas tu sapienter, docte et cordate et cate
> mihi reddidisti opiparas opera tua.
> —(*Poenulus*, 129-132.)

Davus and his sort are therefore indispensable figures in Roman comedy. They are the contrivers of its plots. "Machinabor machinam" says one of them (*Bacchides*, 232). Like all of them, his special office is to engineer the intrigue. To succeed in this, he requires all the ingenuity, the unscrupulous cunning and the quick-witted shiftiness traditional in his kind. Chrysalus expounds the essentials of the craft:—

> nequius nil est quam egens consili servos, nisi
>   habet multipotens pectus:
> ubicumque usus siet, pectore expromat suo.
>   nullus frugi esse potest homo,
>   nisi qui et bene et male facere tenet.
> improbis cum improbus sit, harpaget furibus,
>   furetur quod queat,
>   vorsipellem frugi convenit esse hominem,
> pectus quoi sapit: bonus sit bonis, malus sit malis;
>   utcumque res sit, ita animum habeat.
> —(*Bacchides*, 651 ff.)

With a real artist's pride in his artfulness, he compares his achievements with those which brought fame in the Trojan war:—

> Atridae duo fratres cluent fecisse facinus maxumum,
> quom Priami patriam Pergamum divina moenitum manu
> armis, equis, exercitu atque eximiis bellatoribus
> mille cum numero navium decumo anno post subegerunt.
> non pedibus termento fuit praeut ego erum expugnabo meum
> sine classe sineque exercitu et tanto numero militum.
> —(*Ibid*, 925 ff.)

The sympathies of rascals like this will naturally turn them from their ageing master to his friskier son, in whose frolics they will find so many congenial pleasures. They will eagerly participate in his riotous drinking and drabbing. The gay life they could hope to lead in such circumstances is set out by one of the sedater sort in his reproach to Tranio, who is typical of the others:—

> nunc, dum tibi lubet licetque, pota, perde rem,
> corrumpe erilem adulescentem optumum;
> dies noctesque bibite, pergraecamini,
> amicas emite liberate, pascite
> parasitos, obsonate pollucibiliter.
>   —(*Mostellaria*, 20 ff.)

As a Tranio, a Davus, a Chrysalus so readily transfers his allegiance from his master to his master's son, our scene is ready set for the machinations that will form the intrigue for out-witting the old man, and will thus provide our play with its plot.

There is no Roman play quite like the one here outlined. But this is their type. This is the type which Shakespeare, borrow-ing his *Comedy of Errors* from the *Menæchmi* and *Amphitruo*, chose for his model. Yet, though he clung closely to Plautus, inevitably he lost much and changed still more of his originals. Transplanting stories to other societies in other and later periods of time is bound to sever them from that which gives them their essential significance. Moreover, these Roman stories are so closely built into the fabric of Roman society and its mind, that a transference of the mere story carries over with it elements, incidents, or scenes, which must remain alien in their new homes. In particular there are these all-important men-servants. The English bourgeoisie of the sixteenth-century had no exact counterpart of them in their households. Hence the Dromios are exotic on the English stage. In Eng-land, menial servants who are soundly kicked at frequent inter-vals are hardly likely to be taken into the confidential personal secrets of the masters; nor does one expect to find such pantry boys whiling away their leisure with sixth-form dissipations. There are, however, moments when their kitchen gossip brings the Dromios nearer home, and the fat cook's amorousness almost domesticates one of the Dromios permanently in England (*Comedy of Errors*, III. iii.). But though she haunted him, he escaped from her and ran back into the theatrical convention in which alone he has his existence. There is spontaneous roguishness in the way in which Dromio of Ephesus, as the climax to his account of the supposed husband's misdemeanours, adds to the husband's words an unspoken and allround contempt for the wife to whom Dromio is telling the tale—"hang up thy mistress" (II. i. 68). But for the rest, if Maud, Bridget, Marion, Cicely, Gillian, and Ginn had been allowed to show themselves at Dromio's call (III. i. 31), neither he nor his brother would have survived comparison with the real native article. Even as merely theatrical conventions, the Dromios are but shadows of their dramatic originals. In their new surroundings on an English stage, circumstance scarcely ever allows them to be the engineers of the story. Almost invariably, they are merely its clowns.

With less important persons of the Plautine plays, figures whose rôle is merely incidental, Shakespeare may effect a complete anglicisation. The man in buff, for instance, and Pinch the quack, are straight from the streets of London. But general naturalisation is impossible. Many of the favoured incidents, which make a Roman intrigue, lose all semblance of credibility when assembled in a modern play. Loss of children by shipwreck, drastic penal laws to safeguard petty economic systems, summary courts of justice at the street-corner—these are details harder to bring to life on a London stage than on one in ancient Rome.

But in taking his story from Plautus, Shakespeare frankly accepted all these limitations. The Dromios are mere stage clowns. Ephesus is a town where Lapland witches delight in playing spookish tricks on men and women. Farce expands to extravaganza. To give the farcical a larger scope, Shakespeare doubled the source of it in Plautus by providing twin Dromios for the twin Antipholi he took from his Roman original. The plot becomes a sort of mathematical exhibition of the maximum number of erroneous combinations of four people taken in pairs. The bustle leaves no room for characterisation, the persons in it enduring their lot as in a nightmare. Even the stock-types of the original are largely useless. The parasite, Peniculus, in Plautus was a genuine property of the Roman stage, and therefore Shakespeare dropped him overboard *en route*, as he would have been an utter foreigner in Elizabethan England. In one point only did the English dramatist find that he could import something of the social application of the Latin play.

In the *Menæchmi*, Plautus plays lightly with the folly of shrewish wives. It is a common theme in Roman comedy. It was an almost inevitable outcome of their marriage system: marriages were marriages of convenience, the wife bringing with her a dowry over which she retained control, and, though divorces were easily procurable, when a rejected wife returned to her parents, she took her dowry back with her. Such marriages must often have proved unhappy bargains; but release was an expensive luxury. Most of the husbands in Roman plays grumble at their hard lot. Demænetus complains that when he married, he sold his liberty: "argentum accepi, dote imperium vendidi" (*Asinaria*, 87); and Simo describes the inevitable consequence:—

> Quom magis cogito cum meo animo:
> si quis dotatam uxorem atque anum habet,
> neminem sollicitat sopor: ibi omnibus
> ire dormitum odio est.
> —(*Mostellaria*, 702 ff.)

Every husband in Plautus seems to have a nagging, shrewish, wife. And genial old bachelors like Periplecomenus rejoice that though with their own riches they could have wived it wealthily, they have been frightened off marrying, lest they should find themselves housed with a yapping bitch—"sed nolo mi oblatratricem in aedis intro mittere" (*Miles Gloriosus*, 681). Free from them himself, Periplecomenus can present a lively picture of the daily torments a husband must endure.

In the play to which Shakespeare turned for his *Comedy of Errors*, there is a wife and she is, of course, something of a shrew. But she is only half-heartedly so. She is, however, reprimanded for her behaviour; and, very significantly, the reprimand comes from the mouth of her own father. He has obviously more sympathy with the husband than with his daughter. He reminds her that it is her duty to be grateful for the material comforts her husband provides for her:—

> quando te auratam et vestitam bene habet, ancillas penum
> recte praehibet, melius sanam est, mulier, mentem sumere.
> —(*Menœchmi*, 801 ff.)

As a father, he reminds her, he has frequently had to urge her to be complacent, not to spy and pry into her husband's affairs:—

> Quotiens monstravi tibi, viro ut morem geras,
> quid ille faciat, ne id observes, quo eat, quid rerum gerat.
> —(*Ibid.*, 787 ff.)

He goes so far as explicitly to approve of the husband's resort to a courtesan in retaliation for his wife's nagging, adding that to complain about the particular sort of pleasure he has chosen is to treat him as one would treat a slave! Only when the wife adds that the husband is stealing her property to provide presents for his mistress, does the old man find the husband clearly in the wrong. The attitude of mind is characteristic. He rebuked his daughter for her feminine inability to understand the material situation: by her blindness to the economic principles of house-keeping, she was causing an uneconomic distribution of the household's wealth between wife and courtesan.

But when a story embodying a situation like this of the *Menæchmi* is brought into sixteenth-century England, it has ceased to be a problem of domestic economy. The question of fidelity in wedlock is primary: and as the plot involves infidelity, Shakespeare is compelled to provide Antipholus with more immediate provocation for his lapse. So he draws on another play, the *Amphitruo*, and only allows Antipholus to resort to the courtesan when he has been locked out of his own house by his own wife who at the moment is entertaining a man whom she mistakenly assumes to be no other than her own husband. But even so, in the English play, the husband's drastic retaliation calls for a much greater emphasis on the shrewishness of his wife, Adriana, than appears in the Plautine counterpart.

Shakespeare's Adriana is doubtless shrew, virago and vixen to boot. She breaks the servants' pates across, though that hardly gives her characteristic distinction in a play in which fisticuffs are the regular means of intercourse. She rails at bed and board, and jealousy gives venom to her clamours, adding to them a virulence of which Plautus could scarcely avail himself, for it is only love in the modern sense "which is full of jealousy." An English shrew, moreover, much more than a Roman one, is hampered by memories of the affection she once had for the man of her choice. Adriana even fondles at times. But her single lapse into the broken-hearted bride who will weep and die in tears is a fall both from type and from character. A more credibly humanising trait appears in her excited enlargement of the tale of her husband's frenzied acts: the duke is treated to a display of rumour's growth, as facts swell with fancy when she recounts the incidents she thought she had seen (V. i. 136 ff.). Yet at the end of the play, the shrew is not so much out of countenance as she was meant to be. One cannot but remember that the person solemnly reproving Adriana for her shrewishness is not, as in Plautus, her own natural parent, but her mother-in-law. Nor does her husband appear to suffer much spiritual disquiet from her moods. A

man who conducts a domestic tiff by calling his wife a dissemb-
ling harlot, and by threats to pluck out her eyes, is not too sensitive a fellow and has a sufficient protection in the thickness of
his skin. Indeed, the general temper of the life depicted in *The
Comedy of Errors* is so crude, coarse, and brutal, that Adriana's
fault appears to be not so much her shrewishness as her undip-
lomatic use of it. Even the abbess accuses her of nothing more
heinous than bad tactics:—

> In food, in sport, and life-preserving rest
> To be disturb'd, would mad or man or beast:
> The consequence is then thy jealous fits
> Have scared thy husband from the use of wits.
> —(V. i. 83 ff.)

But there is one person in the scene for whom this explanation is entirely inadequate. Luciana, sister of Adriana, breaks in
on the abbess's reproaches:—

> She never reprehended him but mildly,
> When he demean'd himself rough, rude and wildly.
> Why bear you these rebukes and answer not?

The challenge is exactly what the woman of to-day would
urge. Yet in the rest of the play, though it is our sentimental
sympathy with Luciana which has reflected on Adriana a deeper
condemnation than has any of the formal charges laid against
her, our sympathy with Luciana is not in the least founded on
a concurrence in her explicit propositions about the relationship of man and wife. It is indeed Adriana who speaks with the
voice of to-day in these matters. "Why should man's liberty
than our's be more?" she asks her sister, adding that none but
asses will be bridled in such fashion by their husbands' will.
But this is Luciana's creed:—

> There's nothing situate under heaven's eye
> But hath his bound, in earth, in sea, in sky:
> The beasts, the fishes and the winged fowls
> Are their males' subjects and at their controls:

> Men, more divine, the masters of all these,
> Lords of the wide world and wild watery seas,
> Indued with intellectual sense and souls,
> Of more pre-eminence than fish and fowls,
> Are masters to their females, and their lords.
> Then let your will attend on their accords.
> —(II. i. 15 ff.)

No mortal in this world of ours now would venture to swear
by such a creed: nor could a subject of Queen Elizabeth have
easily dared to do so. And yet though Luciana's terms are
mere relics of the past, she secures from the moderns more
instinctive sympathy than does her sister, despite the almost
Georgian modernity of Adriana's views on conjugal equality.
For Luciana brings into the play a range of sentiment utterly
incompatible with the atmosphere of this *Comedy of Errors.*
When Antipholus of Syracuse woos her as

> mine own self's better part
> Mine eye's clear eye, my dear heart's dearest heart,
> My food, my fortune, and my sweet hope's arm,
> My sole earth's heaven, and my heaven's claim.
> —(III. ii. 61 ff.)

he is putting into words a way of looking on the relationship of
man and woman different fundamentally from the point of
view expressed in Roman comedy and in its English imitations.
Between Plautus and Luciana are the centuries in which
chivalry and its achievements in life and letters had evolved the
love which, like God, makes earth and man anew. The world
which is enshrined in mediæval romance was embedded in the
inherited experience of the sixteenth century. Even when he
was recoiling from romanticism, Shakespeare could not divest
himself of the romantic. And so these alien elements are stuffed
within his imitation of a classical play. Adriana is the shrew
realistically sketched in the routine of housewifery, complain-
ing, bullying servants, seeing to dinner, and querulously shout-
ing her troubles to the street. Luciana is a singing mermaid,

spreading o'er the silver waves the echoes of her song and wisps of golden hair as a bed whereon her love may lie. Not even Shakespeare can make sisters of two such beings. They are of different family, and indeed of different race, if not of different species.

But Luciana is not the only romantic intruder into the gross Roman world of the *Comedy of Errors*. Old Ægeon and the abbess never lived in Rome. The father in the Plautine story died when he lost his sons, and not a word is heard of their mother. But Shakespeare's Ægeon brings into the story memories of tragic instances of harm reaching all but to the extremity of dire mishap. With echoes of mortal and intestine jars, he strikes a full note of pathos, the pity of age, and suffering, and frustrated hope. And these are plangent cries with which the heedless rollicking brutality of the comedy makes nothing but discord. Old men in Ægeon's sad situation are not unfamiliar to Roman comedy. But children were lost in Plautus, not to provide him with exhibitions of broken-hearted parents: they were lost simply that their finding might restore social status to such of the girls in a brothel as his young fellows might wish to marry. The old parent and his broken heart are useless to Plautus. As a rule, he will not even allow the bereaved parent a place in the play: and when he does, it is a parent who carries his bereavement lightly. There is Daemones, for instance, in *Rudens*, who has lost his daughter in infancy. The play tells of her miraculous restoration to him— or rather to the young man who has fallen in love with her whilst she was in the keeping of an old procurer. But as old Daemones has a wife, he has to be a Plautine husband, playing his part in the traditional comedy of the shrew, and presenting his wife as a prating torment:—

> redeo domum.
> iam mens opplebit aures sua vaniloquentia.
> —(*Rudens*, 904 ff.)

Clearly, there can be no pathetic and romantic picture of the reunion of a lost daughter to a man like Daemones for whom there are no domestic sanctities at all. When the daughter is restored, we hear him commenting on his wife's revolting behaviour: she is even hugging and kissing the child so marvellously brought back to her as from the grave:

> quid conspicor?
> uxor complexa collo retinet filiam.
> nimis paene inepta atque odiosa eius amatiost.
> —(*Rudens*, 1202 ff.)

As there is neither the love of romanticism in Plautus, so neither is there its pity, except for the little of it which oddly creeps in to that abnormal play, the *Captivi*. But as love, so pity comes incongruously into the *Comedy of Errors*. Doubtless, much of the incongruity is hidden by Shakespeare's adroit use of Ægeon, who is not so much a figure in the play as a prologue and an epilogue to it. But at odd moments, the incongruity obtrudes itself. One is stupefied to learn that Antipholus of Ephesus, the thick-skinned man-about-town, has rendered knightly service in the field to his feudal overlord, bestriding him in battle, and taking in this deed of chivalric devotion, as deep a scar as ever hero won in mediæval romance.

> Justice, most gracious duke, O, grant me justice!
> Even for the service that long since I did thee,
> When I bestrid thee in the wars, and took
> Deep scars to save thy life: even for the blood
> That then I lost for thee, now grant me justice.
> —(V. i. 190 ff.)

The *Comedy of Errors* is indeed a recoil, but a recoil which amply indicates that the recoiler will soon be turned again towards romance. It is in his blood and in the spirit of his times. The problem of reconciling romance and comedy was not to be avoided. It would have to be faced.

IV

The Taming of the Shrew

I HAVE put myself down to talk to you to-night on *The Taming of the Shrew*. It is the third of Shakespeare's early comedies which I have been privileged to make the subject of a Rylands lecture. For this occasion, therefore, I have presumed to take liberties with the advertised topic. Instead of presenting to you a general view of all the more important critical questions which emerge from *The Taming of the Shrew*, I have sought to use the play only as a further development of the argument I tried to lay down in my previous lectures to you, to make my treatment of it, if the arrogance of the claim be overlooked, the third chapter in a study of the evolution of Shakespearian comedy. Hence I have jettisoned much which the fashion of current Shakespearian scholarship makes most interesting in *The Taming of the Shrew*, and have, for instance, allowed myself no concern with the textual problems which are raised by the play. I mention this in particular, because, although my argument will require me to make use of another play of shrew-taming, *The Taming of A Shrew* as well as of Shakespeare's *Taming of the Shrew*, I shall entirely omit any consideration of their textual relationship, occupying myself exclusively with the way they stand to each other in the idea of comedy. Fortunately, the proposition I shall put forward does not appear to depend at all on whether one accepts the modern view (and I confess myself unpersuaded) that *A Shrew* is a textual adaptation of Shakespeare's play, or whether one retains the older opinion that *A Shrew* is an older play which

Shakespeare used as a source for *The Shrew*. And if in phrase I may seem to assume a historical priority for *A Shrew*, I trust that such an assumption has been without influence in my general argument. Similarly I have assumed that *The Taming of the Shrew* is Shakespeare's play; and though for my own part I am disposed to lament the concessions which such a stalwart as Sir E. K. Chambers has made to the disintegrators of Shakespeare, again I am not aware that my faith in it as a play by Shakespeare has any essential bearing on my handling of it for the present purpose.

That purpose, briefly, is to consider what light is thrown by the *Shrew* play on the growth of Elizabethan comedy, and in particular to see how far it carries Shakespeare towards the idea of comedy which he realised most triumphantly with such of his maturest achievements in comedy as *Twelfth Night*, *As You Like It*, and *Much Ado*. Though there is ample justification for our continuing to label as romantic comedies these consummate embodiments of the Shakespearian comic spirit, the romanticism in them has been submitted to a severe discipline since it wrought such dramatic havoc as we found in *The Two Gentlemen of Verona*: it has indeed made its submission to that tradition which ancient Roman dramatists passed on to modern Europe, but it has secured such concessions in the settlement as amply satisfy its own romantic intuition. England and Shakespeare obtained the best terms possible in this compromise between Renaissance romance and the enduring classical realism which still persists through and informs the comedy of twentieth-century Europe. England drove the hardest bargain: but other European countries were consciously or unconsciously affecting in their own comedies the compromise between romanticism as they felt it in their own time and the dominant classicism or the enduring realism embodied in comedy as it had come to them. The history of sixteenth-century comedy in Europe is a record of the encroachment of romance on the ancient domain of comedy. But the invasion is almost entirely the result of circumstance, and hardly at all the consequence of deliberate attack. The gap between Plautus and *Twelfth Night* seems at first an unbridgeable chasm severing irreconcilable opposites. But, in fact, the way from one to the other was solidly laid by dramatists who never realised how far circumstances were leading them from the beaten track. When Bibbiena in his *Calandria* (1513), whilst modern comedy was in its swaddling clouts, seized on the Plautine motive of lost twins, he took the first decisive step towards Shakespeare by making a boy and a girl twin out of Plautus's boy twins.

This may sound like a cryptic or a paradoxical remark, or even a ludicrous proposition, in view of the palpable differences between the comedy of Shakespeare and that of Plautus. In spirit, the Latin type is realistic, satiric, earthy; Shakespeare's, poetic, sentimental, romantic. Plautus is full of sex; Shakespeare is all for love. Plautus weaves plots of cunning intrigue; Shakespeare chooses simple tales of wooers and their wooing, "it was a lover and his lass." In the people of their plays there is striking difference in the types characteristic of the one and of the other, and an equally marked difference in the characteristic importance assumed by corresponding figures in the two sorts of play. With Plautus, it is the old men and the rascally men-servants who come first to mind: then the young sparks lusting for illicit liaisons or trafficking without delicacy for possession of attractive concubines; and the girls they pursue flit across the scene, mere accessories to the plot, permitted to make our personal acquaintance only in direct proportion with the extent of their alleged impropriety. In Shakespeare all is different. Old men withdraw to the wings. Cunning servants, deprived by his plots of extensive opportunity to acquire skill in scheming, survive mainly as natural clowns. It is the young folk who occupy the centre of his stage, and the hero, gaining grace in the mysteries of wooing, discards many of the traits of his Plautine ancestor, and replaces them by the finer susceptibilities of feeling, the nobility of mind, and the sweetness of soul which more closely reflect the romantic ideal of manhood. An even greater change is suffered by the girls of the older tradition. They are transmuted both in quality and in significance. They are promoted from super-numerary parts to play the all-important rôle,—the heroine, in the technical sense, now first emerges. Moreover, that she may worthily acquit herself in her new office, she is gradually taking on a personality for which the whole of ancient comedy had no proximate parallel. The clue to the history of sixteenth-century comedy is to watch for this heroine's appearance in its drama, to follow her through the century, noticing how she increases her sway over the plays in which she appears, and how, as time goes on, she acquires those qualities of hand, of heart, and of head which are at length to be most magisterially embodied in a Rosalind, a Beatrice, or a Viola. For then the heroine has in fact become the very incarnation of the spirit of Shakespeare's comedy.

This is the process by which Elizabethan comedy evolved. In manner, it was largely unconscious, but in determining its direction, the part played by the comic dramatists of Italy has hardly received adequate notice. However, *The Taming of the Shrew* directly prompts an attempt to estimate Italy's share in the formation of a type of comedy like the romantic variety which our Elizabethans made peculiarly their own. The sub-plot of *The Shrew* is one of the few English plots immediately traceable to a sixteenth-century Italian comedy. The Bianca episodes in *The Taming* are taken over either straight from Ariosto's *Suppositi* (1509) or from Gascoigne's English version *The Supposes* (1573-75).

At the outset, however, it is well to remember that no Englishman reading *The Taming of the Shrew* would at first incline to think of it as having any conceivable bearing on the development of any kind of comedy which could be called romantic. Its prevailing temper is so rollickingly anti-romantic that one may well take it as Shakespeare's boisterous revenge on the romantic spirit which had led him the terrible dance he had trod in *The Two Gentlemen of Verona*. One might indeed be persuaded to regard *The Shrew* as Shakespeare's antidote to his *Two Gentlemen*. Valentine in the latter avows his capacity to dine, sup, and sleep upon the very naked name of love. But in *The Shrew*, such ambrosial menus are unknown. From beginning to end there is a hearty appetite for bread, beef, and beer. Sly knows by instinct that a pot of even the smallest ale is no inconsiderable item of well-being; stone jugs and duly sealed quarts are the palpable pillars of his universe. Petruchio, too, has a native intuition of the stomach's sway, and a sure sense of its strategic uses; he deploys adroitly the promise of good eating and drinking. But most marked of all is Gremio's instinct for gastronomical realities. He is the forlorn suitor, rejected by his lady and mocked by his rivals. But his broken heart is amenable to culinary recipes; and we take leave of him at the end of *The Shrew*, reconciled to the loss of a lady by the prospect of a feast, stumping off eagerly, though it be to the wedding breakfast of his fortunate rival.

> "My cake is dough; but I'll in among the rest;
> Out of hope of all but my share of the feast."

Although he is cast for a dotard, Gremio excellently serves our immediate purpose. For he belongs, not to the story of Katherine's violently unromantic taming, but to the germinally romantic story of the wooing of Katherine's sister, Bianca. It is this wooing which forms the sub-plot of the Shakespearian play; and it is this which Shakespeare took from Italy. This is the part of *The Taming of the Shrew* which links it most closely to the development of sixteenth-century comedy in Europe.

There are in English three dramatic handlings of this tale. There is Gascoigne's translation of Ariosto's *Suppositi* in which it is the main and only plot. There is *The Taming of A Shrew*, in which it is substantially the main plot, bulkier than the other set side by side with it, the plot of the taming of her ladyship's sister. And there is Shakespeare's *Taming of the Shrew*, in which the wooing of the Shrew's sister is a sub-plot, of which the subsidiary nature is more evident in its quality and its function than in its bulk, for although it suffers little diminution in length as compared with its size in *A Shrew* it is markedly subdued to the temper of the main taming plot. Between them, these versions offer a unique illustration of the progress of sixteenth-century comedy and of the circumstances most vitally effecting that progress.

Of the first of these plays, *The Supposes*, there are, so to speak, four texts. Ariosto wrote it first in prose, calling it *Gli Soppositi*, and in that form it was acted in 1509. Later he re-wrote it in verse, this time under the title *I Suppositi*. Gascoigne, knowing and using both the verse and prose versions of the original, made his translation, *The Supposes*, which was acted in 1566, published pseudo-surreptitiously in 1572 or '73, and this text, "corrected, perfected, and augmented by the Authour," was issued again in *The Posies of George Gascoigne*, 1575. We need not, however, concern ourselves with these bibliographical differences. For our purpose, the four versions are one play, and that one play will adequately illustrate the circumstances in which Renaissance comedy was born.

Ariosto's *Supposes* is primarily a play of masquerading, the plot turning on a scheme of disguise to bring about mistakes in identity, whereby a young man may secure access to his mistress. The young man changes place and clothes with his own servant; then hires himself as a servant into the household of his mistress's father. When the play opens, this liaison has subsisted in secret for a considerable time. But it is now threatened with exposure; an elderly and wealthy suitor has found favour with the girl's father, and the plan for playing against him another pretended suitor (in reality the young man's disguised servant) is becoming more difficult to main-tain, for the father of the young man himself is shortly due to arrive. Here clearly is much Plautine and Terentian matter: "vi confessa," wrote Ariosto in his *Prologue*, "vi confessa l'autore havere in questo et Plauto et Terentio seguitato." The plot is a succession of dilemmas from which only cunning devices and intrigues can rescue the hero. In temper, too, it is sufficiently classical; and though one need not be alarmed to find that its first performance was at the charges of a Cardinal, one is somewhat surprised to learn that a spectator, reporting the performance to a distinguished lady, the Marchioness of Mantua, strongly recommended the play to her as "piena di moralità." For though its dialogue is comparatively inoffensive, the whole situation depends on securing the sympathy of the audience for clandestine lovers whose love has dispensed with the normal sanctions of the moral code.

The Supposes does not, indeed, break very considerably from the Latin comic tradition. But there are features in it which point to the future. It is, for instance, a play of love rather than of sex: the lovers mean honest matrimony and would welcome the ceremony which circumstance forbids. It is, however, not a play of wooing. The young people had lived in irregular union for some time, and in the play itself there is not a single scene in which they are together. Yet there is in the play something of the comedy of wooers; the lady has three wooers,— her unofficial husband, his servant who is pretending to woo, and the third, the traditional elderly lover of the comic stage, deprived, however, of the goatishness, if not of the folly, of that genus. Clearly, modern sentiment has not eaten deeply into Ariosto's play. Even so, it has at least brought about certain changes which are making along the line of the future development of comedy. The germ of romanticism is beginning to leaven the classical tradition. The heroine is not yet installed; but she is beginning to qualify herself for the part: "it pitieth me to see the poore yong woman how she weepes, wailes, and teares hir heare: not esteming hir owne life halfe so deare as she doth poore Dulipos; and hir father, he weepes on the other side that it would pearce an hart of stone with pitie" (Act III, sc. v). And she has already earned a public reputation altogether different from the kind which any of Plautus's girls could have claimed or would, indeed, have aspired to: "Aske the neighbours, and you shall heare very good report of hir: marke hir behaviors, and you would have judged hir very maydenly; seldome seene abroade but in place of prayer and there very devout, and no gaser at outwarde sightes, no blaser of hir beautie above in the windowes, no stale at the doore for the bypassers: you would have thought hir a holy yong woman" (Act III, sc. iv). Moreover, though older folks bulk as largely in Ariosto's play as in Latin drama, and often, too, for the same comic purpose, that is, to be gulled in the interests of gaiety, yet one or two of them here have affections and sentiments which anticipate the more benign function to be found for them in future comedies. Naturally one will not expect a Countess Rousillion or a Lafeu; for to no motive did the comic tradition stick more tenaciously than to this of the folly of old fools. But the father of Ariosto's young man shows the metamorphosis beginning. He tells of the plans he had had for his son: "I thinking that by that time he had sene the worlde, he would learne to know himselfe better, exhorted him to studie, and put in his election what place he would go to. At the last he came hither, and I thinke he was scarce here so sone as I felt the want of him, in suche sorte as from that day to this I have passed fewe nightes without teares. I have written to him very often that he shoulde come home. . . . I would not be without the sighte of hym againe so long for all the learning in the worlde. I am olde nowe, and if God shoulde call mee in his absence, I promise you I thinke it woulde drive me into disperation" (Act IV, sc. iv). The young lady's father, too, is different. He is not merely enraged at his daughter's seduction, he is heartbroken by it, in the modern way: "Yea, what should it prevayle me to use all the punishments that can be devised? the thing once done can not be undone. My daughter is defloured, and I utterly dishonested: how can I then wype that blot off my browe? and on whome shall I seeke revenge? alas, alas, I myselfe have bene the cause of all these cares, and have deserved to beare the punishment of all these mishappes. Alas, I should not have committed my dearest darling in custodie to so carelesse a creature as this olde Nurse: for we see by common proofe that these olde women be either peevishe or pitifull: either easily enclined to evill, or quickly corrupted with bribes and rewards. O wife, my good wife (that nowe lyest colde in the grave), now may I well bewayle the wante of thee, and mourning nowe may I bemone that I misse thee! If thou hadst liven (suche was thy governe-ment of the least things) that thou wouldest prudently have provided for the preservation of this pearle . . . etc." (Act III, sc. iii). Even the man-servant of *The Supposes*, required by the plot for the Davus-like trick of fooling his old master for the profit of his young one, is given to quite un-Plautine qualms of conscience and sentiment: "Alas, he that of a litle childe hath brought me up unto this day, and nourished me as if I had bene his owne: and in deede (to confesse the trouth) I have no father to trust unto but him" (Act V, sc. i).

Clearly, changed habits of mind and different ideals of con-duct are inevitably creeping into sixteenth-century plays; and though at the outset the traditional classical machinery of the comedies will confine their action to devising assignations, out-witting rivals, and overcoming other material obstacles, they will in time throw off the formal inheritance which denies them opportunities to exhibit the whole ritual of wooing, and to express the spiritual ecstasies of the beloved. So far at least, they are providing the situations which in due course will serve as an essential setting for romance. The process will naturally be gradual and largely unintentional. One can indeed see developments of that kind even within the course of Ariosto's brief career as a comic dramatist; and the *Scolastica* which he left unfinished might have led him to an even more clearly romanticised completion than the one which was given to it by his son. Here, at all events, love was discovering its own romantic terms, and the heroine was growing in the grace by which she would reach her romantic triumph in the future.

The future clearly was with her. It is doubtless very difficult nowadays for us to realise how serious were the obstacles which stood in the way of woman's power over comedy. We recognise her dominion in Shakespeare's maturest comedies,

and take our Rosalinds and our Violas for granted. Sometimes a Beatrice, by the plenitude of her wit, the adroitness of
her intellect and her relative independence of what we choose
to call the attributes of femininity, leads us to suggest, half-
mazedly, half-apologetically, that Shakespeare's women were
made to be played by boys. But such implication of restraint
is in part delusory, and in part inadequate. It is a general plea
that the girls of Plautus were what they were because no
Roman could present a decent girl in the spectacle of public
life required by the stage-conventions of his day. Thinking of
famous or notorious women of the sixteenth century, Tudors
or Borgias or Medicis, Duchesses of Malfi or Moll Cutpurses,
knowing, too, of Renaissance ideals in the education of
women, one is disposed to assume that sufficient emancipation
was a recognised fact of the social system. Yet even in Italy,
which was giving Europe the first of its modern women,
dramatists were still hampered by the persistence of older
taboos both in the traditions of drama and in the conventions
of society. The emergence of the heroine was still impeded by
the conscious and unconscious habits of the general will. Even
as late as the middle of the century, one of the acutest of Italian
men of letters, Cinthio, who was critic and dramatist, comedian
and tragedian, and whose critical insight had much to do in
determining the direction of sixteenth-century tragedy in Italy
and thence in Europe, recognised the difficulty and sought a
way out of it. In his *Discorso sulle Commedie e sulle Tragedie*
(1554) he records that in comedy it is as an article of religion
("serva la comedia una certa religione") that no well-born,
well-mannered, and innocent girl shall be allowed to act and
speak in the play. He admits that there is ample warrant for the
proscription, since in the main comedy traffics with the lasciviousness of disreputable folks—"e però non pare che convenga
al decoro di una giovane vergine, venire a favellare in tale
scena, e tra queste persone." Even if a particular comedy is
without the customary nastiness of matter, the prohibition still
holds: "e ancora che la comedia fosse onestissima, come noi

veggiamo essere i Captivi di Plauto, non vi s'introdurrebbe anco vergine alcuna; perchè è già così impressa negli animi degli uomini che la comedia porti con esso lei questi sorti di genti, e questi modi di favellare, pieni di licenza che ciò non sarebbe senza pregiudizio della polcella." But Cinthio had already urged that tragedies on ancient themes would not strike directly to the hearts of his contemporaries; they must reject ancient mythologies and turn to more vital sources in contemporary love-stories. A critic like this was not likely to accept a perpetual prohibition of romantic tales of lovers from the scope of contemporary comedy. He had, incidentally, protested against Bibbiena's perpetuation of the ancient Roman trick of making the elderly lover a senile idiot: "dee adunque l'amor del vecchio non esser di mal essempio. E quantunque sià egli innamorato e cerchi di goder della cosa amata, non gli si debbono però far far quelle sciocchezze per venire al fine del suo amore che fe' fare al suo Calandro il Bibbiena, e hanno dopo lui fatto alcuni altri de'nostri tempi, perchè è fuori di quel che conviene." Naturally, one who had qualms about profaning the display of love even when it was an old man's passion, would eagerly seek for opportunity to exhibit it in its congenial atmosphere, the ideal passion of noble girl. His solution was, in effect, the establishment of tragi-comedy, the acceptance of plays he calls "tragedie di felice fine," "tragedie liete," tragedies with a happy ending. "E non tengo io biasimevole che'n questa specie di tragedie vergine reale sfoghi in iscena da sè (per esser tutta la scena di persone grandi, e per farsi per la maggior parte le cose nella corte) le passioni amorose, dogliendosi o lamentandosi onestamente." Plays of this kind are really Italy's nearest approach to our English romantic comedy: Greene's *James IV. of Scotland* is built on one of Cinthio's own novels, just as Cinthio himself dramatised certain of his own prose tales. In these, the heroine had full dignity of status and the whole armoury of romantic charm. She had, however, paid for her admission to the stage in such dignified company by forswearing the simpler, more natural, more domestic, and even more worldly attributes which are an indispensable part of the power of Shakespeare's heroines in comedy.

Cinthio conferred a stage-right on the romantic heroine, and went some way towards equipping her to exercise it effectively, though, on a mere matter of terminology, he still regarded comedy as outside her liberty. One has therefore to see how she fared in comedy itself. Ariosto's immediate successors, like Bibbiena and Machiavelli, can hardly be said to mark any decisive change. The motive of sex-disguise used by Bibbiena in his *Calandria*, whereby twin brother and sister each dresses in the clothes of the other sex, is not employed by the dramatist to evoke particularly romantic sentiments, though future borrowers of the device found it a prolific source of such congenial material. Bibbiena's hero can pay tribute to the new sense of love—"i compagni d'amore sono ira, odii, inimicizie, discordie, ruine, povertà, suspezione, inquietudine, morbi perniziosi nelli animi de' mortali. . . . Alla potenzia sua ogni cosa è suggetta. E non è maggior dolcezza che acquistare quel che si desidera in amore, senza il quale non è cosa alcuna perfetta nè virtuosa nè gentile" (Act I, sc. ii). But the idealism is mainly the matter of a few phrases. The hero is carrying on an intrigue with a married woman, who in her turn can also utter the hallowed phrases, but she is almost Plautine in her plans to make for her own son a marriage which will give her lover ampler opportunity to enjoy her company.

Nor will one expect much concession to romantic sentiment in the comedies of Machiavelli. His merit rests rather in the sting of his satire, and for this he found the older Roman tradition a sufficient comic instrument. But even Machiavelli endeavours to add a kind of moral recommendation to the unmoral figures he takes over from his Latin models. His *Clizia*, for instance, is the *Casina* of Plautus: but the young hero of it is not only given a much more extensive part to play, he is also favoured by a persistent moral justification. In his most effective comedy, *Mandragola*, Machiavelli's story is as salacious as antiquity had demanded. But the lascivious persons in it are not held out for our approval; their doings are generally the occasion for direct satire. The plot tells how a husband is duped into urging his wife to accept the embraces of a lover; and it is at least significant of the times that Machiavelli, who could easily have made the wife a conventional consenting party, is at pains to have her trapped into innocent infidelity by the lying injunctions of her confessor.

It is in these ways that the prevailing sentiments and the current ideals of society were gradually creeping into comedy. In the upshot they transformed its governing spirit. Hardly ever are serious changes in Italian comedy consciously instituted. Yet in a generation or so, dramatists saw that the plays they were writing were in a sense new dramatic kinds. A dramatist like Gelli admits in the dedication to his *La Sporta* (1543) that he imitates Plautus as much as is possible ("il quale io ho il più ch'io posso imitato"); he confesses in the Prologue that there is ground for saying "ch'egli ha tolto a Plauto e Terenzio la maggior parte de le cose che ci sono." But he immediately goes on to say that he brings into his play nothing but things which are a common feature of the life of his own time ("non tratta d'altro che di cose che tutto'l giorno accaggiono al viver nostro"). He commends himself especially for omitting such things as the conventional mistaken identities and the recoveries of long lost children. "Non ci vedrete riconoscimenti di giovani o di fanciulle, che oggidì non occorre." In practice, however, his plays are not dissimilar from those of his contemporaries—and they are the majority— who acclaim themselves for novelty, and for not stealing from Plautus and Terence. Occasionally their plea has considerable substance in it. Grazzini, for instance, in almost all his prologues, attacks those who stick to the mechanical devices and conventional situations of Latin comedy. He claims credit for his *Gelosia*, "perchè in essa non sono ritrovamenti. Chè, a dirne il vero, è gran cosa, gran meraviglia, anzi grandissimo miracolo, che di quante comedie nuove dallo assedio in qua, o publicamente o privatamente si sono recitate in Firenze, in tutte quante intervengano ritruovi, tutte forniscano in ritrovamenti: la qual cosa è tanto venuta a noja e in fastidio ai popoli, che, come sentano nell'argomento dire che nella presa d'alcuna città o nel sacco di qualche castello si siano smarrite o perdute bambine o fanciulli, fanno conto d'averle udite, e volentieri, se potessero con loro onore, se ne partirebbero; sapendo che tutte quante battono a un segno medesimo. E di qui si può conoscere, quanto questi cotali manchino di concetti e d'invenzione, veggendosi per lo più le loro comedie stiracchiate, grette e rubacchiate qua e là: e peggio ancora, che essi accozzano il vecchio col nuovo, e l'antico col moderno, e fanno un guazzabuglio e una mescolanza, che non ha nè via nè verso, nè capo nè coda; e faccendo la scena città moderne, e rappresentando i tempi d'oggi, v'introducono usanze passate e vecchie, e costumi antichi e tralasciati: e si scusano poi col dire: Così fece Plauto, e così usarono Terenzio e Menandro; non si accorgendo che in Firenze, in Pisa, in Lucca non si vive come si faceva anticamente in Roma e in Atene. Traduchino in mal'ora, se non hanno invenzione, e non rattoppino e guastino l'altrui e il loro insieme: il senno, e la prudenza degli uomini è sapersi accomodare ai tempi." There is a briefer statement of the same point of view in his prologue to *La Spiritata*, which was one of the few plays translated into the corpus of Elizabethan comedy. And *La Strega* has an introductory scene between Prologue and Argument as interlocutors in an almost Jonsonian manner, which is a comprehensive plea for modernity and for a proper independence of ancient authority, whether that of critic or of dramatist. The case turns on the fundamental claim that the whole object of comedy is to give its hearers an immediate and recognised pleasure: "oggidi non si va più a veder recitare comedie per imparare a vivere, ma per piacere, per spasso, per diletto, o per passar maninconia e per rallegrarsi." So modern times must have modern comedies, adapted to contemporary habits. "Aristotile e Orazio viddero i tempi loro, ma i nostri sono d'un 'altra maniera: abbiamo altri

costumi, altra religione e altro modo di vivere, e però bisogna
fare le comedie in altro modo: in Firenze non si vive come si
viveva già in Atene e in Roma; non ci sono schiavi, non ci
usano figliuoli adottivi; non ci vengono i ruffiani a vender le
fanciulle; nè i soldati dal dì d'oggi nei sacchi delle città o de'
castelli pigliano più le bambine in fascia, e allevandole per lor
figluiole, fanno loro la dote, ma attendono a rubare quanto
più possono, e se per sorte capitasser loro nelle mani, o fanciulle
grandicelle, o donne maritate (se già non pensassero cavarne
buona taglia), torrebbero loro la virginità e l'onore."

After such an emphatic assertion of the comic dramatist's
liberty, it is disappointing to find that his comedies avail themselves so little of the rights claimed. Grazzini was fond of
writing prologues, and his *Gelosia*, amongst its three, has one
specially addressed to the ladies in the audience, which, despite
the conventional phrases in it, excellently indicates the probable
consequences on comedy of the kind of society for which it
was written. It compels conjecture about the influence of
such "bellissime e onestissime donne" as appear to have pre-
vailed in the audience. Italian comedy, one suspects, would
inevitably adapt itself to the conditions which were bound to
make room for the romantic heroine, the ideal, that is, of contemporary womanhood. She is indeed almost ready to step
into the scenes of such a notorious unromantic as Pietro
Aretino. His *Ipocrito* ends with a quintuple peal of wedding
bells—"consento che Porfiria, Tansilla, Angizia, Sveva et
Annetta siano mogliere di Corebo, di Artico, di Tranquillo, di
Prelio e di Zefiro" (Act V, sc. xxiii)—the very names defy the
prosaic customs of the world; and in the course of the play its
people have ardently delivered themselves of ecstatic romantic
sentiments: "a chi ama è facile l'impossibile." Zefiro speaks of
his Annetta as "vita, luce et anima de la mia anima, de la mia
luce e de la mia vita": and seems to mean it. Naturally, Aretino
must occasionally thrust his tongue into his cheek; but the
smile is not necessarily a sceptic's nor a mocker's, for one of his
own characters, devoutly reciting the articles of his faith, admits

the place of laughter in the service of love: "ma tornando a Cupido, non lo prenda a servire chi non ha valore e pazienza, perocchè egli è un Dio che si alimenta non meno di generosità e di fatica che di riso e di pianto" (Act II, sc. iv). And the speaker goes on to recount how he has served love with propitiatory quests and ventures which would have qualified the bravest mediæval knight to expect reward from the most exacting mediæval maiden: Aretino, indeed, clearly merits the casual epithet our Gabriel Harvey applied to his "courting" comedies. But with all his audacity, Aretino too easily accepts the restrictions which kept the parts of his ladies small in extent and insignificant in effect, although he allows himself at times the sixteen-century device which was meant to accept the traditional usage and yet extend to women a larger liberty for appearing in comedy: they are debarred from a free appearance on the streets of the stage, but they may appear freely at the windows of their houses and discourse with those below.

In fine, then, though Italian comedy in the sixteenth century never emancipated itself sufficiently from its inherited Roman tradition and from its conventional schemes and practices, to become the mirror of the contemporary ideals and sentiments which were freely reflected in English romantic comedy, it nevertheless provides ample indication of the trend in development, and of the inevitability of some such accommodation as was attempted in the romantic comedy of Shakespeare.

Not many English comedies of the sixteenth century are built directly on Italian models. But besides the three printed in Mr. Warwick Bond's *Early Plays from the Italian*, there is a fourth, *The Two Italian Gentlemen*, printed probably in 1584, and translated with considerable adaptation from Pasqualigo's *Il Fedele* (c. 1575) which had also served Abraham Fraunce as a source for his Latin play, *Victoria* (c. 1583). The remarkable fact about the English translators' adaptations is that in almost every respect they excise the more squalid and unromantic episodes of the original, to convert the story into a romantic play of love, rivalry and reconciliation. The juxtaposition of the Italian and the English versions excellently indicates the rôle of Italian drama in the sixteenth century. Debarred by its own conventions from achieving a definitively romantic comedy, it is nevertheless providing an assortment of circumstance and situation which cry out for such romantic development as English dramatists were congenially inclined to supply. This makes no particular claim for *The Two Italian Gentlemen* as a play; it is indeed a crude and unsuccessful attempt to impose romantic sentiment on a tale originally invented to express the coarser animal passions of men and women.

But there are in Italian one or two plays, apart from the so-called tragi-comedies, in which the movement towards romantic comedy is particularly marked. There is Piccolomini's *Amor Costante* (1536) and the anonymous *Gl'Ingannati* (1537). *Amor Costante* is literally what its title implies, the representation of ideally constant lovers. The academicians who presented it, duly avowed themselves corporately "esser schiavo, servo affezionato e sviscerato di queste donne" who were their guests at the performance, and for whom the comedy was written. Their choice of theme is in accord with the principle enunciated in the play:

"Oh felicissima coppia d'amanti! oh amor costante! oh bellissimo caso da farci sopra una comedia eccellentissima!" (Act II, sc. iii).

The comedy is not, however, well provided with essentially dramatic matter. There is much discourse at length, and a deal of sentimental narrative. But it represents its heroes and their ladies as true patterns of lovers in romance. Ferrante, one of its heroes, has suffered adventures in the right romantic key. "Con questa resoluzione, montati, una notte, in una barchetta preparata da due amici miei, per gran pezza di mare felicemente navigammo. Ma la fortuna, che sempre s'oppone ai bei disegni de li inamorati, volse che, come fummo nei mari di Pisa, fussemo assaliti da quattro fuste di mori da le quali fummo messi in mezzo e, doppo che i miei compagni, valorosamente combattendo, furon morti ed io gravemente ferito, venne ogni cosa in man de' mori. E già, in quel mezzo che combattemmo, avea una fusta di quelle, in mia presenza, rapita per forza la mia Ginevra e portatala via, non giovando alla meschina el pregarli o che l'uccidessero o che non la dividessero da me" (Act II, sc. iii). Love is the object of life, and its manifestations, its effects, and its obligations are told much in the way of Shakespeare's *Two Gentlemen of Verona*. Of one young hero we hear from his servant—"egli pochissimo mangia, la maggior parte del tempo piange e si lamenta; sempre sta fisso in un medesimo pensiero il quale, profondissimo, continuamente gli rode l'animo; non dorme un'ora di tutta la notte, e quella in mille pezzi, perciochè non prima è addormentato che, farneticando, si sveglia" (Act I, sc. ii). The young man himself tells us how he feels: "Io so pur ch'io l'amo quanto amar si possa già mai. Io so pur che non è rimasto altro pensier in me che di servirla e odorarla con quella nettezza di fede che per me sia possibile, tener sempre spogliata l'animo dell' amor di ogni altra donna, aver fermo proposito, o bene o male ch'ella mi faccia, che tanto duri in me l'amor di lei quanto la vita, esser sempre diffensor dell' onor suo, non pensar mai cosa che le dispiaccia, spendere tutti quegli anni che mi restano per amor suo, con tanta fermezza che in rarissimi si troverebbe" (Act I, sc. ix). And another of these fine young men rhapsodises of himself—"che tu sei pur el più felice uomo del mondo. Oh beato te! oh consolazion grandissima! lieto, divino, fortunatissimo! oh allegrezza incomparabile! O Dio, o stelle, o sole, o luna!" (Act II, sc. iii). Though we are not vouchsafed much direct knowledge of the heroines of the play, we are given to understand that they too live for true love alone. Suited to this exalted sense of fidelity in love, there is an absolute recognition of other loyalties in life, private and political, and friendship imposes a lifelong and unquestioning devotion: "non si trova al mondo il maggior tesoro che la pura, vera e libera fedeltà" (Act III, sc. xiii). There is a soldier in *Amor Costante* whose service to his friend and whose shock at the suspicion of his friend's disloyalty is not unlike that of the sea-captain who brings Viola into *Twelfth Night*. A no less striking feature of *Amor Costante* is that, as in Shakespeare's comedies, the lower characters are allowed to display their inferiority by humorous mocking of the faith in which their masters live. The parasite Squazza, for instance, is almost Falstaffian in his contempt for what to him are the unsubstantial recompenses of a life of love. "Quanto io mi rido di questi locchi innamorati che si lassan perdere tanto in questa lor pazzia che non mangiano e non beon mai! Oh poverelli, di quanto ben son privi! . . . Questa è la beatitudine che si può aver in questo mondo. Tutti gli altri piaceri son cose vane. Perché, se tu pigli la musica, tutto è aria e fiato, che niente t'entra in corpo. L'aver denari confesso che gli è piacere, perché con quelli tu puoi proveder da mangiare; ché, altrimenti, io non saprei che farmene. Se noi parliam dell' amore, peggio che peggio; ch'io non so, per me, considerare che consolazion che s'abbin costoro di spender tutto il lor tempo in andare stringatelli, sprofumati, con le calze tirate, con la braghetta in punto, con la camiscia stampata, con la persona ferma acciò che, torcendosi una stringa, non toccasse l'altra; fare una sberrettata alla dama, dirgli un motto per una strada cogliendola all 'improvista ad un cantone, mirandola un tratto sott 'occhio, e lei miri te, gittarli quattro limoni, farsene render uno e baciarlo . . . etc. Tutte queste cose io no so a che diavol di fine che se le faccino, i merloni . . . Ma del mangiare tutto el contrario interviene, ché tuttavia ti sa meglio" (Act II, sc. viii).

In some ways, *Gl' Ingannati* is even closer to the English type. Like *Amor Costante*, it is an offering by an Italian academy to the ladies of its district. At points it is so close to the English kind that Shakespeare is alleged to have reflected something from it in his *Twelfth Night*. But the matter of it had wide European currency. It was translated into French (1543), adapted for the French stage (1549), and for the Spanish (1556). A Latin version appears in England as the *Laelia* played at Cambridge in 1595, whilst its story is also to be found in the novels of Italy and France and in our English *Historie of Apollo-*

nius and Silla, by Barnabe Riche (1581). It is, perhaps, the best of sixteenth-century Italian comedies, early in date though it be. Not only does it employ its story to excellent dramatic effect; it infuses into its romantic incidents something of the sanity of a mature comic spirit. Its Cesario, moreover (who, of course, is not so called), not only has the active rôle assigned to Viola by Shakespeare, but has also something of Viola's capacity for profiting from her rich and romantic intuitions without endangering the native sanity of her comprehension of circumstance.

But now to return from the Italians to our English plays, and particularly to the Shrew series, or at least to that part of the Shrew plays which tells of the wooing of the shrew's sister. It is in this part that *The Taming of A Shrew* differs most extensively from *The Taming of the Shrew*. The non-Shakespearian version is artistically the crudest kind of medley. Though its other half is the boisterous taming of a shrew, its wooing plot is in the most flagrant or even fatuous romantic manner. The shrew in it has two sisters, not one, as has Shakespeare's Katharine. These two are wooed in stilted romantic sentiments by two conventional lovers. There is no dramatic rivalry, nothing to impede the steady flow of high falutin' literary devotion. It includes from *The Supposes* the further motive of a servant deliberately disguised as an additional wooer; but he is only employed to pay suit to the shrew, and so leave her sisters free to enjoy the uninterrupted cooing of their lovers. Every comic incident of its original in Ariosto is either dropped or clumsily perverted to a use which enlarges the fatuous romanticism of its dominant temper. The lover's old father, for instance, is taken over; but only to add to the conventional harmonies of the concluding marriage feast. And already one has endured a surfeit of these romantic wooings. This, for instance, is how they do it:

> *Polidor.* Come faire Emelia my louelie loue,
> Brighter then the burnisht pallace of the sunne,
> The eie-sight of the glorious firmament,

In whose bright lookes sparkles the radiant fire,
Wilie Prometheus slilie stole from Ioue,
Infusing breath, life, motion, soule,
To everie obiect striken by thine eies.
Oh faire Emelia I pine for thee,
And either must enioy thy loue or die.

Emelia. Fie man, I know you will not die for loue.
Ah Polidor thou needst not to complaine,
Eternall heaven sooner be dissolvde,
And all that pearseth Phebus silver eie,
Before, such hap befall to Polidor.

Polidor. Thanks faire Emelia for these sweet words,
But what saith Phylena to hir friend?

Phylena. Why I am buying marchandise of him.

Aurelius. Mistresse you shall not need to buie of me,
For when I crost the bubling Canibey,
And sailde along the Cristall Helispont,
I filde my cofers of the wealthie mines,
Where I did cause Millions of labouring Moores
To undermine the cauernes of the earth,
To seeke for strange and new found pretious stones,
And diue into the sea to gather pearle,
As faire as Iuno offered Priams sonne,
And you shall take your liberall choice of all.

(Sc. vi.)

Or in more settled moods of unmitigated rapture:

Polidor. Faire Emelia sommers sun bright Queene,
Brighter of hew then is the burning clime,
Where Phœbus in his bright æquator sits,
Creating gold and pressious minnerals,
What would Emelia doo? if I were forst
To leave faire Athens and to range the world.

Emelia. Should thou assay to scale the seate of Ioue,
Mounting the suttle ayrie regions
Or be snacht up as erste was Ganimed,
Loue should give winges unto my swift desires,
And prune my thoughts that I would follow thee,
Or fall and perish as did Icarus.

Aurelius. Sweetly resolued, faire Emelia.

and so on for fifty more lines of golden syrop as glucosic and as sticky, ending:

> Sweet Phylena bewties mynerall,
> From whence the sun exhales his glorious shine,
> And clad the heaven in thy reflected raies,
> And now my liefest loue, the time drawes nie,
> That Himen mounted in his saffron robe,
> Must with his torches waight upon thy traine,
> As Hellens brothers on the horned Moone,
> Now Iuno to thy number shall I adde,
> The fairest bride that ever Marchant had.
>
> (Sc. xiv.)

Even the two gentlemen of Verona are nearer humanity than these, and the ludicrousness of their performance is emphasised by its juxtaposition with such men and women as a tamer and a shrew to be tamed. Yet even at the end of *The Taming of A Shrew* the taming makes not the slightest diminution of her sisters' conjugal felicities.

There is a far finer dramatic instinct in Shakespeare's *Taming of the Shrew*. Bianca is never set adrift in the wide ocean of romantic emotion. She is not allowed to grow too far beyond the stock from which she springs, the heroine of Ariosto's *Suppositi*. Her retinue of admirers is a little larger than is that of Ariosto's lady, for all her three are genuine wooers. But almost as much as Ariosto's, her wooers are deprived of the licence, so riotously enjoyed by those in *The Taming of A Shrew*, to dissolve their sugary hearts in luscious volubility. Bianca's lovers are indeed granted somewhat larger liberty of romantic utterance than are their counterparts in Ariosto's *Suppositi*. Lucentio is enthralled when he sees her coral lips to move: everything attaching to her is sweet and sacred, and the very air about her is perfumed by her breath. Hortensio, loving with all affection, and with his lute, has but two notes of the gamut—"show pity, or I die." But clearly these Anglo-Italian lovers are not yet initiated into the full ritual. They are mostly occupied with planning opportunities to express a faith which has not yet become articulate. Love remains more an intrigue than a religion. Hence the convenience of the classical machinery. Wily, scheming men-servants, disguises to procure mistaken identifications, inopportune coincidences to be encountered by still further reaches of unfeeling cunning—these are the traditional weapons of classical comedy. Though the old men of the piece are much more sympathetic and amenable than Latin comedy made them, they are still treated with the brutal callousness which formerly had its legitimate occasion. Fathers in Roman comedy deserved the disciplinary measures which Vicentio has now to suffer, though here his behaviour is exemplary. Tranio is straight from Plautus and from Terence, still practising his customary rôle of beguiling the old folks in the interests of their amorous sons and daughters. If at the outset of the play Lucentio allows Tranio less initiative than is commonly possessed by his ancient prototype (for the disguise is Lucentio's own idea, and his having the wits to come by it, is part of the unconsciously increasing importance of the amorous young man as he grows from his subordinate part in Roman comedy to the predominant one in modern plays) yet the course of the incidents draws more and more largely on Tranio's own ingenuity. Grumio and Biondello bear their Roman origin unmistakably stamped on their features. Theirs is the traditional stupidity of "fond reasoning," and of clumsy and occasionally unclean quibbling. Theirs, too, are the customary rewards of their type, good sound thwackings with stick or rope. Grumio is Petruchio's servant, however, and not Lucentio's. But his fellowship with Tranio is a strong link between the wooers of Bianca and the tamer of Katharine. Through such alliance, Tranio is a curb on their romantic sentiments. His natural task is to stir his master from futile trances of ecstatic adoration:

> I pray, awake, sir, if you love the maid,
> Bend thoughts and wits to achieve her.

It is Tranio, too, who encourages the rival lovers frequently to dispense with prescribed forms of jealous enmity, for the more congenial ways of passing an afternoon in quaffing carouses to their lady's health:

> Do as adversaries do in law,
> Strive mightily, but eat and drink as friends.

There is virtue in this plan. For even though the rival lovers who maintain it so far forth as friends are not completely cured of the desire to have to't afresh in the conventional tilts of rivalry in love, there is bound to be some mitigation of their knight-errantry. Gremio will find a feast no little compensation for the loss of a mistress, and Hortensio will discover that a widow who is wealthy and loving, if not a paragon of beauty, is nevertheless a worthier prize than a disdainful maiden who gives her favours elsewhere. Thus is Thurio of the *Two Gentlemen of Verona* so soon justified of his descendants. Bianca herself suffers a surprising metamorphosis when she frames her manners to the new regime. She begins as the retiring maiden whose modesty and silence stand as pattern of "maid's mild behaviour and sobriety." She cowers timorously before her cantankerous sister, humbly subscribing herself in a quite uncovenanted submission to Katharine's pleasure. Yet in the end, she has acquired a most unmaidenly taste in repartee, and a stiff-necked reluctance to do anything her lawful husband lovingly entreats her to do.

But if romance in Bianca's wooing is thus largely attenuated, it is completely destroyed in Katharine's. Pollution penetrates to the innermost sanctum of romantic holies. The ritual of wooing is exposed to boisterous mockery. It was a stroke of audacious profanity to take the brutal rollicking temper of classical comedy which knew not love, and to impose it as the ruling air on a story which comprises nothing but the incidents of courtship. Love becomes a matter of business, not of sentiment. "Wealth is the burden of my wooing dance," declares Petruchio, who has come to wive it wealthily in Padua. Courtship should be set within a lawyer's office, not in moonlit pleasaunces. "Let specialties be therefore drawn between us, that covenants may be kept on either hand." Wooing itself is not with flowers and song and sonnet, but with discordant argument and fisticuffs. At times in the procedure the wooer may find it opportune to use the traditional flattery of the code, but this is merely a matter of tactics, not of faith. The atmosphere of devotion has entirely disappeared. Even the marriage ceremony is riotously profaned. Obviously there is here no bid for love, but for subjugation.

Naturally, a tale of taming makes both the tamer and the tamed more like dwellers in a menagerie than in the polite world. Yet even such a brutal insistence on the animal in man is no unhealthy symptom in an author whose Gentlemen of Verona had been built on the facile assumption that men are near allied to angels. Petruchio is a madcap ruffian and a swearing Jack. His life has been a boisterous one. An adventurer on land and seas, whose music is the roar of lions, the chafe of waves puffed up with winds, great ordnance in the field and heaven's artillery thundering in the skies, he has the swaggering insouciance, the brutal strength, and the animal preferences which fit him for the taming. Katharine is less intelligible. She is intolerably curst and shrewd and froward so beyond all measure, that although her extravagant bullying of her sister and of her teacher is within her physical compass, her complaint that her father is committing her to an old maid's life, and her lament that she will sit and weep until she finds occasion of revenge, seem widely out of character. Even more disconcerting are the tears she sheds because she anticipates that Petruchio will fail her at the church, or will surely overlook some item or other of the arrangements ordained by fashionable propriety for a bourgeois wedding. A Katharine of such nature needs no taming. She needs a dietary. After that, a moderate dress-allowance will bribe her into absolute submission. She will place her hands below her husband's foot in token of her duty.

Petruchio is different from the wooers of romance, because

he remembers the grocer, the butcher, and the tailor. He drags love out of heaven, and brings it down to earth. To the chivalrous, love is a state of worship; to him, it is a problem of wiving. Its object is not primarily a search for spiritual bliss in the contemplation of the beloved. It seeks merely a guarantee of domestic comfort, by securing a Kate conformable to other household cates, a wife who will be as "his house and as his household stuff." A condition of this is naturally, that he must be master of what is his own. Courtship is merely incidental to the attainment of this ease and settlement. It is not of itself the business of a life-time—"I come not every day to woo." And as the world knows, it may be the matter of a casual moment—"I knew a wench married in an afternoon as she went to the garden for parsley to stuff a rabbit." But casual or deliberate, it keeps a main eye on the state to which it is itself merely preparatory—"there be good fellows in the world, an a man could light on them, would take her with all her faults, *and money enough.*" Whether it proceed by sweet words and by kisses, or by combing noddles with a three-legged stool, the test of its worth is invariable and plain; it is its worth as a method of securing a guarantee of "peace and love and quiet life" at the domestic hearth of man and wife. The mind which takes its love and courtship so is one which claims to take the world for what it is and to accept the conditions life imposes on the living of it. It is a matter-of-fact recognition of the practical and the expedient. It is rudimentary common sense—rudimentary, however, because though at some stage in his development, man may have been able to conduct his wiving so, it is apparent that, except in moments of temporary revolt, no Elizabethan and no modern could really hold to the underlying assumption that marriage is mainly an economic arrangement. *The Taming of the Shrew* gives Shakespeare momentary ease of the burden of romance; but only by denying its existence. It does not solve his problem; it merely shelves it. But he will return to the facts of Elizabethan experience in the more characteristic mood which we shall find in *A Midsummer Night's Dream.* In the meantime, this at least can be claimed: that though for the moment his mood was to exhibit the love of woman more in the spirit of the Roman market-place than in that of his own modern Europe, he has at least allowed his artistic sense to make the proper accommodation in the temper of every part of his play. No such claim can be made for the author of *The Taming of A Shrew.*

V

A Midsummer Night's Dream

ON the previous occasions when I have talked with you on Shakespeare and his comedies, we have been dealing with a dramatic apprentice—with one who was thrilled by the kaleidoscopic procession of life, and who was as spell-bound with the power of words over the mind of man as with his own genius for manipulating that magic spell. But nevertheless with one who, as a dramatist, was still serving his apprenticeship. As a poet, one may safely say, he had at the outset given pledges of a triumph to come. If *Love's Labour's Lost*, his first comic offering, be regarded, not as a drama, but merely as an exercise in the play of words, it is palpably the diploma piece of one born for mastery. The words in it are clearly more important than are its men and women, and all their deeds. It is the work of a poet who is born into an age of drama,—but who as yet is only vaguely cognisant of the demands of drama as distinct from those of poetry. He is bewitched by the magic of words and revels in his dexterity to manipulate sound and symbol. Every mode of expression is a delight or a snare for him; all are exercises in the fascinating game of word-play. Sparkling taffeta phrases flash in scintillating wit. Choice new-minted expressions strut in spruce affectation. Heavy ink-horn terms waddle by in mock solemnity. Vulgar and clownish perversions blunder into humorous nonsense. At times, too, there is the sweet and musical harmony of bright Apollo's lute. But all this is the revelry of poetry, the amazing craft of a young poet, for whom words are the power of life, the

mighty instruments through which his mastery may be displayed, or perhaps by which he may himself be mastered.

But the poet gives the dramatist little or no opening. Only
at the end are these spruce affectations forsworn for honest
kersey yeas and nays. So the folk of his play walk on to the
stage, not to display themselves in the human predicaments
which are the matter of drama, but merely to add another
dialect to the feast of languages. The courtiers are the brilliant
and witty euphuists, Armado is the gongorist, Holofernes the
disgorger of scholastic pedantries, Costard the canny lout whose
misprisions of the Queen's English are all to his own bodily
profit. But in *Love's Labour's Lost* all of them have but one
function—they are pedlars of wit. Shakespeare's indifference
to character, to anything but the tongues of his people, and his
utter lack of interest in the story which should involve them in
the chances and mischances of human circumstance, are plain
proof of his blindness to what soon was to provide the stuff of
his and the world's greatest dramas. For drama lives on its
interest in human action, in man's moulding in the maze of
incident, in his response to his environment, his strife with
destiny, either to achieve control of circumstance in comedy, or
to meet destruction in tragedy by opposing the facts of his
fate.

Yet even *Love's Labour's Lost*, because it is artificially and
arbitrarily cast into the shape of drama, broadly indicates what
features of man's contact with the world were, for Shakespeare's day, the crucial and decisive moments of his mortal
existence. They were his apprehension of what for the sixteenth century was the problem and the opportunity by which
man's destiny was most richly to be realised—his aptitude for
the disciplinary experiences of love.

The sixteenth-century dramatist, depicting the dilemma and
the triumph of life, was mainly moved to discover man
achieving happiness or sorrow through his relationship with
woman, through his liability to love. There is talk of love in
Love's Labour's Lost: there is no dramatisation of its operation

on life as a vital energy. And the plays after *Love's Labour's Lost*, already looked at in earlier lectures in this series, have shown Shakespeare the poet slowly becoming Shakespeare the dramatist, finding a technique or a manner by which, as in the *Comedy of Errors*, the theatre may be competently used as the dramatist's instrument for expressing whatever for the moment he may have to say, or as in the *Two Gentlemen*, using that technique to express what in the prevalent temper was assumed to be the proper thing to say in respect of man's capacity for the happy mastery of his life.

But at length in *The Taming of the Shrew* there appeared a Shakespeare who had acquired a certain control over his instrument, the theatre, but who apparently was completely baffled by the inability of that instrument to play the tune which was the music of his own times. He had set the *Two Gentlemen* to the key which was the song of the sixteenth century, the music of lovers and of their romantic loves; but the dramatisation of it grated with strident discords, and so in *The Taming of the Shrew* he seems to fall back on drama as a mode of expression, a kind of orchestration, which is not fitted to utter the delicious and exquisite notes of lovers proving all the pleasures of their love. *The Taming of the Shrew* is an evening's amusement in which Shakespeare is running away from the inevitable dramatic problem of the life of his own day.

But of course the story of *The Taming of the Shrew* is so built that it solves, or seems to solve, Petruchio's problem. Yet in fact it does not rescue Shakespeare and his contemporaries from their predicament. It does not mirror an Elizabethan facing and grappling with the dilemmas of Elizabethan man; it is not therefore comic drama, it is farce. It succeeds, not by its representation, but by its distortion of life. The play in our programme to-night, the *Midsummer Night's Dream*, with all its appearance of fairy, with its apparent revelry in the stuff of which dreams are made, with its alluring unreality, and its evident riot of fantasy, is yet the first play in which Shakespeare reveals his promise as the world's comic dramatist, the first exhibition of his power to use comedy for its proper function, to show real man encountering the real problem of the world in which he was really living—in other words, for Shakespeare's day, the first play in which he showed contemporary man buffetted by the power felt then to be the primary factor of his existence, his response to the quality and the might of love. *A Midsummer Night's Dream* is admittedly Shakespeare's first masterpiece. But the attributes of it often put forward as the features determining its excellence are rather the results than the cause of its supremacy. Critics note the wonderful dexterity with which three evidently alien kinds of matter are woven into a single composite picture, three distinct and unrelated worlds shaped into one consistent universe. The anachronistic court of a pre-Homeric Athens, the realistic population of a contemporary English countryside, and the realm of a fairy land in which ancient, mediæval, and modern have broken through the limits of time to exist together in one and the same timeless moment—here are seemingly indissoluble incongruities, apt only to the unintelligible confusions of a nightmare. Yet Shakespeare welds them into the form of a credible society; and all, one is asked to believe, by his technical expertness in plotting, and in particular, by his marvellous employment of the pansy's philtre. But in fact, this skilful workmanship in plotcraft, in forging links to bind the incidents of three different stories into one, is but the outward execution giving visible unity to a body of matter of which the real harmony has been shaped by imaginative insight. These three separate worlds are moulded into one by a controlling point of view, by an idea, not by a philtre. The unity of the comic idea, not the joinery of episodes, is what makes the greatness of *A Midsummer Night's Dream*. *A Midsummer Night's Dream* is not Shakespeare's first masterpiece because in it he is technically more expert than hitherto in such qualities as deftness in structure; it is because in it he has seized more securely on the vital temper of his generation and embodied with it more of the essential spirit of his time. Though this security shows itself through a surer control of his plot and a greater ease in effecting the progressive relationships of his characters, the most distinctive mark of it is that his matter has now acquired a more searching significance for life, and a closer bearing on the facts of existence. As an artist, Shakespeare is attaining a comic idea, but attaining it as an artist, through his imaginative apprehension, not through his work-a-day reason. Even in *A Midsummer Night's Dream* it is not by any means fully evolved; and the sign of its imperfection is that as yet it has not fully apprehended the part to be played in the comic idea by the sense for character; and so, technically, the weakest part of the play is its characterisation. But sufficient progress in other respects is obvious by ready reference to its forerunners.

Thus, once the guffaws over *The Taming of the Shrew* have died down, it becomes clear that Petruchio's is a specious triumph. If man can be like Petruchio, if, like Petruchio, he can choose his mate on strictly economic principles, if the object of wiving is wealth and domestic comfort alone, then there is no more to be said. *The Taming of the Shrew* is the last word of wisdom. But none of these qualifications held good for Shakespeare or for his contemporaries. They were different in temper from Petruchio. Wiving for them was wooing. They clamoured for romance, because they themselves had become romantic. They were different in spiritual kind from the men of the older world where Petruchio would have been congenially at home, and their world itself was different. They clamoured for the romantic representation of love because they had learnt, in the meantime, that love was a romantic experience. Reading in the chronicle of wasted time the description of fairest wights, hearing beauty making beautiful old rhyme in praise of ladies dead and lovely knights, they had added to their own spiritual susceptibilities; they had inured in themselves the habit of experiencing the pains and the pleasures of love as a romantic ecstasy, the most decisive and the most significant episode in human life. Turn at random to any anthology of Elizabethan poetry. The vast bulk of it is mainly the song of the lover, of his passion and of his plaint; but whether one or the other, the poet is enthralled by the attitude of man to maid. His most frequent question is "What is Love?" and though he may in devouter moments recognise its implications in eternity, he is above all concerned with its significance to his present state. There is Shakespeare's light-hearted answer:

> What is Love? 'Tis not hereafter;
> Present mirth hath present laughter;
> What's to come is still unsure:
> In delay there lies no plenty;
> Then come kiss me sweet and twenty,
> Youth's a stuff will not endure.

Lightly, too, Peele (*Hunting of Cupid*, 1591) asks—

> What thing is love? for, well I wot, love is a thing.
> It is a prick, it is a sting,
> It is a pretty, pretty thing;
> It is a fire, it is a coal,
> Whose flame creeps in at every hole;
> And as my wit doth best devise
> Love's dwelling is in ladies' eyes:
> From whence do glance love's piercing darts
> That make such holes into our hearts;
> And all the world herein accord
> Love is a great and mighty lord.

Or Sir Walter Raleigh opens a poem by expressing his sense of the enormous issues involved:

> Now what is love, I pray thee tell?
> It is that fountain and that well
> Where pleasures and repentance dwell.
> It is perhaps that sauncing bell
> That tolls all into heaven or hell.
> And this is love, as I here tell.

If the last line foreshadows the cynical anti-climax of the

poem, that is but the hall-mark of Raleigh's own temperament.

So largely, then, did love bulk in the consciousness of life; there was no escape from it. Hear, for instance, a minor poet, one, therefore, likely to speak the common voice and tell of everyman's sentiment:

> Except I love, I cannot have delight,
>   It is a care that doth to life belong:
> For why I hold that life in great despite
>   That hath not sour mixed with sweet among,
> And though the torments which I feel be strong,
>   Yet had I rather thus far to remain
> Than laugh, and live, not feeling lover's pain.
>   (*Mirror of Knighthood*, 1583).

It was an experience—inevitable, universal, omnipotent—and whether it brought immediate joy or present pain, it was the experience to be desired above all others:

> Amid my bale, I bathe in bliss,
>   I swim in heaven, I sink in hell;
> I find amends for every miss
>   And yet my moan no tongue can tell.
> I live and love, what would you more?
>   As never lover lived before.
>   (Gascoigne, *Posies*, 1575).

Even in the full consciousness of probable suffering through it, man could not control his nature and foreswear it:

> But if the love that hath, and still doth burn me,
>   No love at length return me,
>   Out of my thoughts I'll set her.
> Heart, let her go: O heart, I pray thee, let her.
>   Say, shall she go?
>   Oh, no, no, no, no, no!
> Fixed in the heart, how can the heart forget her?
>   (Davison, *Poetical Rhapsody*, 1602).

And if most of these laments and raptures tinkle like sweet nothings or nothings which are bitter-sweet, if they sound but as a passing fashion, a mannerism of an epoch rather than a habit deeply graven in its consciousness, one may turn to profounder expressions, which tell how love fills the mind of man and permeates the whole of his universe. There is Donne with his sense that love is old as time itself: he longs to talk with some old lover's ghost who died before the god of love was born. Or again, he can conceive no significance for a world in which love has no existence:

> I wonder, by my troth, what thou and I
> Did, till we loved: were we not weaned till then?
> But sucked in country pleasures, childishly?
> Or snorted we in the Seven Sleepers' den?
> 'Twas so; but this, all pleasures fancies be;
> If ever any beauty I did see,
> Which I desired, and got, 'twas but a dream of thee.
>
> And now good-morrow to our waking souls,
> Which watch not one another out of fear;
> For love all love of other sights controls,
> And makes one little room an everywhere.
> Let sea-discoverers to new worlds have gone;
> Let maps to other, worlds on worlds have shown,
> Let us possess one world; each hath one, and is one.
>
> My face in thine eyes, thine in mine appears,
> And true plain hearts do in the faces rest;
> Where can we find two better hemispheres
> Without sharp north, without declining west?
> What ever dies, was not mixed equally:
> If our two loves be one, or thou and I
> Love so alike that none do slacken, none can die.

And then his (or Hoskin's) magnificent apprehension of love's triumph over time and life:

> Who loves a mistress of such quality,
> He soon hath found
> Affection's ground
> Beyond time, place, and all mortality.
> To hearts that cannot vary
> Absence is present, time doth tarry.

But these are enough to show how mightily love bulked in what the Elizabethans found life to be. To them, for better or for worse, to live was to love, and to love was to love romantically. That was for them a fact of existence. Whether, of course, it was a fact ultimately giving man cause for joy, or whether it constituted a danger to humanity was a further question. It was precisely one of those questions pertinent to the comic dramatist. For comedy, necessarily leading to a happy denouement, showing its heroes attaining their joy by a successful management of circumstance, must equip its heroes with the qualities apt to triumph over the hindrances and troubles which are part of such life as is reflected in comedy. "What is love?" or rather, "What is the place of love in life?" is the question underlying *A Midsummer Night's Dream;* and as the play is a comedy, life in it will necessarily be life as men are finding it, life which is the thing men such as author and audience find themselves destined to live. And in their direct and daily experience of it, the power of love was an undeniable fact. So Petruchio in *The Taming of the Shrew* achieves only a false victory. He triumphs because he denies love. But his denial is simply a mark of his own limitation, and in no wise dismisses love from the consciousness of the sixteenth century. He is a less complete man than is any of his audience, and the world he knows is less than is theirs. His orbit does not reach beyond the knock-about, workaday world of merchandise and merchant venturings, in a phrase, the world of the city. He never sees beyond the horizon of Roman comedy. Petruchio brings love down to earth, but only to a small corner of it, to the quarter still known as "the city," or that "about town." And even before the Roman comic dramatists were born, Greek poets in Sicily had explored vastly different regions, rural scenes where "there is spring and greenness everywhere," "rivers and vales, a glorious birth," "pastures and rills, a bounteous race." These woodlands of Theocritus echo to the piping of Menalcas and to the songs of Daphnis, surpassing those of nightingales in sweetness. And even the earliest

singers of this new country were dimly aware that the novel
sensations they felt when they were moved by their rural
surroundings, betokened a new faculty for sentiment; and that
this faculty was stirred into consciousness by other than the
inanimate manifestations of the simple nature in which they
lived. They were becoming a new race of men and women,
having new eyes and new hearts. Most deliciously novel of all
was the discovery that

All things that are young have life anew
Where my sweet maiden wanders; but parched and withered seem
When she departeth, lawn and shepherd too.

Love in these haunts is beginning faintly to be what a later
world would find it to be:

She cometh, by the quivering of mine eye.
I'll lean against the pine tree here and sing.
She may look round.

Here is wooing in its earliest efforts. And although in these
idylls of Theocritus, courtship does not grow beyond the
piping of a ditty and the offer of a goat with its twin kids, yet
the skies and the winds, the fountains and the rocks, the grapes
and the flowers of his Sicily—

Sea-blue swallow-wort, and there
The pale-hued maidenhair, with parsley green
And vagrant marsh-flowers—

these are tuning the young Sicilian shepherds and shepherdesses
to modes of amorous susceptibility more mysterious and more
perturbing than anything of which the Roman citizen was to
become conscious. The Sicilian shepherd might well be
wrought to urge that as the net is the bane of the stag, so love is
that of man: but he would not dream of denying its power.

Still less could Shakespeare dispose of love in Petruchio's
way. For by Shakespeare's age the faint experience of Sicilian
shepherds had been widely extended, largely diversified, and

substantially deepened by mystic and by knight, by courtier and by poet, until men were now so born that to love romantically was a natural prompting. In Virgil's day, a man might break faith with his love, and yet preserve his virtue without spot. What the Romans meant by loving occupied us extensively when the *Comedy of Errors* was our theme. Before them, even amongst the classic Greeks, love was not what later ages found it to be: once one overcomes the shock of a brutal phrase, one might agree that even Sappho's is but a sublimation of physical sensation. But Roman love bears still more potent signs of its nature. In the modern sense, the Romans were lovers hardly at all; they passed too easily from animal man to the status of men of the world. Love was a bodily experience of sex or a fashionable manner of gallantry, and even if the shade of Catullus should hear such a description, he more than another would understand its meaning. Nothing could more simply indicate the immeasurable distance between Roman and Elizabethan sentiment than their titles for Æneas, who to the Romans was the predestined founder of their race, and to the Elizabethans was the paramour of Dido. To the one people he is "pius Æneas"; to the other, he is "the false Troyan." Theocritus permits us to guess how the world will move from one of these judgments to the other which seems its antipodes.

Shakespeare's country was even more potent than the countryside of which Theocritus had sung, to prompt in man the fancies and the sentiments which turn him easily to love. Here, as in Sicily, were hill and dale, bush and brier. Here were banks

> where the wild thyme blows,
> Where oxlips and the nodding violet grows,
> Quite over-canopied with luscious woodbine,
> With sweet musk-roses and with eglantine.

England's cowslips were golden cups, spotted with rich rubies, and a pearl of dew hung in each. Its woodlands were carpeted

with thick primrose beds, and its springtime outrivalled that of
Theocritus in greenery: the song of the lark in the season when
wheat is green and hawthorn buds appear, roused English
villages betimes to do observances to the month of May. The
fields are asparkle with the dewdrop's liquid pearl: the woods
are lighted with the fiery glow-worm's eyes. Morning has
mountain top and western valley filled with music of the
hounds,

> So flew'd, so sanded, and their heads are hung
> With ears that sweep away the morning dew:
> Crock-knee'd and dew-lapp'd like Thessalian bulls;
> Slow in pursuit, but match'd in mouth like bells,
> Each under each. A cry more tunable
> Was never holla'd to, nor cheer'd with horn,
> In Crete, in Sparta, nor in Thessaly.

Its skies are swept with flight of wild geese, startled by the
fowler, or with russet-pated choughs, rising and cawing at the
gun's report. And evening ushers in the midnight revels on
hill, in dale, forest or mead, by paved fountain or by rushy
brook, or in the beached margent of the sea, where ringlets are
danced in quaint mazes to the whistling of the wind. This is
the land of *A Midsummer Night's Dream*. But it is none the less
England because it is a land of enchantment, where all between
the cold moon and the earth is filled with fairy strains. Here
the ploughman, lost in sweat, the village maiden skimming
milk, and the busy housewife breathless at the churn, are
familiar with fairies as with each other. They need but look
around, or sit upon a promontory, to hear a mermaid on a
dolphin's back, uttering such dulcet and harmonious breath
that the rude seas grow civil at her song, and stars shoot
madly from their spheres to hear the sea-maids' music. Here
indeed is fairyland itself. Even in Sicily, Corin could not but
play all day on pipes of corn, and verse his love to amorous
Phillida. But in England, every wood is decked with the very
spring of romance, the irresistible source of love itself, the

pansy, the little western flower "before milk-white, now purple with love's wound," on which the bolt of Cupid's fiery shaft had fallen. The spell of love was in our countryside, and none could stand against its strange but mighty influence.

It is this which gives meaning to the fairy realm of *A Midsummer Night's Dream*. It prepares a place for poets and for lovers. Its world is fairy-ridden, and its inhabitants are apt to the witchery of love. Its natural instruments are magic philtres and mischievous Pucks. It is evanescent as a dream, a midsummer fantasia. Yet at the end, its fairy haunts are native England, its people are compatriots of Shakespeare, and under the dominion of Puck and philtre, they are lovers no more volatile and variable than in actual life they were, acting amazedly as if half-asleep, half-waking, seeing things with parted eye when everything seems double. The poet's world of fairy and the lover's rural England are indistinguishably one. Fancy, dream, and fairy are lightly woven for a toy, but, transfigured so together, "they witness more than fancy's images, and grow to something of great constancy." The dream, even the *Midsummer Night's Dream*, takes on a more profound significance for the actual world than any of Shakespeare's earlier plays had had. It recognises the reality of romance. Men must love; and their love is power and charter to break all opposing ancient privileges. And love refuses to go hand in hand with reason. Its moods and whims are exempt from all constraint but destiny. But providentially, a period is set to its fiercest dominion. It is an episode, a growing pain which cannot be avoided, but which will be outgrown with the ending of the salad days. It passes as the fierce vexation of a dream. The wise man lets his trial teach him patience; and the doting madness of unhardened youth gone by, he tunes his wedding to another key from that wherein he wooed, changing the feverish intoxication of amorous idolatry for the lasting bond of fellowship in marriage.

A Midsummer Night's Dream is a play of love and of lovers, but it opens only when the nuptial hour is drawing on apace, and Theseus' courtship is already past. Even the Athenian lovers have but a brief four days' nightmare of wooing before they too pass into a maturer life. Theseus has had his wilder gallivantings; echoes of a Perigenia, a fair Aegle, an Ariadne, and an Antiope sound faintly through the glimmering night of years gone by. But the fever has worked itself out of his blood. He stands now as the normal member of the society of men, still conscious of the natural pulsings in the veins, and choosing the earthlier-happy state of wedlock in preference to mortifying the flesh in thrice-blessed but inhuman tasks to master blood and chant faint hymns to the cold fruitless moon. Theseus stamps his mind on the play. He admits love because it is natural; but he circumscribes its scope to lead to marriage, because that has become second nature and so is natural too. From such a point of view, the most romantic lover is no mere freak, and his vagaries present a mirror to the real world. But if at the end of his green youth, he cannot fit his fancies to the will of the world, then a natural experience has occasioned in him a condition of disease. He has cut his teeth, but the gums have festered. One part of life, and that but incidental to the whole of it, is claiming to be the whole, and is thereby damaging other, and certainly no less essential, features of it.

But though Theseus strikes the temper of the play at the outset, and summarises the trend of it at the close, the main incidents in the play present the fashion of romantic love and the ways of romantic lovers. The order of the medley of the *Comedy of Errors* is inverted: there, romantic matter frames a realistic picture, but exercises no control over it. Here a normal temper sits president, whilst romance displays its quality in furious dance, before finally coming up for judgment. So much change is there since the *Two Gentlemen of Verona*. The lovers now are not they who impose their valuations of life upon the play. They are themselves on trial, and their scheme of values is submitted to correction at the hands of Theseus. They are in the dock, not on the bench. And though to the unhuman eye of Puck their crime is flagrant folly, to the normal human Theseus it is a kind of foolishness to which all human flesh is heir, and which all mortal eyes will see with sympathy. Hermia and Lysander, Helena and Demetrius as devoutly dote, and with as much romantic idolatry as did ever lovers of whom tale and history tell. They interchange their rhymes and their love-tokens as the manner is. They serenade by moonlight, and employ each coin of the hallowed currency— "bracelets of hair, rings, gawds, conceits, knacks, trifles, nosegays, and sweatmeats." Their love makes heaven of hell, and hell of heaven. Crosses and hellish spight render its course unsmooth. They spend their passion on misprised moods. Their faith is ardent.

> I'll believe as soon
> The whole earth may be bored and that the moon
> May through the centre creep, and so displease
> Her brother's noontide with the Antipodes,

says Hermia. This is faith indeed, absolute—and absolutely misplaced. So with the other lovers. Their passions and their preferences are entirely inexplicable. Things base and vile to common view, their love has transposed for them to form and dignity. They sway from deepest loathing to intensest rapture, merely as the blood within them burns or freezes—"hot ice, and wondrous strange snow," very tragical mirth.

Yet despite it all, these lovers do not leave the common earth so entirely as do their earlier romantic counterparts. Antipholus reclines on wisps of Luciana's golden hair spread floating on the sea. Hermia has a firmer couch on yellow primrose beds. Hermia's invocation is not by all the protestations of true lovers in the past, but "by all the vows that ever men have broke, in number more than ever women spoke," an infinitely more substantial body of experience. Indeed, the love of these Athenians is much more a natural mood than a prescribed attitude. It shows itself in jealousies and wranglings as frequently as in devoted protestations. It has its Billingsgate as well as its liturgy: cat, burr, vile serpent, tawny Tartar,

dwarf and minimus are as current as goddess, nymph divine
and dear, precious, celestial. The lovers themselves know what
a frail and fleeting thing true love has been:

> if ever there were sympathy in choice,
> War, death, or sickness did lay siege to it,
> Making it momentary as a sound,
> Swift as a shadow, short as any dream;
> Brief as the lightning in the collied night,
> That, in a spleen, unfolds both Heaven and earth,
> And, e'er a man hath power to say "Behold,"
> The jaws of darkness do devour it up:
> So quick bright things come to confusion.

There is little to choose between Demetrius and Lysander;
Demetrius is at first suspect of disloyal escapades, but Lysander's metal is not without good sound dross. Hermia and
Helena are much more distinct. They are Shakespeare's first
real flappers, straight from a lady's seminary. Helena has sat at
her sampler like the prim young maiden of the Pre-Raphaelites,
weaving her first love into silken dreams, and endeavouring
to restrain her more mettlesome companion from stealing out
of the window to try kisses on the mouth. But school-days are
over when the play begins, though assuredly not very far
behind. Helena is pale and tall, the traditional emblem of
forlorn maiden love, a sweet lady, sweetly doting upon
inconstant man. All she asks is to be allowed to fawn and follow her lover as his spaniel. But she is just woman enough to
begin to realise that life under such terms is scarcely worth it:

> What wicked and dissembling glass of mine
> Made me compare with Hermia's sphery eyne?

The "sphery eyne" look backward to the tapestried samplers
and their hallowed archaisms. But the tradition is making way
for phrases, modes, and ideals more applicable to the needs
and situations of the moment. Helena herself has had enough
of it:

> And now, so you will let me quiet go,
> To Athens will I bear my folly back
> And follow you no further.

But her disillusionment has taught her much of the world. When fate turns love at length towards her, she is worldly-wise enough now to demand effective guarantees before accepting it:

> You do advance your cunning more and more. . . .
> Weigh oath with oath, and you will nothing weigh.
> Your vows to her and me, put in two scales,
> Will even weigh, and both as light as tales.

Hermia, small, dark and quick of tongue, is even more alive. She is soon driven out of maiden patience, though she is schooling herself to bear with customary crosses. Her temper is as sharp as is her tongue, and excites itself most touchily in matters of her stature and her complexion. She was a vixen when she went to school, and even in the drawing-rooms of the politer world she has not quite mastered her instinct to bring her nails into the fray. The customary comic play of misapprehension and unexpected confusions in the scene where the four lovers are at odds, is enormously enhanced by the sprightly sketch of the girlish moods and the feline attitudes of Hermia's jealousy.

But when the lovers have played out the fond pageant of youth, their human nature will be the power which brings them to health and natural taste.

> The country proverb known
> That every man shall take his own,
>   Jack shall have Jill,
>   Nought shall go ill,
> The man shall have his mare again and all shall go well.

At all events, so much are we bidden to take on trust. As an article of faith, it is made easier of acceptance when Titania and Oberon have revealed the disadvantages of houseless, undomesticated fairyland. Their term of courtship is ended. But, inhabiting the air from pole to pole, they are exempt from the constraints of housekeeping. Acorn-cups impose no fellowship. There is nothing to compound mere whim and vagary. In a house on earth, presumably it little matters whether the Indian boy be known as master's or as mistress's servant. But in fairyland such problems do not settle themselves. Mere personal preference and mood are left in entire control of fairy life. Affection follows fancy, and the consequent state of sentimental anarchy is never ordered by obligation to the world. Titania and Oberon are, of course, the better fairies for their lack of human principles in their behaviour. But the more fairy, the less fitted for the responsibilities of the settled human institution of marriage.

The exposure of Oberon and Titania's conjugal relationship is comedy fulfilling its natural function, glorifying those settled institutions of man's social existence which owe their persistence to mankind's experience that such as these make for his welfare in the substantial problem of living life in the world as the world is. Marriage is to the comic dramatist the beneficent arrangement through which mankind achieves a maximum of human joy and a minimum of social disability. Of course, at a later stage comedy may look to proportionately minor disadvantages in the social habit of marriage and monogamy: but its first law is to insist on the common sense of the settled habit, and only later will it suggest possible and relatively minor modifications of that habit. Shakespeare will justify the world's practice, Shaw will suggest minor adaptations, or even plead that the real world itself has developed qualities requiring, on the same grounds of common sense, a complete overhauling of hitherto conventional and fixed practices. At all events, in *A Midsummer Night's Dream*, wedlock and housekeeping are imposed on man for his advantage; and the advantage as a social being he gains thereby is made patent by setting beside him the undomesticated irresponsible beings of fairyland. Fairy whim was not even to be trusted to prefer its own authentic king to the monstrous, gross Bottom with the ass's head. And even so, its precious Bottom would have soon revolted against a fairy wife, who, when he pined for bread, offered him a stone—emerald, pearl, or diamond, though it should be.

Hence it comes that Bottom and his fellows are as much a part of the play as are Titania and Oberon, or the Athenian lovers. The spirit of the earth which stirs men's sentiments for nature, producing thence the fairies of its folk-lore, and the springtides which turn men's thoughts to love, has brought forth also, as its most material children, these rustics of the countryside. Like Costard, they are straight from the bosom of Mother Earth, and though, for the nonce, they have left the plough for mechanic labours on Athenian stalls, they are still but countrymen and villagers.

And Bottom is sufficient assurance that, though nature makes men liable to love, it gives them also so much mortal grossness that man can never distil himself to a mere airy spirit. Sublimation has its visible limits. Bottom, transported to the lap of an adoring queen of faery, has enough of earth about him to preserve his native self. He is at home anywhere, and turns fairyland to his own needs as Shakespeare has now learnt to turn romance to his. Nothing finally perturbs Bottom. The strangest and most perplexing experiences have no power to alter his essential nature, but merely serve to give additional strength to it. The fairy queen may stick musk-roses in his sleek, smooth head, but he will only take advantage of the scene to call up Peaseblossom, and Cobweb, and Mustardseed to ease him of an itching. No dulcet sound of fairy song will lure him from his preference for tongs and bones. And although he will regale himself on fairy dishes of apricocks and dewberries, he will not fail to order the complementary course, the pecks of the provender on which he naturally subsists. He is, of course, a clown. But it is clownage sufficient for its day. It completes the guarantee for the world's security which Theseus has offered.

From the earliest days, Bottom has been accepted as the best piece of characterisation in *A Midsummer Night's Dream;* the Restoration, in fact, cut the play to the pranks of bully Bottom. But he is the most substantial character because Shakespeare's apprehension has laid more certain hold of him than of the other figures in the play. That is another way of saying that, as a man, he means more to Shakespeare than do the others. He is, to the dramatist, the tangible person who provides in the flesh and in life what the mind of Theseus was to provide in theory and in conjecture about life.

Sanity, cool reason, common sense, is the pledge of Theseus against the undue ravages of fancy and of sentiment in human nature. But in Bottom the place of this intellectual temper is supplied by the crude native matter of human instinct. Bottom is a bigger part of the world than is a Lysander or a Demetrius, and always will be, for he has, above all, the instinct which makes for the preservation of his species. He will take command in any the most unexpected situation, and will impose his will on his fellows or on his superiors. Even when he has been killed upon the stage he will rise again with his "No, I assure you," and set the world to rights. He has supreme confidence in himself, and in his ability to play any part in life or in theatricals. And this is no mere overweening conceit, for schemes collapse when he withdraws. The world is safe so long as it produces men like Bottom, for its inhabitants will never be permitted to get completely out of touch with earth, will never be allowed to forget the conditions which real life imposes on actual livers of it. Earth and the world take visible human form in his huge bulk before men's eyes, and in such way that it sharpens their sense of humour, of the difference between what man is, and what he vainly pretends himself to be.

Hence the substance in the seemingly unsubstantial cloud-world of *A Midsummer Night's Dream.* At first glance it appears but as a light excursion into the realms of pure romance, where fairies dance and lovers woo, and magic philtres are the dispensers of fate. Yet the intellectual foundations of it all are embodied in the unromantic worldly realism of Theseus. But it is the realism of an English and an Elizabethan mind, not one of classical Roman comedy. It is the temper of a landed gentry, rather than the outlook of a man about town. It is more humane, more representative, and more sympathetic. Roman comedy bolstered a limited society; it was a defence of the customs and conventions of a narrow social group—the citizens, who even so, were only a minority of the inhabitants of their city. But the comedy in *A Midsummer Night's Dream* looks to the preservation of the whole human race as human beings rather than to the maintenance of a particular social caste. It comprehends the court, the city, and the country. It seeks for what contributes to this larger fellowship of man, rather than for what is discordant with the conventions of a class. It values the normal in mankind at large much more than mere propriety in a particular clique. It lifts comedy from concern with the merely unconventional in manners to envisage the more vital incongruities in personality itself.

> Lovers and madmen have such seething brains,
> Such shaping fantasies, that apprehend
> More than cool reason ever comprehends.
> The lunatic, the lover and the poet
> Are of imagination all compact:
> One sees more devils than vast hell can hold,
> That is the madman: the lover, all as frantic,
> Sees Helen's beauty in a brow of Egypt:
> The poet's eye, in a fine frenzy rolling,
> Doth glance from heaven to earth, from earth to heaven;
> And as imagination bodies forth
> The forms of things unknown, the poet's pen
> Turns them to shapes, and gives to airy nothings
> A local habitation and a name.
> Such tricks hath strong imagination,
> That, if it would but apprehend some joy,
> It comprehends some bringer of that joy,
> Or, in the night, imagining some fear,
> How easy is a bush supposed a bear.

In this speech, Shakespeare formulates in set terms his first conscious notion of the comic idea, and adds tersely a summary illustration of its value by recalling one of the homeliest, most familiar and most general of common experiences. Grown man, as the play has shown us, is liable to be distracted by vagaries whose source is his fancy or his emotion. For these are apt to subdue his cool reason and his intuitive common sense. They distort his view of things as things are; like a lover, he sees Helen's fair classic beauty in a gypsy's coarse brown visage; or like a lunatic, he not only sees real things awry, but imagines he sees things which are not; or like a poet, subject to the ills of both, he gives substantial reality to mere figments of his uncontrolling brain. But even the most commonplace of mortals, one neither born to be a great lover nor destined to utter a line of verse, may from his own life realise the harm of poets' and lovers' qualities. He will recall the evening in his childhood when at dusk he had the last half mile of a country lane to traverse in the gloom; he will remember the starts and the shocks endured when the shade of a tree took the shape of lurking footpad, when the rustle of the leaves seemed like pursuing footsteps—and all the myriad other perturbations he suffered through the false creations of his own fancy and of his own fears.

> Or in the night imagining some fear
> How easy is a bush supposed a bear—

These, his common sense will clearly tell him, are features arising from his inability at the moment to control his fancy and his feeling by his cool reason: they are disturbances likely to prevent his competent dealing with circumstance, whether that circumstance be a walk along a country lane at dusk, or whether it be a major episode in a bigger life. Indeed, he may go beyond Shakespeare's illustration. He may recognise that the erratic vision which makes a bush a bear, is just as likely to fail in the converse situation, and mistake a bear for a bush. It needs no imagination at all to grasp at once, not how perturbing, but how fatal such an error is likely to be. At once, he sees that mere survival in the world depends upon man's ability to differentiate rapidly and certainly between bears and bushes, and thus perceives that the attribute of supreme value in the world is the "cool reason" which comprehends things as things are: that men without cool reason, who are the sport of seething brains and of the tumultuous frenzies of fancy and of sentiment, are the victims of the world, and the butts of its comedy. Comedy, leading its action to a happy ending, leaving its characters at the end in harmony with the world, is bound to put its highest values on qualities which make for worldly happiness and success. With Theseus, the philosophy of comedy is finding its voice, and his "cool reason" is its prevailing spirit.

A Midsummer Night's Dream is Shakespeare's first comic masterpiece. In its technical aspect, it is the work of a master of language and of plot: but its greatest attainment is that embodied in it, the controlling power shaping its form and texture, there is this first considerable apprehension of the enduring attitude of comedy, the spirit which gives to comedy its vital significance for man and endows it with the permanence of a fine art.

VI

Shakespeare's Jew

THERE is, I fear, a catchpenny ring about the title by which I have described the subject of my talk with you to-night. It may suggest that topics are to be handled which are at the moment of grave concern to all who wish for peace and progress in Europe. I want therefore to make it quite clear that this evening's subject was chosen without reference to any problem beyond those which belong to the study of Shakespeare. It was, in fact, chosen four years ago, to take its place in due course as the fifth in a series of talks on Shakespeare's comedies. That is why I deal with *The Merchant of Venice* to-night.

I regret therefore that circumstances have given to its theme certain extraneous interests of a topical origin. I am no politician, and I freely acknowledge an utter incompetence to handle political questions of international significance. My concern is with Shakespeare. With his work, as with that of every other artistic genius, the aim of the critic is to see it *sub specie æternitatis*, divesting himself, as far as fallible mortal may, of the biases and the prejudices which distort our ephemeral judgments. It is a mere accident that Hitlerism has intervened at this moment, and made it even harder to exercise dispassionate judgment on the place of *The Merchant of Venice* in the organic growth of Shakespeare's creative genius. But at least I may honestly assert that the interpretation of Shakespeare's Jew which I am venturing to put forward this evening is an interpretation which I have been propounding for many years in the semi-publicity of University classes, from a time indeed long before Hitler's name had been heard outside his own village. I do not claim any peculiar perspicuity on that account; I merely state it, lest I should be accused of desecrating the platform of our John Rylands Library by using it for what may perhaps seem like propagandist purposes. And I should be loath to appear even remotely guilty of profaning the privilege of addressing a Rylands audience. Yet, at the outset, of one thing I must make unconditional declaration. I have said that I regret the complications which give a topical interest to this lecture; that the opinions in it were formulated at least a dozen years ago; that on their restatement for the present occasion, I trust I have guarded against modifications directly due to to-day's affairs. I will add to that, too, that as a student whose postgraduate days were spent in pre-War Germany more than twenty years ago, I grew to a fondness and admiration for the German people which even the War did little to mitigate. But I should be unfair to myself, and, what is more important, I should be exposing the name of academic scholarship to improper hazards, if I did not state categorically here and now, my own personal sense that Germany's persecution of the Jews is an entirely indefensible exhibition of those animal passions which it has been the trend of civilisation to subdue, and of which the gradual elimination is our firmest hope for a future in which humanity will live in brotherhood together and will devise for themselves a practicable parliament of men and a substantial federation of the world.

These explanations made, I resume my immediate task. With the object of suggesting an æsthetic of Elizabethan romantic comedy, I have in previous winters spoken to you of four early comedies of Shakespeare, regarding them as Shakespeare's experimentations with types, and watching for his election of the sort most congenial to the sensibilities of his generation. The trend of development is not difficult to distinguish, and the main outlines of Shakespeare's comic scheme are already becoming apparent. Its chief concern is with lovers and with love-making, and the lovers whose wooing is his main interest are youths and maidens endowed with those gifts of body and of spirit which are the tradition of a cultured aristocracy. Alongside the high comedy which is conceived in sentimental and poetic manner runs a subsidiary low comedy providing the realistic homeliness or the farcical buffoonery contributed by the indispensable rustic or the clownish serving man. In the interplay of these two components, there is still much for Shakespeare to discover; but the essential pattern is determined already. He has chosen his protagonists, a hero and a heroine, and their primary obligation is to woo or to be wooed. Wherefore, the long procession of lovers in Shakespeare's comedies, from Rosaline and Biron, and Sylvia and Valentine, of the early ones, to Rosalind and Orlando, and Beatrice and Benedick of the greatest.

But despite the moonlit gardens of Belmont, *The Merchant of Venice* will not be forced into this march of Shakespearian comedy. It has, of course, its lovers and there is elaborate ritual in its wooing. But of its wooers, Portia is more adept in the badinage than in the poetry of love, and indeed, in the action of the play, her technical triumph is not in love, but in law. And Bassanio is palpably relegated to the subordinate characters. Nor is the wooing itself in the way of Elizabethan sentiment; the symbolism of the caskets surrounds it with picturesque ceremony, but deprives it completely of that passionate reality whereby the Elizabethans recognised the lordship of love. And indeed, though perhaps not by a mere arithmetical computation of lines, yet certainly by the estimation of men's memories of its people, there can be no doubt that the wooing of Portia by Bassanio is not the main stuff of the play. It is an episode, an expensive undertaking which will therefore serve as pretext to introduce a scheme for guaranteeing overdrafts. The Bond story, not the tale of the caskets, is the backbone of *The Merchant of Venice;* and Shylock and Antonio, not Bassanio, nor even Portia, are the real protagonists of the piece.

The Merchant of Venice, then, is hard to fit into a progressive series of Shakespeare's comedies. The story of the play would not appear to offer much opportunity for comedy of the kind to which his preference was apparently running; nor does it seem in any way to illustrate the approach to life in terms of which the idea of comedy had already been formulated in the creed of Theseus. Just where Shakespeare got his story is not exactly known. The likelihood is that *The Merchant of Venice* is his re-shaping of the play, "The Jew . . . representing the greedinesse of worldly chusers and the bloody minds of usurers," which Gosson had seen sometime before 1579. That play is unfortunately lost. But at such a date in the history of the Elizabethan stage, it can hardly have exhibited much of the romance of love-making, though Gosson does in fact name the caskets before the bond. In all probability, it was a heavily moralised interlude, and, Gosson specifically and puritanically adds, nowhere "with amorous gesture" did it wound the eye. It is possible, though in my view unlikely, that Shakespeare knew other versions of the story, the one for instance in *Il Pecorone* of Ser Giovanni, written a little before 1400, and published in Italian in 1558. Ser Giovanni himself was telling an oft-told tale, and the two earlier archtypes of it are the versions in *Dolopathos* (*c.* 1200) and in *Gesta Romanorum* (1342). Though in all these versions, the man's pursuit of the wealthy wife is in a sense the main story to which the tale of the bond he signs with a usurer is subsidiary, yet in all of them the manner of the pursuit and the characters both of the pursuer and of the pursued are in nowise of the kind most obviously congenial to romantic treatment. In all of them, there is no wooing: the lady, in fact, sets herself up as an unregistered private prostitute, extracts her fee from her client, drugs him, and then adjudges him unworthy of her because of his proved impotence. But the story had gone at least a stage nearer to romance when some one or other between Ser Giovanni and Shakespeare cut out this salacious testing and substituted another familiar theme of mediæval tale, the choice of caskets.

I see no reason why we should not credit this amendment to
the author of *The Jew*, whose concern for morality is sufficiently certified, and who would certainly find apt material for
moralising in the mottoes of a row of caskets. It is not impossible to imagine that Shakespeare might somehow have seen
his way to use material like this of *The Jew* for comedy such
as comedy was becoming in his hands. Yet it is obvious that
in fact he did not use the material in that way at all.

There can be little doubt that in determining to write a
play like *The Merchant of Venice*, and in choosing the particular
matter from which to make his *Merchant of Venice*, the decision
came not from Shakespeare's artistic impulse but from his
conscious deliberation. Hitherto, in the growth of this genius
for comedy, his deepening insight has appeared in his choice
of this or that material for comic projection, in his sense for
matter most apt to express the spirit of comedy. But in choosing the story of *The Merchant of Venice*, Shakespeare the artist
is not asserting himself. It is Shakespeare the Elizabethan, with
the political and racial prejudices of the average man, or of the
mob, of his own day. About 1594, public sentiment in England was roused to an outbreak of traditional Jew-baiting; and
for good and evil, Shakespeare the man was like his fellows.
He planned a *Merchant of Venice* to let the Jew dog have it, and
thereby to gratify his own patriotic pride of race.

It is not open to serious question that this was Shakespeare's
purpose. The text itself preserves sufficient evidence of the
author's fixed intent to exhibit his Shylock as an inhuman
scoundrel, whose diabolical cunning is bent on gratifying a
satanic lust for Christian flesh, the Jew, in fact, who was the
ogre of mediæval story and the cur to be execrated by all
honest men. This, indeed, is how Shylock is described by
every character in the play who is cast to secure the sympathy
of the audience, Portia, for instance, and Antonio, in particular.
And those who knew him nearest, his daughter Jessica and his
servant Launcelot, are enrolled to heap up the ignominy. This
is particularly remarkable because these two are invented

characters, not in the original story.[1]   Another invention—
the penalty finally imposed on Shylock, that he become a
Christian—is a sufficient indication not only of the dramatist's
intention to expose Shylock to shame, but, by the callousness
of the punishment, of his unrelenting antipathy to the figure he
had been minded to create. It is most likely that in his racial
passion, he never consciously meant his Shylock to be entitled
to more sympathy or to less callous cruelty than is meted to
him when Salarino and Salanio allow themselves to be merry
with him over the flight of Jessica, a disgusting exhibition of
sheer heartlessness (Act III, sc. i). Indeed, when one thinks of
the recipe for an Elizabethan comedy, so much admixture of
buffoonery in every play, and when one remembers that
Gobbo is the slenderest and most pointlessly fatuous of
Shakespeare's clowns, one cannot resist the thought that the
instincts in an audience which buffoonery satisfies, were meant
to be provided for by Shylock himself—"*The Comicall
History of the Merchant of Venice*," as the half-title of the first
Quarto (1600) has it.

Shakespeare, it would seem, meant to make, and never
doubted that he had made, a Shylock fit only for exciting
execration and opprobrium. But it is no less certain that
Shylock has become a different figure. There has been a
strange redistribution of sympathies; and Shylock the ogre
becomes Shylock the hero. Since Irving's day, and indeed
from the earlier times of Macready and even of Kean, Shylock
totters from the stage, a pathetic frustrated figure, broken by
callousness and insensate stupidity, to make an Elizabethan
holiday.

[1]They may, of course, have been in the anonymous play, *The Jew;* Jessica
almost certainly was. Dr. Cardozo (*vide infra* p. 20, n. 1) speculates inter-
estingly about the authorship of the play, taking its writer to have been a
good Hebrew scholar, since the four Jewish names in the play all occur in
reasonable proximity in the Old Testament, two of them occurring once
only in the Bible, where their English form is not as in Shakespeare, though
the Shakespearian ones are not incorrect, but only alternative, translitera-
tions of the originals.

It is not impossible, of course, to accuse the actors of distorting Shakespeare's text: or one may account for the transformation of Shylock by alleging that racial prejudices are no longer as virulent as they were nor as right as they were assumed to be. But these explanations are utterly inadequate to account for the facts. The Shylock of whom the Elizabethan pit, and Shakespeare amongst them, made such hearty mockery, and the Shylock who wrings the withers of a modern audience are both in the play. The one is Shylock as he was meant to be, the other is Shylock as he became through Shakespeare's unconscious dramatic instinct. Moscovitch, describing his own performance of Shylock, says that "he gropes his way like a blind man from scene to scene, playing all the contradictions, it being the duty of an actor to be faithful to his author."

There is nothing peculiar in a situation such as this. Shakespeare the Elizabethan, the man of his day, addicted to the thoughts, the prejudices, and the passions of his fellows, felt like them a bitter hatred of the Jews. Shakespeare the typical Elizabethan could determine that an anti-Jew play should be written. But only Shakespeare the artist could write it. Writing it, his dramatic genius shaped it at the direction of his creative imagination. Precisely how the creative faculty operates remains a mystery, the great mystery of art—

But here is the finger of God, a flash of the will that can,
  Existent behind all laws, that made them and lo, they are!
And I know not if, save in this, such gift be allowed to man,
  That out of three sounds he frame, not a fourth sound, but a star.

The mystery is admitted. The artist apparently has a dual personality. He is his conscious self, and he is an artist. On the one hand he has like the rest of us his normal nature and his familiar mind, functioning not differently from the minds of the rest of us. On the other hand, he has the artist's gift; he possesses a faculty of apprehending and of bodying forth the forms of things not known to his rational self. It is a faculty which works by laws of its own; and both its processes and its findings may remain unknown to the other side of the artist's personality, his normal self.

A parallel illustration suggests itself. There is Milton the puritan determining to write a poem to the glory of God. But Milton the poet has to write it; and *Paradise Lost* emerges almost as a pæan to Satan. Milton the man certainly never meant this to happen; and further still, it is certain that if Milton had for a moment realised that Satan would triumph in men's minds because of his *Paradise Lost*, he would un-hesitatingly have torn the manuscript to shreds.

> Amphora coepit
> Institui; currente rota cur urceus exit?

The problem is not merely the old and arid dispute, "Natura fieret laudabile carmen an arte?" It is not a matter of whether technical accomplishment may be attained through discipline and instruction. There are, it would seem, behind the distinc-tion between poet and normal man, fundamental differences in modes of apprehending reality, differences in faculties for grasping at truth. That deeper distinction is what the late C. H. Herford argued before the British Academy, when an analysis of Lucretius and Dante amongst others, led him to propound the view that there is in fact 'a poetic view of the world,' which it is the poet's prerogative to contribute to the sum total of human knowledge. It may be that there is a subtle connection between the vision which the poet owes to his creative imagination, and the faculty by which as a creator he has a sense of the forms within which he creates. It is possible, for instance, and up to a point demonstrable, that the formal conditions of drama to which a dramatic genius adapts itself are themselves influential in determining the nature of the thing dramatised, quite independently of the deliberate will of the dramatist. Even so conscious an artist as Mr. Shaw admits somewhere that whilst he always knows what sort of a play he means to write and what intellectual proposition it is meant to support, once the making of the play begins, the direction of it is taken over from his reason by some other force, and he is never certain how it will work out. His dramatic genius, not his sociological reason, determines that.

It may be easier with drama than with other arts to trace the working of some of the influences which determine the final character of the drama, and, therefore, of the thing dramatised. With *The Merchant of Venice*, the circumstance appears to be this. Moved by his intelligible prejudices as nationalist and politician, Shakespeare the man wished to write a play embodying a Shylock who had been created down the ages by the mob, the diabolical bogey of racial antipathies. How far, it must be asked, how far in the making of the play did Shakespeare the dramatist's intuitive sense of the necessities of drama, albeit unconsciously and perhaps quite unrecognisably to his contemporary audiences, modify the nature of the Jew he was dramatising? Is there in drama any obvious power to effect such unwitting transformations?

Mediæval legend told of the diabolical Jew who trapped a Christian merchant into a bond to surrender a pound of Christian flesh, on which the Jew could glut his devilish hatred. The tale was popular, because as a tale, it was good. Stories are much more thrilling when they tell of unusual, wild, and extravagant incidents than when they confine themselves to the familiar common round. Hence the romances are our finest tales. But story-telling and play-making are different undertakings. The story-teller is not impeded by his actors and by his stage; he can, for instance, make his Green Knight's headless trunk stoop down and pick up its severed head. But the dramatist has not this liberty. A dramatist works not only with words which range the free spaces of his reader's imagination: he has actors who act, and a stage whereon they act. His actors cannot but look more or less like men and women, and, in the main, his stage presents a semblance of a world more or less like the world we know. Inevitably therefore an audience in a theatre finds itself demanding some sort of realism. It is idle to try to determine categorically the degree of this demand: but at least it requires that its stage shall not depict episodes flagrantly contradictory of its sense of what may conceivably happen in a world where the participants in the action are apparently human beings. Hence the paramount significance of characterisation in modern drama as a means of securing the effect of probability and therefore of credibility. Putting living men upon the stage to represent the persons of his story, the dramatist confines himself to figures who act as men may act; he is tied to an appearance of truth to human nature. The actions he presents must seem to be within probability, and his persons must palpably belong to the race of man.

The bond story demands a Jew who is a monster; but the dramatised version of it must exhibit a Jew who is a man, a figure who will be accepted as a possible man by the men whose company the play compels him to meet. That is Shakespeare's difficulty in *The Merchant of Venice*. His Shylock is a composite production of Shakespeare the Jew-hater, and of Shakespeare the dramatist. Sometimes in the play the figure is clearly the Shylock of mob prescription; at other times, it is the Shylock which the play itself is making. Very frequently it is a Shylock whose traits may satisfy the desires of either Shakespeare. It is particularly noteworthy that Shylock as he was meant to be is more often to be found at the outset of scenes in which he appears, or at other moments in the action where the dramatic tension is relatively low and at which therefore the poet's dramatic intuition has not been excited to function in its own proper mode. On the other hand, Shylock as he was becoming at the instigation of the dramatic artist is more frequently apparent where the drama is reaching tensions in the interplay of human beings which in themselves excite the genius of the dramatist. The outstanding example is, of course, the trial scene. But there is much to be said before that is reached.

Dramatically, the crucial moments of the bond story are

two. At the beginning Shylock presents a revolting bond for sealing; and at the end, he comes with devilish anxiety to claim the forfeit stipulated. Possibly at the outset of his story, the dramatist is entitled to impose whatever assumptions he likes upon his audience: and an Elizabethan audience would certainly not feel itself unduly taxed in being invited to take a Jew for an inhuman monster. Shylock at the beginning, purposing his bond, may be taken as a mere fiend without disturbing the credulity of the audience. But as the story moves along to its climax, as the dramatist's imagination is increasingly excited by the matter passing through it, the figure who at first relies for his reality on prejudice will be born again; he will of necessity acquire a reality of his own to give dramatic conviction to his deeds. Shakespeare can dispense, and indeed must dispense, with prejudice to secure dramatic conviction for the Shylock at the end of the play. The figure who appears at that stage of the story has been driven to a paroxysm of hatred by the circumstances revealed in the preceding incidents of the story. The demon in the court scene is in fact created by the drama itself, and not imposed on it by the racial passions of the pit, although even here, an intermittent feature or two harks back to his origin in mob frenzy.

Critics with one voice have pointed to the power of Shakespeare in these scenes between the sealing and the forfeiture of the bond. They have recognised therein his genius in securing convincing probability for the raging Jew of the trial scene. There is agreement, too, that Shylock in his most demoniacal fury becomes more convincing because he becomes more human. His claim to reality is not that, such as he is, he does not exceed the limits of ideal possibility, but that, being what he is, he is within the bounds of human probability. Truth of abstract science is one thing, truth to human nature another. One is reached by reason and systematic research; the other is grasped by the artist's instinct for life. A monster is not beyond the scope of speculative possibility; but a monster is outside the community of the human race.

Shylock at the end of the play is humanised, because Shylock at that point is in fact the creation of the drama and the dramatist. He has already lived through three acts of the world of which he is a part, where he speaks and feels and walks in semblance of a man, and where he encounters other beings moving and acting even by express intention as men do move and act. To make the world in which Shylock lives, the dramatist has intuitively exerted his genius and his apprehension of the world of man. In the process, the character of Shylock has taken on new traits to naturalise it amongst human beings. He has acquired them by his immersion in the play. But even as the play begins, its own laws may not improbably operate to colour the initial and pre-dramatic assumptions of the story.

Of course, an audience which assembles in the fervid consciousness of its racial prejudices may thereby be willing to adopt the wildest of congenial assumptions as the starting-point of its play. It is as yet politically and not æsthetically conscious. But as the play winds itself into its audience's imagination, the æsthetic conscience will awaken and demand satisfaction. Shakespeare and his fellows were willing to adopt the ogre of popular story, and at the outset to accept without question a devilish Jew intent on tricking a benevolent Christian into a diabolical bond. Their prejudice appears to have blinded them into a ready acceptance of the play's account of the origin of the bond as a plain instance of the Jew's consummate and implacable devilry.

Even here, however, there are signs of the dramatic re-fashioning of given material to mould it to dramatic purposes. And though it remains possible to read the scene in which the bond is proposed and sealed without importing into it a Shylock much different from the devil the mob took him to be, a closer reading begins to shake the easy assumptions which were all of which it was necessary to remind the Elizabethans to secure their ready acceptance.

The bond story requires the participation of two main people, debtor and creditor, Antonio and Shylock. Moreover in all three stages of the preliminary action, the propounding of the bond, its acceptance and its sealing, there must be a semblance of reasonable and probable action. For if an audience is prepared to take a diabolical propounder without much question, its sympathies will be all the more alert to acquit the acceptor of such crass folly as would be implied in the acceptance of palpably outrageous terms.

So the dramatist shapes the origination of the bond as an episode springing naturally out of the normal circumstances of the society whose ways of life he is depicting. Shylock is first encountered in conversation with Bassanio. It is a matter-of-fact business interview, neither of the parties wasting words. With the curt but not impolite manner of the professional banker, Shylock simply reiterates the sum requested—"Three thousand ducats." But he is a business man. There is no reason for him to fall on Bassanio's neck and express his eagerness to do a deal. He must go cautiously, and see how urgent Bassanio is, and how much therefore he can increase his own gains in the deal by stipulating a more or even a much more profitable rate of interest. So "Three thousand ducats"— and, playing for time by letting the client show his hand— "well?" Bassanio's urgency is immediately apparent in his curt eagerness—"Ay, sir, for three months"; which, in its turn is suitably parried by the same non-committal stroke— "For three months; well?" Wherefore Bassanio raps out the primary inducement—"For the which, as I told you, Antonio shall be bound." It is all going as Shylock's business acumen would have it go. It is still worth his while to keep his client in the suspense which may increase the profits. So, as yet, no outright acceptance—"Antonio shall become bound: well?" But by now Bassanio, with all his thoughts on the next boat for Belmont, is played out as a bargainer. He loses patience and politeness in his brusque anxiety to get the money and put an end to an unpleasant interview. "May you stead me? Will you pleasure me? Shall I know your answer?" That is exactly the mood into which Shylock desires to reduce his clients: they are then more likely to accept any terms he may propose. But it is not his habit to show his hand: and so the technique is still exploited—"Three thousand ducats for three months and Antonio bound." Out of all patience, and as if hearing the siren of the packet-boat, comes Bassanio's contemptuous exasperation—"Your answer to that!" But again, it is exactly as Shylock the business man would have it: his customer is working himself into the mood which will pay any price demanded. And so, astutely, he maintains the non-committal but partly consenting attitude: "Antonio is a good man." At once the attitude of Gentile to Jew flares out in the angry stupidity of Bassanio's misapprehension; arrogance and contempt blind him to the plain sense of Shylock's comment, and his "Have you heard any imputation to the contrary?" is so naively inept, that Shylock can only put it aside with a muttered expression of perplexed surprise—"Oh no, no, no, no"; and by a simple restatement of what he had already clearly said—"My meaning in saying that he is a good man is to have you understand me that he is sufficient"; sufficient, that is, for a bond, ample security, in fact. But this explicit affirmation of Antonio's goodness as security into which circumstances have forced Shylock is hardly the best business strategy. It seriously handicaps further bargaining for substantial interest. So Shylock follows up his explanation by accumulating every conceivable mitigation of Antonio's soundness as a security. His wealth is at the hazard of the seas—"His means are in supposition: he hath an argosy bound to Tripolis, another to the Indies; I understand, moreover, upon the Rialto, he hath a third at Mexico, a fourth for England, and other ventures he hath, squandered abroad." And, warming to the argument, he clumsily elaborates the speculative risks of traffic, making a portentous hazard of mere commonplace—"Ships are but boards, sailors but men": and multiplying the other incidental chances by his crude catalogue of synonyms for thieves: "there be land-rats, and water-rats, water-thieves and land-thieves, I mean pirates," he rises to a peroration which summarily includes the assembled perils of navigation—"there is peril of waters, winds, and rocks." But Shylock knows that on this count he is not playing a strong suit. And so—"The man, notwithstanding, is sufficient: I think I may take his bond"—which still leaves him a chance for further bargaining. But Bassanio's thick-skinned arrogance and his natural impetuosity make him still perceive nothing but an implied imputation against a Christian friend and boon-companion: "be assured you may." There is nothing left for Shylock but to defer a final agreement, and to get into touch with Antonio himself. But that in itself signifies so much of willingness, that Bassanio sees himself likely to be provided: it is therefore an occasion to celebrate in the way of his kind, a convivial commemoration. And so, to Shylock's question— "May I speak with Antonio?" Bassanio's bonhomie suggests the appropriate occasion—"If it will please you to dine with us." Thinking to get what he wants he means the invitation in a kindly way. But its heedlessness is its sting. It touches Shylock's religious and racial sensitiveness to the quick. It symbolises the course of his life. His fate is to dwell in an alien world, encountering at every turn the deliberate hostility of the men amongst whom he lives; and even at the rare moments when for their own advantage they mean kindly, their off-handed tolerance bites more deeply than their avowed ani-mosity. "Yes, to smell pork; to eat of the habitation which your prophet the Nazarite conjured the devil into." His memory is stirred to a vivid review of the continuous torments incidental to his daily life in Venice: "I will buy with you, sell with you, talk with you, walk with you, and so following." But there are a few moments in each day when he can with-draw into the secluded domain of his own spiritual life, and in the sanctuary of his own house, protect himself from profana-tion by the Gentiles: "but I will not eat with you, drink with you, nor pray with you," The collocation of phrase, eating, drinking, and praying, sufficiently indicates the intensity of Shylock's spiritual sensitiveness. But a moment later, he relapses into the self-possession and the conventional demeanour of the part he has schooled himself to play in a hostile world—"What news on the Rialto?"—buying and selling amongst a people alien in race, in custom, and religion, and making his own life amongst them only tolerable by practising a disciplined imperturbability for the public hours of the day, in the strength that he secures for himself in the privacy of his own home where he may realise the instinctive demands of his own spiritual life.

Then enter Antonio: and the stage is set for the first time for its protagonists. At an initial juncture of this kind, Shylock is called upon by the prescription to exhibit himself as the unrelieved villain he was taken by the audience to be. His soliloquy aside as a sort of diploma piece, his qualification for the rôle he had been brought in to play. And Shakespeare does it well. Shylock utters an incoherent jumble of furious revilings, urging confusedly religious, racial, and commercial rivalry as his promptings to revenge, just, indeed, as popular prejudice willed him to do.

But the very first line of his speech, as set down in both quartos and in the folio, and perpetuated in all modern editions, is an excellent example of the uncritical prejudice with which the audience were ready, without question, to take anything apparently opprobrious as proper to Shylock, more opprobrious even than Shakespeare in his own prejudice had offered them. For it is hardly credible that Shakespeare made Shylock say of Antonio—"How like a fawning publican he looks!" Shylock would hardly use the term 'publican;' and in its developed Christian sense, "an extortioner," it has no apparent application to Antonio, even from Shylock's point of view. Moreover, so far as Shylock's acquaintance with Antonio has gone, it has never shown him a "fawning" Antonio. On the contrary, it is Antonio's arrogance and high-mindedness and self-righteousness which have marked their encounters. It is perhaps not a little ironic that once, and once only, in the play, Antonio does 'fawn,'—when, after habitually calling

Shylock a dog, but at length finding himself in Shylock's power, he addresses him as 'Good Shylock' (III. iii. 3); yet perhaps 'fawning' itself is too dignified a word with which to describe this turn in Antonio's manners. A generation ago Moulton saw that 'fawning publican' would in every way be a proper description for Antonio to apply to Shylock. To Antonio, Shylock was a publican, an extortioner, who consorted with fellow sinners, and was obliged by nature or circumstance to adopt gestures which might well be described as "fawning." But even, if by a displacement of the opening line, the texts outdo Shakespeare in antipathy to Shylock, it hardly affects the obvious tenour of Shylock's opening speech. With the deliberately characterising soliloquy over, Shylock responds to Bassanio's invitation—"Shylock, do you hear?"— and applies himself with a lie to the business in hand. But once he is again brought into a dramatic situation, once he is again involved in the interplay of a group of men, the specifically dramatic sense of the playwright is stimulated, and once more two Shylocks cross each other's shadows.

> I am debating of my present store,
> And, by the near guess of my memory,
> I cannot instantly raise up the gross
> Of full three thousand ducats. What of that?
> Tubal, a wealthy Hebrew of my tribe,
> Will furnish me.

Shylock is obviously temporising. But what is at the back of his mind? A scheme to inveigle Antonio, according to the legend. But his actual question, "How many months do you desire?" is exactly what he would be turning over if he were calculating possible profits, and preparing to stipulate such and such a rate of interest. Antonio's entry, however, gives a fresh direction to his thoughts. In substance, and in form, Antonio's first remarks to the Jew are a pattern of unconscious effrontery and of half-conscious offensiveness. Self-righteously, he protests against usury in the act of asking a loan from a usurer: and his excuse for his breach of principle, 'to supply the ripe wants of a friend,' enhances the unpleasant savour of his self-righteousness. It is as if, dashing during closed hours into the bar of a public house, one preached to the landlord a complacent sermon on teetotalism, prior to demanding brandy from him for a fainting friend. The contemptuousness in Antonio's attitude is emphasised by his turning from Shylock to Bassanio for a piece of information, as if to save himself further contamination from the Jew's mouth—

> Is he yet possess'd
> How much ye would?

But a new and exciting notion is fermenting in Shylock's mind: to catch Antonio on the hip, of course, according to the story—but one must await its utterance to distinguish its real character. It is, at all events, a notion which makes it urgent for Shylock to maintain direct contact with Antonio. So, neglecting the slight, he himself replies to the question which has not been addressed to him: "Ay, ay, three thousand ducats." Antonio peremptorily names the other relevant term—"for three months." The only point left for agreement is the rate of interest. But, his mind running along that line, Shylock is struck by a new notion. He speaks absent-mindedly—"I had forgot, three months, you told me so: well, then, your bond."

The new notion is beginning to take definite shape; and, of course, in the old tale, it is in some such way that he devises his diabolical plot. But that hardly squares with the plain sense of the immediate text. Shylock's thoughts are running on the question of rate of interest. The morality of usury is, as his own bitter experience daily teaches him, a fundamental consideration which sharply divides Jew from Gentile. Christian doctrine and law traditionally forbade the lending of money at interest. But here now is Antonio, a representative Christian, proposing to borrow money at interest. The occasion suggests itself at once to Shylock as a proper one for trying to get Antonio to see the moral problem of money-lending from the Jew's point of view:

Methought you said you neither lend nor borrow
Upon advantage.

It is Shylock's bid for mutual understanding; but Antonio's
brusque "I do never use it," hardly promises a willingness to
try to understand. Yet Shylock persists in the attempt. He
wants some common ground from which to start, something
with common authority for Jew and for Gentile. Hence the
Old Testament example of Jacob's "thrift."

It is strange that commentators have almost invariably
missed the point of Shylock's illustration. Antonio, of course,
misses it; and perhaps Shylock is not at his happiest in rab-
binical exposition. But his argument is particularly cogent.
He is, in fact, exposing the fallaciousness of the formal principles
underlying the Christian condemnation of usury.

The law of England did indeed permit usury in Shakespeare's
day, limiting the maximum legal rate to ten per cent. But
despite Calvin's pronouncement on the morality of interest,
even in Protestant countries the traditional view remained
what it had been through the Middle Ages. Dante labelled
usury a sin; and canon law categorically condemned it. The
ethical case against it rested queerly on a passage in Aristotle's
Politics (I. x. 4; xi. 1) in which Aristotle discusses the "useful
parts of money-making." "The art of money-making out of
fruits and animals," by knowledge of livestock, by husbandry,
tillage, and planting, is of course, approved. But Aristotle's
approval is oddly phrased: "the art of money-making out of
fruits and animals is always natural." He examines other
modes of money-making, barter, service, and so on; amongst
them, "the most hated sort and with the greatest reason, is
usury." The reason given is that "usury makes money out of
money, as if money could be born of money"; usury is therefore "most unnatural."[1]

[1] I owe these quotations to an extraordinarily interesting thesis by a
Dutchman, Dr. J. L. Cardozo, *The Contemporary Jew in Elizabethan Drama*
(Amsterdam, 1925), written at the instigation of my friend, Professor A. E.
H. Swaen. Dr. Cardozo's book first drew my attention to the connection

The argument was generally familiar to the sixteenth century. And not everybody who knew the form of it, "a breed for barren metal," was as stupidly blind to its implications as was Antonio. Frances Meres, who knew his Shakespeare well in 1598, expresses the whole theory in brief: "usurie and encrease by gold and silver is unlawful, because against nature: nature hath made them sterill and barren, usurie makes them procreative." And Thomas Overbury, characterising a Devilish Usurer, says; "He puts his money to the unnatural act of generation."

But how does Jacob's exploit bear on the argument? It is meant to undermine the factitious differentiation between "natural" and "unnatural" kinds of money-making, by quoting an established case in which, though the 'productivity' is by natural procreation, yet the quality of the production and the producer's profits are controlled by the exercise of human skill and ingenuity. Jacob's device was in accord with the law of nature and the law of God—

> This was a way to thrive, and he was blest,
> And thrift is blessing, if men steal it not.

Shylock's exegesis, however, is too subtle for Antonio, (probably also for Shakespeare who very likely took it confusedly from the old Jew play), who brushes it aside with unintelligent contempt: "this was a venture, sir, that Jacob served for." He disregards the clear sense of the biblical story, denying that Jacob's scheme had succeeded:

> A thing not in his power to bring to pass,
> But swayed and fashioned by the hand of heaven.

And so, of course, he has not even a glimmering notion of the relevance of Shylock's argument:

> Was this inserted to make interest good?

between Shylock's argument and the Aristotelian proposition. I differ, however, from Dr. Cardozo very widely in estimating the dramatic implications of the material.

He has not even perceived that the theory is built on a dis-
crimination of livestock from barren metal:

> Or is your gold and silver, ewes and rams?

Shylock's whole point is that, for the argument in question,
gold and silver are exactly in the same kind as ewes and rams.
But he must have seen that it was useless to press an abstruse
point with Antonio; he ends the argument with a last despair-
ing remark which does at least express the one practical common property of animal and mineral possessions: "I make it
breed as fast."

His bid for understanding has failed, how abjectly appears
from the characteristically pharisaic complacence of Antonio's
comment:

> Mark you this, Bassanio
> The devil can cite Scripture for his purpose—

and more to the same effect.

There is apparently nothing for Shylock to do further than
to complete the transaction as a mere business undertaking:
"then, let me see, the rate." But he is moved to another kind
of appeal by Antonio's irritable anxiety to have done with the
irksome affair as quickly as possible—"Well, Shylock, shall we
be beholding to you," in which the formal phrasing, 'beholding,' cannot but make Shylock consider what obligation indeed
he can be thought to owe to his clients. He has failed in his
appeal to Antonio's intellect; now that other sanctions are
suggested, will it be possible to reach him on the broader
grounds of mere humanity? Hence Shylock's moving recital
of the sufferings of his tribe, and of the ignominies daily heaped
upon them. Yet now the oppressors come uninvited and ask a
favour of the oppressed:

> *You* come to me, and *you* say
> Shylock, we would have moneys: *you* say so.

What in such circumstances can they expect for an answer? Shylock is evidently leading to an offer of friendly accommodation. But it seems destined to fail, for the recital awakens no spark of tolerance in Antonio:

> I am as like to call thee so again,
> To spit on thee again, to spurn thee too.

The offer is indeed rejected before it has been formally made. And Antonio himself, Antonio, not the Jew, suggests that the transaction be conducted by a bond incorporating as harsh a penalty for default as may be devised:

> If thou wilt lend this money, lend it not
> As to thy friends; for when did friendship take
> A breed for barren metal of his friend?
> But lend it rather to thine enemy,
> Who, if he break thou mayst with better face
> Exact the penalty.

It is Shylock's great opportunity, whether he be the mob's Shylock, or the artist's. Even the mob's Shylock has so far shown little initiative in arranging circumstances to secure the bond for which he is supposed to be lusting; Antonio, in fact, is determining circumstances which are thrusting a bond on Shylock. But Shylock's great moment has come. So far he has never hinted that he has thought of foregoing interest; he has indeed from the beginning exercised himself as to the rate he might impose. But now, Antonio's phrasing of the Christian condemnation of interest, "a breed for barren metal," provides Shylock with an opening for a supreme gesture:

> I would be friends with you and have your love,
> Forget the shames that you have stained me with,
> Supply your present want and take no doit
> Of usance for my moneys.

The Jew will take a leaf from the Christian's book, and in friendship's name, will break a custom. He will out-Christian

Antonio, for he will forego his legitimate and reasonable profit in favour of one who has nothing but scorn and contempt for him. "This were kindness," Bassanio cannot help but say. And Shylock, jumping at this first expression of sympathy ever spoken to him, will settle the thing at once. Let them immediately devise a bond, and, remembering the general terms suggested previously by Antonio, but glossing them as if they could now be taken with friendly humour, let the bond include a forfeiture penalty, never likely, of course, to fall due, which will be a sort of extravagant parody of the contractual forfeits customary in bonds. The naming of the pound of flesh is "a merry sport": it is so put by Shylock; it is so accepted by Antonio:

> I'll seal to such a bond
> And say there is much kindness in the Jew.

It is, may be, a poor sort of joke; but Shylock has had little practice in developing his sense of humour. At once Bassanio, whose friendly word has called forth Shylock's offer relapses into the usual distrust and enmity. And Shylock, the mood of magnanimity shrivelled within him, sinks despairingly from the high level on which he has been contemplating the transaction; as if desperately realising that no noble sentiment can touch a Christian heart, he translates his offer into a purely material form, feeling by the need to do so, that its chief intention is doomed to fail:

> If he should break his day, what should I gain
> By the exaction of the forfeiture?
> A pound of man's flesh taken from a man
> Is not so estimable, profitable neither,
> As flesh of muttons, beefs, or goats.

Therefore, if Antonio will take the bond, "so: if not, adieu."

As the scene closes, Bassanio's remark, "I like not fair terms and a villain's mind," brings us sharply back to the original outline of the Shylock of mediæval story. But the scene has run its course under our eyes without need for these assumptions; the situations of the drama have made the characters appropriate to the essential incidents.

To the mob and to Shakespeare when he was part of it, the scheming for the bond and the terms of it were the outcome of malignant hatred in the alleged Shylock. In the play, the bond has evolved itself naturally out of the situation, and its contrivance has at no point involved the necessary intrusion of a demon's malice. The original plot, of course, required that Shylock should disguise his hatred so consummately that the Christian should be gulled. His actions were to be taken by the eye at their presumed value, and the audience would supply the unseen motive from its prejudice. But the dramatist has unwittingly depicted a sequence of events which make for the destruction of the prejudice. The mood of the unskilful merry jester is liker life than is its presupposed motive. Existing prejudices absolved the dramatist from creating sympathy for the Christians, and the prejudicial sympathies already in existence fatted themselves on tales of punishment inflicted on the Jew. But in the absence of prejudice, these very tales heap up sympathy for the Jew and antipathy for the Christians. The mind reverts to incidents intended to exhibit Shylock's devilishness, and questions anew their real import. It finds a Shylock who largely belies his author's description of him. An Elizabethan Jew-baiter could still find enough in him to corroborate his prejudice. He would take, as he was intended to take, the merry sport as a grim pretence; and he would have no difficulty in so doing.

But on closer scrutiny, Shylock's proceedings show little sign of cunning. He defends usury; but his bond dispenses with usury. He recounts his sufferings, and the story of them is hard to fit into any scheme of diabolical strategy. If the retort it brings from Antonio be taken as a lash which roused fury in Shylock, then even less intelligible is Antonio's acceptance of the Jew's offer. The terms of the bonds were, of course, determined centuries ago in mediæval legend; yet in the play they have the air of arising from the situation without pre-arrangement, and their general tenour is not Shylock's, but Antonio's proposal.

Though, let it be said again, the dramatist's formulation of the actions which lead up to the bond still preserves in isolated detail this or that feature which is sufficient to keep the pit in its unquestioning assurance that it was getting the odious Shylock it desired, yet in retrospect one realises that the drama-tist's re-creation of the sequence of incident has, in one vital respect, destroyed or at least completely transformed a main assumption of the original story.

Shylock's discourse with Bassanio shows him fully informed of the extent of Antonio's resources. He knows, therefore, that it is the highest degree unlikely that a situation can arise in which Antonio's forfeit will fall due. Of course, as we saw, in his bargaining with Bassanio, Shylock tried to exaggerate the risks to which Antonio's fortunes were subject; but that was plainly his proper move. He knows, and Antonio himself knew, that save by the intervention of a malicious fate to raise storms simultaneously on all the seven seas of the world just at the very place where Antonio's ships happened to be, and at a time, too, when they happened simultaneously to be in proximity to rocks or to pirates, save by some such series of miracles as this, indeed, he knows that Antonio will be able to pay on the appointed day. Even with the signed bond and its forfeiture clause in his possession, Shylock's chances of demand-ing the forfeit are in fact almost equal to the chances of a first prize through the holding of one ticket in the Irish Sweepstake. A Shylock diabolically bent on ensnaring an enemy for whose blood he lusted might surely have shown sufficient ingenuity to scheme for shorter odds: or if he were satisfied with chances so remote as to be almost non-existent, then the poor plotter is his own weak victim, a pitiful, maundering madman, but certainly no mighty demon of guile and craft.[1] The only

[1]Note also that the sum, three thousand ducats, is in itself no really con-siderable item for a 'royal merchant' to be wrecked on. Shylock, without a

madness visible in this Shylock of the early scene is the madness of supposing that Antonio may be persuaded to extend to him a common human sympathy and understanding.

But if the making of the bond does not in the dramatist's version necessarily presuppose the mob's Shylock, and if, on the contrary, it provides the outlines of another Shylock who is to be made by the play, how far will the mob's Shylock impose himself on the action after the bond has been signed? There is, indeed, a long interval before Shylock appears again, and then (II. v.), it is merely for a few moments in a scene between Shylock, Jessica, and Launcelot. This is a scene primarily needed to carry on the plot by disclosing the preparations for Jessica's elopement, and therefore the dramatic tension in it is slight: there is easier access for the Shylock of popular belief:

> But yet I'll go in hate, to feed upon
> The prodigal Christian

he says, although the earlier and impassioned Shylock had avowed his determination neither to eat nor drink nor pray with Christians. Yet even here, as will be seen when his dealings with Launcelot are considered, the dramatist's Shylock is not altogether missing.

But a scene or two later (III. i.) brings in a Shylock completely caught up in the turmoil of significant action. Jessica has eloped, and the effect of her elopement on Shylock had already been gleefully depicted by Salarino and Salanio:

> I never heard a passion so confused,
> So strange, outrageous, and so variable,
> As the dog Jew did utter in the streets.

moment's hesitation, knows that Tubal will have it by him. Portia is aghast at its smallness. But as these are points, unlike the ones adduced above, which emerge sporadically in later parts of the play, their significance has not been relied on as evidence for the interpretation of the scene in which the bond is proposed and accepted. Yet they do confirm that interpretation.

Shylock has been visited by all the torments of mob hilarity:

> all the boys in Venice follow him
> Crying, his stones, his daughter, and his ducats.

But even in this description Salanio's unintelligent version of Shylock's outcries needs the qualification of closer examination:

> My daughter! O my ducats! O my daughter!
> Fled with a Christian! O my Christian ducats!
> Justice! the law! my ducats, and my daughter!

What indeed is running through Shylock's distracted mind, and particularly the values in it of the alternating cry of daughter and of ducats, will be more truly measured when they come to us not in the callous version of Salanio, but from the mouth of Shylock himself: and as yet, since his daughter's elopement, he has not been seen on the stage.

When he appears Salarino and Salanio are already there, lamenting the rumour that certain losses have befallen the "good Antonio, the honest Antonio." As Shylock enters, they immediately try to see how much he knows—"What news among the merchants?"—that is, of course, the news they have been lamenting, the news which, for the Shylock of the original legend, would naturally have been the only thing which mattered. But the Shylock of the play is different; he has a daughter, as his original had not, and she has eloped. His mind, under the shock of the elopement, has no recollection of the bond at all. It is full of his daughter's flight; and so, instead of answering the pertinent question concerning his assumed hold over Antonio, in his agony he has nothing to say about forfeits and bonds. All that matters is his daughter:

> You knew, none so well, none so well as you, of my daughter's
> flight.

Seeing his agonised distress, Salanio and Salarino are elated, and his misery is merely an opportunity to them for the cruellest jokes and for the salacious witticisms of the smoke-room. Shylock has been pierced to the heart: his most sacred tie has been ruthlessly severed—"My own flesh and blood to rebel," to which in reply the heartless jest—"Out upon it, old carrion, rebels it at these years?" But brutal as they are to Shylock, their bonhomie and esprit-de-corps make Salanio and Salarino concerned about Antonio: "but tell us, do you hear whether Antonio have had any loss at sea or no?" Shylock's reply is of the utmost significance. It is necessary even once again to recall the presuppositions of the story: Shylock is plotting diabolically to trap Antonio by a bond. His scheming may or may not succeed, and, as the play had modified the chances, Shylock's hopes for getting Antonio into his claws were extremely remote. But fate is working marvellously for him. It is a moment when Shylock should be hilariously elated that despite the enormous odds against, his speculation is to be a winner: possibly, and against all reasonable expectation, Antonio is to prove a defaulter. And yet, at the very moment, with this miraculous turn of fortune in his favour, what does Shylock say? Not, as the legend required him to say—"my wildest hopes are coming true, my outsider's chance is to win, a very good bargain indeed"—but, on the contrary, what he says is "There I have another bad match, a bankrupt, a prodigal, etc." The badness of the bargain is all Shylock is aware of; and the bargain is only bad if Shylock had meant it merely in the way of ordinary business. If for a second he had thought of it as a means to gratify his hatred—the only way in which in the legend he ever did think of it—he could never have described it as a 'bad bargain,' but clearly as an unbelievably fortunate one.

Of course, as an inevitable dramatic development of the situation, once his hold over Antonio is brought to his mind, he naturally turns to the fact of the bond in the distraught mood of the moment—"Let him look to his bond." It is the first time he has ever considered the possibility of forfeiture; and for the first time, it will now be made, not a nominal pretence, but a substantial gratification. "Why," says Salarino, "I am sure, if he forfeit, thou wilt not take his flesh: what's that good for?" In reply, Shylock is moved to a revelation of his profound humanity, his sense of the community of Jew and Gentile, though now that sense expresses itself distortedly as a partly demented sufferer's opportunity to wreak bitter revenge on those who have narrowed the bonds of human sympathy by excluding from it the race to which he belongs. What is the pound of flesh good for? he is asked. In a wave of compelling passion, he replies:

"To bait fish withal: if it will feed nothing else, it will feed my revenge. He hath disgraced me, and hindered me half a million; laughed at my losses, mocked at my gains, scorned my nation, thwarted my bargains, cooled my friends, heated mine enemies: and what's his reason? I am a Jew. Hath not a Jew eyes? hath not a Jew hands, organs, dimensions, senses, affections, passions? fed with the same food, hurt with the same weapons, subject to the same diseases, healed by the same means, warmed and cooled by the same winter and summer as a Christian is? If you prick us, do we not bleed? if you tickle us, do we not laugh? if you poison us, do we not die? and if you wrong us, shall we not revenge? If we are like you in the rest, we will resemble you in that. If a Jew wrong a Christian, what is his humility? Revenge. If a Christian wrong a Jew, what should his sufferance be by Christian example? Why, revenge. The villainy you teach me, I will execute, and it shall go hard but I will better the instruction."

At length, the idea that with the bond, he has a means of righteous vengeance against Antonio and the Christians at large has entered Shylock's mind. But even yet it is not implanted there. Tubal enters, and eagerly Shylock questions him—"What news from Genoa?" Not however, news about Antonio, but about the infinitely more pressing preoccupation—"Hast thou found my daughter?" When he hears of Tubal's failure to track her, his desolation returns; an impossible frame of mind, be it remembered, for a Shylock who, bent on

Antonio's flesh, now has his first promise that he may get it—
"The curse never fell upon our nation till now: I never felt it
till now." This is not the mood of a man whose far-flung
contrivances are proving successful. It is the desolate mind of a
man whose nearest and dearest possessions are torn from him,
daughter, diamonds, ducats, and his loss harries his mind to a
frenzied and confused iteration of what he has lost—"two
thousand ducats," and "other precious, precious jewels," as
well as his daughter. To a modern ear, doubtless, this joining
of daughter and ducats argues something of heartlessness in
Shylock: and no doubt it was meant to do so. But ducats are
more to Shylock than mere material possessions. They are the
only means by which, in an alien world, he preserves a refuge
for the true life of his own spirit:

> You take my house when you do take the prop
> That doth sustain my house; you take my life
> When you do take the means whereby I live.

They are the guarantees of his house, as Jessica was its only
pledge: and the two hang together as the sole joy in which his
Hebrew soul may delight itself in a hostile community. Moreover, even in this speech, in which ducats and daughter are
intermittently spoken, Shylock is patently above and beyond
the merely material valuation of material assets. He has lost all
that satisfied his deepest religious instincts, his sense of Judaism.
His Jewish daughter has deserted the faith: to avoid that, he
would have buried her and all his wealth in her grave: "I
would my daughter were dead at my foot, and the jewels in
her ear! I would she were hearsed at my foot, and the ducats
in her coffin." And this is palpably no miser's placing of the
things of this world above those of the spirit. Here is Shylock's
great sorrow, and in the throes of it, merely accidental affairs
like Antonio's fortunes have no place in his mind. So much so
that Tubal has to bring Antonio's misfortunes to Shylock's
notice—obviously a Shylock different from the prescribed
one. "Yes," says Tubal, "other men have ill luck too; Antonio

... hath an argosy cast away." It is only by the gradual and interrupted account from Tubal of Antonio's losses that Shylock is brought to full consciousness of his opportunity for condign vengeance. Daughter and ducats are alternative and successive stabs in Tubal's tale. In the course of it Shylock is moved to his deepest being by the story of Jessica's bartering of a ring—"Out upon her! Thou torturest me, Tubal: it was my turquoise; I had it of Leah when I was a bachelor: I would not have given it for a wilderness of monkeys." Immediately following on this desecration of his most sacred memories, pat comes Tubal's "But Antonio is certainly undone," and Shylock is irrevocably committed to his vengeance. Yet even in the moment of the avowal, it is a vow bound by the holiest sanctions: "Go, go, Tubal, and meet me at our synagogue."

Clearly the Shylock who has been brought to his determination in this way is a Shylock who has been wrought by circumstance to an impassioned mood of frenzy. He has been transformed into the intelligible fanatic who with perfect naturalness may play the pathetically demented rôle he must fulfil in the trial scene. He provides an admirable example of the way in which the dramatist's instinct secures dramatic reality.

The play exhibits many other strokes of this intuitive sense in operation. Even from the beginning, Shakespeare's picture of Venice and of the Venetians is the representation of a world in which a Shylock would suffer the extreme torments of racial antipathy. The Venice of Bassanio, Lorenzo, Salanio, and the rest is an opulent world, inhabited by high-spirited men of affairs, who live richly, and with the reckless gaiety which is the privilege of those whom blood or experience has endowed with a competent *savoir-faire* as with a second nature. The youths of Venice are the stock from which later generations have recruited their proconsuls and their colonial administrators. They are the aristocracy of regal merchandise; they inherit the confident, efficient culture of the dominating middle class. They are destined to rule the world by virtue of their limitations as much as by their qualities. Their pre-

judices serve them as well as do their abilities. Vigorous
bodies prevent their minds from over-development; *sang froid*
saves them from the torment of deep feeling; social camaraderie
breeds in them a contempt for the outsider. Life is good to
them, and they live it eagerly and gaily, revelling in the warmth
of their blood and in the opulence of their estate. They have
vigour, audacity, and assurance: and these qualities, which their
fathers employed successfully in the world of business, they
devote with no less success to the social occupations of life.
But they have also ease and manner, wit and culture and ele-
gance, and above all, the luxury of freedom from immediate
responsibilities. They are at liberty to enjoy the mirth and
the large laughter of the world without concern for its seamier
and more serious sides. They participate in a merry fellowship
of health and high spirits, and are bound together as a class by
a sense of good form and of the sportsman's fair play. They are
prodigal by habit, and endeavour to come fairly off from their
great debts. Obligation is a due of honour rather than a moral
sanction. Prompted readily by the sentiment of camaraderie,
they give lavishly to help another of their own set out of his
temporary embarrassment. But of larger sympathy they have
none. For all that runs counter to their own code of life, they
have a careless and a robust contempt. They are incapable of
even a superficial understanding of the strange fellows whom
Nature in her time hath framed with solemn countenances and
a disposition to jaundice. They are, in sum, a society destined
to make intolerable the life of an alien in their midst.

Yet one amongst the Venetians, Antonio, seems to have a
deeper understanding and a more compassionate heart. His
friends are beginning to remonstrate with him for a growing
disposition to sadness. It is withdrawing him from the right
uses of company and of the world. He is marvellously changed
from what he was, and being neither in love nor yet in debt,
he is held to be afflicted by a causeless charge. He is taking life
more seriously than they think meet, and is losing touch with
their manners and their interests. But the increasing aloofness

does not impair his regard for his friends' worth; he is indeed more ready to sympathise with their needs, even to the full extent of his purse, his person, and his extremest means. He is palpably intended to reflect a soul of noble honour. On every count, he is the one member of Venetian society who might understand deep suffering. Yet it is no other than Antonio who wounds the Jew most deeply by his blunt contempt.

As the play runs its course, we have seen, even more effective means suggest themselves to the dramatist for hounding Shylock into madness. The most powerful, as we have seen, is Jessica's elopement, and this brings in, not only Jessica and Lorenzo, but the instruments of the elopement, Launcelot on the one hand, and Lorenzo's friends on the other.

Launcelot's desertion of Shylock is doubtless meant to add to the Jew's ignominy. But Launcelot's testimony to the truth of circumstance carries little weight. His most reasonable excuse for running from the Jew to the Christian is that Bassanio "gives rare new liveries," and that, in Bassanio's service, there is better chance of his coming by eleven widows and nine maids, "a simple coming in for one man." How one of these unfortunate female domestics suffered from Launcelot's transfer is learnt a little later—"the Moor is with child by you, Launcelot." Launcelot has no doubt been frequently upbraided by Shylock for being a huge feeder, snail-slow in profit, and a great sleeper by day. But what is seen of him serves rather to justify Shylock's reproof than to convict Shylock of an evil disposition. It is Shylock himself who says "the patch is kind enough."

The behaviour of Lorenzo and his friends in scheming the elopement is no less likely to wound by its flippant callousness. Shylock is invited to dinner by Bassanio. The friends of Bassanio are planning to steal away his daughter, and as a perfectly gratuitous piece of cruel fun, are bringing her disguised as torch bearer to the very banquet where her father is a guest. All that prevents the enactment of this revolting joke is not anybody's thought for Shylock's feelings, but a mere veering of the winds which makes it necessary to put off the masque and get aboard. The veering wind, however, does not save him from the loss of his daughter.

But the worst stab of all comes from Jessica's own action in her elopement. Her lie to her father who sees Launcelot whispering the arrangements to her is perhaps forgiveable on the romantic assumption that all is fair in love and war. But it is no less a lie. Yet perhaps one need not try Jessica too scrupulously for her use of words, for she has already shown with what a flippant laxity she employs the English tongue. Taking farewell of Launcelot, who is leaving for Bassanio's service, she pleasantly says to him:

> I am sorry thou wilt leave my father so.
> Our house is hell, and thou, a merry devil,
> Didst rob it of some taste of tediousness.

It sounds like a convincing exposure of the horrors of Shylock's devil's kitchen, since it comes from his daughter's mouth. But words, after all, are not absolute in their meaning: they must be interpreted in their context. Perhaps, at this stage of the story, not enough is known of Jessica to provide a key to her terminology. But it is clear that her words have not a simple dictionary meaning. "Our house is hell" is a comprehensive expression of disapproval and disgust. But what does it really mean? "And thou, a merry devil, didst rob it of some taste of tediousness." Notions of hell certainly do differ and differ very widely. But into whose idea of hell before Jessica's did the expectation of tedium ever enter? Indeed, her phrase says more of Jessica's frivolous nature than of the repulsiveness of her father's house. Shylock's is admittedly a sober house, without gramophone or wireless and other "sounds of shallow foppery." But that hardly makes it "hell," although it may explain Jessica's tedium in it.

Her elopement strikes the same note. She appears at the upper window disguised in a boy's suit, and, oblivious altogether of the tremendous significance of her flight to her father and to her own faith, she bandies sweet dalliance with those below, and then lightly plays the cross-word tricks of conventional lovers—

> And now who knows
> But you, Lorenzo, whether I am yours?

But with this brief prelude, she comes to the solid part of the undertaking—"Here catch this casket, it is worth the pains," a strikingly flippant temper in robbing her father of his wealth, and a cruel indifference to her destruction of his family happiness. How indifferent she is appears in her next words, for she goes on into an otherwise mildly charming play with lovers' badinage:

> I am glad 'tis night, you do not look on me,
> For I am much ashamed of my exchange—

the exchange, be it noted, which brings shame to her, is not her change of faith, but merely her change of clothes:

> But love is blind and lovers cannot see
> The pretty follies that themselves commit;
> For if they could, Cupid himself would blush
> To see me thus transformed to a boy.

She is in fact in mock modesty preening herself in her new costume, a boy's suit, and that reminds her that, although she has already purloined a well-stuffed casket, she now has more pockets than she has ever had before; she cuts off the talk with a remark that she'll stuff them full of more gold pieces from her father's stock:

> I'll gild myself
> With some more ducats, and be with you straight.

Such is Jessica, not unworthy, in the values which are beginning to pierce through the play, of Gratiano's appraisement:

> Now by my hood, a Gentile, and no Jew.

A Jessica who does these things in this way and so unexpectedly, is clearly a girl whose revolt will strike to her father's heart. She flippantly desecrates all that Shylock holds sacred. She destroys the foundations of his universe. His frenzied comprehension of her elopement, and of her actions after the elopement, drives him from distraction to maniacal frenzy. He is now ready to settle into the fixed madness which, despite argument and circumstance, will insist on the one retaliation left to his soul—

> An oath, an oath, I have an oath in heaven.

That is the mood in which he is made apt for the trial scene. He is now irrevocably "a strong adversary, an inhuman wretch incapable of pity." But the fury of his wrath has also brought out his cunning. The Duke's invitation to him to show human gentleness and love only reminds him of the cruelty he suffered when he made his gesture of friendship. He becomes the chosen vessel of his tribe's vengeance, sworn to it by "our holy Sabboth." The law of the Gentiles and their interest, the charter of the city's freedom, are now in his hands the instruments of the greater laws of his Prophets. To stand for judgment he will sacrifice all thought of his own selfish and material profit. He is impervious to entreaty and unruffled by abuse, a towering figure, dominating over the little men who spit at him—until Portia enters, charged by the story, of course, with the office of outwitting Shylock. But he has become too portentous a figure to be merely tricked out of his own, and Portia's is an unenviable task. At first, she rises magnificently above the petty part she is destined to play. She attempts to lift the issue to a higher plane of mercy and humanity. But Shylock is by this beyond the sense of all but justice, and with frenzied fanaticism he sees in the plea nothing but a temptation to lay perjury upon his soul. Portia, incapable of understanding, is blind to his motive and to his state of mind. Her dallying with the manuscript of the bond, her trifling with the preparation for the judgment, aimed apparently at giving Shylock

further chances to show mercy, are merely further practices to
make the littleness of the formal decision appear more adequate
to an occasion larger altogether than its nominal scope. In
retrospect, they suffer even more. For the passion for Jew-
baiting imposes a further task on Portia, and this makes her
moral exaltation little better than a pose. Her hesitation to give
judgment appears exactly opposite to its intention. Instead of
an attempt to lead the Jew to a sense of higher things, it seems a
callous trifling with a certain victim, a cat toying with the poor
mouse it is about to kill. She leads him from hope to hope, to
cast him more desperately down. But the Elizabethans in their
racial hatred went further. Portia had to invent a law by which
the broken victim could be still more tormented. "The law
hath yet another hold on you." The office puts her in a false
position. It is strange that the Duke and all the law officers of
Venice had been ignorant of a positive enactment so material
to the constitution of their state. But Portia's knowledge of its
existence is not merely strange. It colours her whole procedure
at the trial. With this trump card in her possession, she could
have won the case with a word. Neither Shylock nor Antonio
need have been stretched so long on the rack of expectation and
despair. The Portia who keeps them so is merely a callous
barrister conducting a case with no more exalted a motive
than what concerns a professional and spectacular triumph. As
such, even her renowned discourse on the quality of mercy,
counts against her character. Its sentiments are unquestionably
noble, but they are for her no more than a pleader's rhetoric.
In the act of glorifying the name of mercy, she is selfishly
inflicting needless suffering on the poor mortals who provide
her opportunity for a mere forensic display. Little wonder that
the play cannot end with the trial scene.

The episode of the rings comes in perhaps to provide what
was covenanted in the comic tradition. It is made out of the
hoariest motive, confusions arising from mistaken identities.
It is but superficial matter after the trial scene. Nor does it
enhance the sense of Portia's nobility. But at least it takes her

back to Belmont and its moonlit gardens. Even hoydenish tricks there are sweeter than questionable devices in law courts. The air of Belmont is restorative. Many of the sufferers in the play are brought by the last act to something near the pleasant disposition they were vainly meant to show from the beginning.

For however one reads the play, it is certain that the intentions of the author were in many ways defeated. Shylock, Antonio, Portia and Jessica do not stand forth as they were meant to do. The parts they were called upon to play by their author's prejudices did not square with those the dramatist worked out for them. There is throughout the clash of rival schemes, the proposals of Shakespeare's deliberate will, and the disposals by his creative imagination. And whatever the conflict makes of the particular play as a single work of art, however much the new Shylock intrudes to the destruction of its artistic unity, the emergence of the new Shylock is undeniable evidence of the incalculable value of the artist's intuition in helping humanity to reach the vital truths which in the end are revealed only through sympathy and on which the world's future welfare is indubitably to be built.

VII

Falstaff

FALSTAFF, you will agree, is a huge subject, a very tun of man: "that trunk of humours, that bolting hutch of beastliness, that swollen parcel of dropsies, that huge bombard of sack, that stuffed cloak-bag of guts, that roasted Manningtree ox with the pudding in his belly, that reverend vice, that grey iniquity, that father ruffian, that vanity in years." God gave him abundantly of the spirit of persuasion, and the words he spoke have moved a multitude of men to make books about him. Perhaps he still retains the receipt of fern-seed, and walks invisible. But the shelves of our libraries are almost as heavy with the Knight as was Mistress Ford's buck-basket. The main task, of course, is to rate his quality within the genus homo which is the common name to all men, to judge how little better than the wicked he may be, to assess precisely what is the virtue in that Falstaff. But there are questions besides these primary points of criticism: there seems to be no remedy against the consumption of print for recording reams of fact and conjecture directly or remotely bearing on the Falstaff saga. Many have sought his ancestors, thinking to lay hold of him there before he had become himself in Shakespeare's imagination. There are those who would find him in the flesh in Elizabethan England—a swashbuckling Captain Nicholas Dawtrey has fairly recently been named for the live Falstaff.[1] Others, starting more directly with a textual problem, are concerned with the name under which Falstaff first

---

[1] *The Falstaff Saga*, by J. Dawtrey, 1927.

came into Shakespeare's plays, Sir John Oldcastle, and with the constraint put on Shakespeare to rechristen him, lest the Elizabethan descendants of the real Oldcastle should resent the tarnishing of their scutcheon. That they did resent it is certain, since in the prologue to another contemporary play, a play with little apparent purpose but to exalt the virtues of Sir John Oldcastle, it is expressly intimated that the hero of it is

> no pampered glutton, . . .
> Nor aged Councellor to youthfull sinne,
> But one, whose vertue shone above the rest,
> A valiant Martyr and a vertuous peere,[1]

and a protest is recorded against the manner in which "forg'de invention former time defac'te." Shakespeare himself admitted his unwitting guilt. "Oldcastle died a martyr, and this [i.e. Falstaff] is not the man."[2]

The dramatist had merely taken over the name Oldcastle amongst the material from the old play of *The Famous Victories of Henry the Fifth* (c. 1588) which he was using for his own Prince Hal plays. But critics agree that there is very little of Falstaff in the Sir John Oldcastle of *The Famous Victories*: he is a minor comic figure amongst the dissolutes whom the reformed prince dismisses from his company. But some curious enquirers into Falstaff's theatrical genealogy find him descended queerly from both the Sir John and from the clown Derrick of this older play.[3] More elaborately, others see him as curiously compounded of the varying figure which a dramatised Oldcastle would cut in popular estimation before, and then after, the Reformation.[4] Further, he has been identified as nothing but the lineal descendant of the vice in the mediæval moralities,[5] whilst an even remoter theatrical origin has been

---

[1] *Sir John Oldcastle* (1600), Prologue.   [2] *II Henry IV.* Epilogue.

[3] Monaghan, J., "Falstaff and his Forbears" in *Studies in Philology* (University of N. Carolina, xviii, 1921).

[4] Baeske, W., *Oldcastle-Falstaff in der englischen Literatur bis zu Shakespeare* (Palæstra 50, 1905).

[5] Spargo, J. W., *An Interpretation of Falstaff* (Washington University Studies, 1922).

claimed for him in the *miles gloriosus* of Roman comedy.[1]

But in much of this, pregnancy is made a tapster and hath his quick wit wasted in giving reckonings; and for the present purpose we can permit ourselves to be troubled with the disease of not listening and the malady of not marking. Our argument is solely with true Jack Falstaff, old Jack Falstaff, Shakespeare's Jack Falstaff; with his forbears, or indeed with his own pre-play proclivities, when he was not an eagle's talon in the waist and could have crept into any alderman's thumb-ring, we have no concern whatever. Yet not all his genealogists have had a limitedly historic object. Behind many of their attempts to trace his family tree, there is a hope that a knowledge of his ancestry may help to interpret the character of the man himself, and that in this way, light may be thrown on what Shakespeare deliberately or intuitively meant him to be. In particular, most of these critics seek to help criticism to extricate itself from a dilemma in which all who are attached both to Shakespeare and to Falstaff find themselves involved, a dilemma which reaches its climax in Henry V's callous rejection of the old man who has been his intimate confederate in an incessant round of escapades—

> the nimble-footed madcap Prince of Wales
> And his comrades, that daff'd the world aside,
> And bid it pass.

It is a scene which has aroused more repugnance than any other in Shakespeare. Henry IV is dead, and Hal succeeds to the Crown. In earlier days there had been much merry talk between Falstaff and Hal, anticipating their gay doings "when thou, sweet wag, art king." Falstaff is at Mr. Justice Shallow's in Gloucestershire when Pistol brings news of Henry IV's death. Falstaff sees all his dreams come true. "Away, Bardolph! saddle my horse. Master Robert Shallow, choose what office thou wilt in the land, 'tis thine. Pistol, I will double-charge thee with dignities." "I know the young king is sick

[1]Stoll, E. E., "Falstaff" in *Modern Philology*, Oct. 1914.

for me. Let us take any man's horses; the laws of England are at my commandment." He comes to London, and without waiting to deck himself for court, puts himself in Hal's way, "to stand stained with travel, and sweating with desire to see him; thinking of nothing else, putting all affairs else in oblivion, as if there were nothing else to be done but to see him." The king and his train enter, to be greeted rapturously by Falstaff. "God save thy grace, King Hal! my royal Hal! . . . God save thee, my sweet boy." But the king does not even speak to him; he commands the Lord Chief Justice, Falstaff's old enemy, to convey the royal message—"My lord chief-justice, speak to that vain man." Falstaff is completely nonplussed. "*My* king! my Jove! *I* speak to thee, my heart." Then he hears from Hal's own lips:

> I know thee not, old man: fall to thy prayers;
> How ill white hairs become a fool and jester!
> I have long dream'd of such a kind of man,
> So surfeit-swell'd, so old and so profane;
> But, being awaked, I do despise my dream.

He hears himself banished in moral strains he has only once heard spoken by that voice before—and then it had been in open fooling:

> When thou dost hear I am as I have been,
> Approach me, and thou shalt be as thou wast,
> The tutor and the feeder of my riots:
> Till then, I banish thee, on pain of death,
> As I have done the rest of my misleaders,
> Not to come near our person by ten mile.

There is a faint speck of material consolation:

> For competence of life I will allow you,
> That lack of means enforce you not to evil:
> And as we hear you do reform yourselves,
> We will, according to your strengths and qualities,
> Give you advancement.

But even this appears in the immediate sequel as a further stroke of callous cruelty. For, at once, the Lord Chief Justice returns and orders his officers to carry Sir John to the Fleet prison. If anything further be needed to make this treatment odious, it is Lancaster's approval of it—"I like this fair proceeding of the King's!" for Lancaster has just previously performed a most opprobrious act of treachery, or rather of Bolingbrokian political strategy: he has deluded the rebels into accepting seemingly honourable terms, to find themselves haled off to execution. It appears indeed as if the family morals are in the blood of all of them, Henry IV, Henry V and Lancaster. Falstaff knew them for what they were. When Lancaster jibes at his capture of Colevile—"It was more of his courtesy than your deserving," Falstaff has the right rebuke ready. "I know not: here he is, and here I yield him: and I beseech your grace, let it be booked with the rest of this day's deeds; or, by the Lord, I will have it in a particular ballad else, with mine own picture on the top on't, Colevile kissing my foot: to the which course, if I be enforced, if you do not all show like gilt two-pences to me, and I in the clear sky of fame o'ershine you as much as the full moon doth the cinders of the element, which show like pin's heads to her, believe not the word of the noble: therefore let me have right, and let desert mount."

Yet he had thought that Hal was different from his family, as indeed Hal had so far been different. "Good faith, this same young sober-blooded boy [Lancaster] doth not love me; nor a man cannot make him laugh; but that's no marvel, he drinks no wine. . . . Hereof comes it that Prince Harry is valiant; for the cold blood he did naturally inherit of his father, he hath, like lean, sterile and bare land, manured, husbanded and tilled with excellent endeavour of drinking good and good store of fertile sherris that he is become very hot and valiant."

With hardly a dissentient voice, the later world has scorned Hal for his offence against humanity. Mr. Masefield lets it colour all Henry V's subsequent deeds, and writes him down for a heartless schemer. "Prince Henry is not a hero, he is not a thinker, he is not even a friend; he is a common man whose incapacity for feeling enables him to change his habits whenever interest bids him. Throughout the first acts he is careless and callous though he is breaking his father's heart and endangering his father's throne. He chooses to live in society as common as himself. He talks continually of guts as though a belly were a kind of wit. Even in the society of his choice his attitude is remote and cold-blooded. There is no good-fellowship in him, no sincerity, no wholeheartedness. He makes a mock of the drawer who gives him his whole little pennyworth of sugar. His jokes upon Falstaff are so little good-natured that he stands upon his princehood whenever the old man would retort upon him. He impresses one as quite common, quite selfish, quite without feeling. When he learns that his behaviour may have lost him his prospective crown he passes a sponge over his past, and fights like a wild cat for the right of not having to work for a living."[1]

There is scarcely a reader who will not sympathise with Mr. Masefield's attitude, though perhaps few would press the case so far. It is indeed hardly thinkable that Shakespeare expected us to feel so bitterly against Prince Hal. Yet it is equally unthinkable that our feelings towards him can remain sympathetically genial.

Doubtless, Shakespeare's problem is inherent in his story. Legend and history affirmed that after a riotous youth, Prince Hal reformed himself into the noble Henry V. The old play of *The Famous Victories* chooses that as its main theme. It opens with the Prince and his associates, Ned and Tom, and, after a second's delay, Sir John Oldcastle also, rejoicing in the pro-ceeds of a highway robbery by which they have relieved the King's Receivers of a thousand pounds. Hal invites them to adjourn to "the olde taverne in Eastcheape; there is good wine, and besides there is a pretie wench that can talke well."[2]

[1]Masefield, *Shakespeare*, p. 112 (Home University Library).
[2]*The Famous Victories*, l. 118 ff.

Later, we hear how they enjoyed themselves. "This night, about two houres ago, there came the young Prince, and three or foure more of his companions, and called for wine good store; and then they sent for a noyse of musitians, and were very merry for the space of an houre; then, whether their musicke liked them not, or whether they had drunke too much wine or no, I cannot tell, but our pots flue against the wals; and then they drew their swordes and went into the streete and fought, and some tooke one part and some tooke another; but for the space of halfe an houre there was such a bloodie fray as passeth."[1] They are arrested and carried to the Counter prison. The King hears of his son's arrest, and forgives the officers for it, though he makes them put in a full plea in extenuation of their audacity—"Althogh he be a rude youth, and likely to give occasion, yet you might have considered that he is a prince, and my sonne, and not to be halled to prison by every subject."[2] He has the roysterers released, after uttering a brief lament over his son: "thrice-accursed Harry, that hath gotten a sonne which with greefe will end his fathers dayes."[3] In a short time, the Prince is bullying a judge who will not acquit one of the Prince's men; he ends by giving him the famous box on the ear, for which the judge has him haled off to the Fleet prison. Soon, however, he is out again, frolicking with his rowdy companions, and vowing what gay times they will have when he is king. He hears that his father "lies verie sicke," and sets off at once for the court, gleefully declaring that" the breath shal be no sooner out of his [father's] mouth but I wil clap the crowne on my head."[4] Going out, he alludes for the first time in the play, to the reformation expected of his character, but does not for a moment countenance the notion; indeed, he roundly scoffs at it. "But thers som wil say the yoong Prince will be 'a well toward yoong man'—and all this geare, that I had as leeve they would breake my head with a pot as to say any such thing."[5] At court, the sick King is lamenting

---

[1]*Ibid.*, ll. 261 ff. [2]*The Famous Victories*, ll. 315 ff.
[3]*Ibid.*, ll. 364 ff. [4]*Ibid.*, ll. 663 ff. [5]*Ibid.*, ll. 678 ff.

his son's dissoluteness. "Oh my sonne! my sonne! no sooner out of one prison but into another? I had thought oncè-whiles I had lived to have seene this noble realme of England flourish by thee, my sonne; but now I see it goes to ruine and decaie."[1] The reprobate prince enters his father's house, noisily, bluster-ingly, wearing a sort of motley and brandishing a dagger. Weeping, his father upbraids him for his deeds and for follow-ing this "wilde and reprobate company." In a flash, the prince repents: "my conscience accuseth me."[2] "And those vilde and reprobate companions, I abandon and utterly abolish their company for ever! Pardon, sweete father! pardon!" When he is afraid that his father will not at once forgive him, he says, "I will go take me into some solitarie place, and there lament my sinfull life; and when I have done, I will laie me downe and die."[3] His penitence is absolute, complete, and permanent. Approaching his sleeping father, and thinking him dead, he reverently carries away the crown, saying that he will weep day and night to atone for his former negligence. The King, however, is not really dead. Missing the crown, he suspects the prince, but is at once reassured of the latter's motives, and determines to crown him forthwith. Doing so, he dies. On the prince's succession, his old friends rush into his presence to secure the anticipated prizes. But it is now a new Henry. "Oh, how it did me good to see the King when he was crowned," says Oldcastle; "Methought his seate was like the figure of heaven, and his person like unto a god."[4] But another of the gang suspects another sort of change; "who would have thought that the King would have changed his countenance so?" They soon know how different things now are—and forthwith are turned off. "I prethee, Ned, mend thy maners, and be more modester in thy tearmes. . . . Thou saist I am changed; so I am indeed. . . . Your former life greeves me, and makes me to abandon and abolish your company for ever. And therefore; not upon pain of death to approach my

[1] *Ibid.*, ll. 713 ff.   [2] *Ibid.*, ll. 764 ff.
[3] *The Famous Victories*, ll. 796 ff.   [4] *Ibid.*, ll. 989 ff.

presence by ten miles space. Then, if I heare wel of you, it may
be I wil do somewhat for you; otherwise looke for no more
favour at my hands then at any other mans."[1]

Such is the stuff of *The Famous Victories* where it is nearest
to Shakespeare's material. But it will be seen that its anonymous author has not caught himself in Shakespeare's difficulties.
He has simply taken successive episodes from the familiar tale
and staged them. At its face value, the story was sufficiently
amusing; he saw no need, and perhaps had no art, really to
dramatise it. Hal's sudden and complete change of character
would be accepted as a sort of Pauline conversion attested by
history. There was no need to prepare for it; indeed, he could
make Hal himself laugh at the mere thought of its possibility.
Credible through legend, there was no obvious obligation to
make it convincing by characterisation. But that was not
Shakespeare's way. With him, the deed was always a trial of
the man. Stage figures, driven hither and thither at the command of the plot, were almost as contemptible in his eyes as
was a brewer's horse to Falstaff, a mere thing which at a tug of
the rein suffers itself to pull away from the delectable and substantial stuff behind it and therefore always behind it. Shakespeare's characters are incessantly striving to break into life.
Dramatically this lends a larger dare to his great enterprise.
But it has its greater hazards. Hal's conversion must be
grounded in character. To make it credible and consonant with
Henry V, it must follow a deliberate motive or an unconscious
but convincing prompting from the stuff of his nature. Hence
the cumulative priggishness of the young roysterer. His
attempts to salve in words the long-grown wounds of his in-
temperance, his plea that he is only upholding the unyoked
humour of his idle confederates for a while, his admission that
he is deliberately experimenting, toying with a political practice to falsify men's hopes, and, by reformation, ultimately to
show more goodly—all this is an offence against humanity,
and an offence which dramatically never becomes a skill.

[1]*Ibid.*, ll. 1018 ff.

The noble change which he has so elaborately purposed is an unconscionable trick. Every time he invites us to weigh his follies with the purpose, he displays a revolting alacrity in sinking from our esteem. His grace is clearly saying that against which our flesh rebels. Retrospectively, even his follies lose something of their savour. To secure a charge of foot for Falstaff, for whom, afoot, "eight yards of uneven ground is three score and ten miles," is a rollicking but a heartless joke, without the zest which was in the hiding of his horse when the job in hand was the highway robbery. It is easy for Hal on a plea that he is of all the humours that have showed themselves humours since the old days of goodman Adam, to demonstrate in act that the drawer is a fellow of fewer words than a parrot. But when triumph is so easily secured, onlookers may remember that the victim is yet the son of a woman, and that, as "his industry is upstairs and down-stairs," Hal is heartlessly endangering the poor drawer's means of subsistence. One prefers to cling to the figure which Vernon saw, the prince who acted with a restrained dignity

> which became him like a prince indeed;
> He made a blushing cital of himself;
> And chid his truant youth with such a grace
> As if he master'd there a double spirit
> Of teaching and of learning instantly.
> There did he pause: but let me tell the world,
> If he outlive the envy of this day,
> England did never owe so sweet a hope.

Or even more pleasantly, one chooses to recall his spontaneous offer to lie his hardest for Falstaff's sake:

> For my part, if a lie may do thee grace,
> I'll gild it with the happiest terms I have.

Perhaps it would have been better if Shakespeare had stinted preparation, letting the conversion come through the stress of present circumstance, almost indeed as it does come, when,

in his new dignity as King, he swears to the Lord Chief Justice
that the memory of the suffering he has caused his father shall
instigate his own regeneration:

> My father is gone wild into his grave,
> For in his tomb lie my affections;
> . . . The tide of blood in me
> Hath proudly flow'd in vanity till now:
> Now doth it turn and ebb back to the sea,
> Where it shall mingle with the state of floods
> And flow henceforth in formal majesty.

But, on his own plea, it is the end which tries the man. The
end is his rejection of Falstaff. And after that, even the wicked
will not readily fall in love with him. It seems a safe guess
that such a Hal, so false to Falstaff, will of that seed grow to a
greater falseness. If indeed, a greater falseness is within the
scope of conjecture.

For Shakespeare's art could not use the semblance of flesh
without vitalising it into life. Hal's reprobates would in their
turn come nearer to humanity than is a shotten-herring or a
stage-puppet. These rascals cannot be swept away to suit the
plot, and one of them in particular, though he would be a fool
and a coward but for inflammation, has pledged himself so
deeply into our affections, that his fate angers us to the heart.

There appears to be no escape from the fact. This huge mass
of flesh, this Sir John, has distorted the drift of the historic
story and of the deliberate plan of Shakespeare's play. He has
converted an intended hero into a heartless politician, and a
happy ending into a revolting conclusion. How is such a
critical predicament to be avoided?

The most specious way is Stoll's.[1] He denies that there is a
real predicament. We only think there is because we are
merely amateur, not 'professional,' critics. We are ignorant
of technique and of historic development; and, feeling the
dilemma, we betray a total misapprehension of dramatic

[1] *Vide supra*, p. 4, n. 6.

methods. Falstaff is a comic character, and nothing more; as good playgoers, we should imitate the Elizabethans and ask no more. Everything that Falstaff does or says is part of the type which Shakespeare is undertaking to exhibit (and presumably has so informed Mr. Stoll directly). It is all so simple, got with much ease. And Mr. Stoll seems impregnable in his panoply of illustrative foot-notes from plays of every age and every nation.

But, one feels prompted to ask, did Shakespeare only write for professional critics? And for those of his day, or those of ours? Is Falstaff a figure for the Elizabethans only, and for those rare people of our own day who have persuaded themselves that they are seeing him historically? And though admittedly the play's the thing, is it a critical sin, when one has seen it and been moved by it, to let the mind dwell on what has been seen? Moreover, even if one can be so certain of what the limits of a dramatic type are, are they so sacrosanct that the characterisation of one of them is merely the adoption of a tradition? Is a dramatist only a stage-carpenter, knocking a play together according to a convention, or is he a creative artist with his own apprehensions of life, and, so far as his material permits, with his own distinctive technique? And why indeed does Falstaff still abide with us of these later times? Why moreover, do we, taking Shakespeare as him to whom we owe our own deepest flashes of insight into human nature, why do we, here and now, protest that he has been untrue to posterity's sense of mortal values? Even to say that Falstaff is a 'comic' character is to state a problem, not to give an answer. Wherein comic, and why one of the greatest of comic characters?

Other exponents of Falstaff, whilst not denying that his rejection is a real and legitimate problem for us, have sought to show that there could be no problem in him for Shakespeare's contemporaries. There is little harm, and little profit, in such demonstrations. It is certain that Mr. Spargo's attempt[1] to explain Falstaff as a survival of the mediæval Vice whose

[1] *Vide supra*, p. 4, n. 5.

rôle it was to be merry and in the end to be punished, involves a wild conjecture about Elizabethan audiences, and has no bearing whatever on the difficulties of a modern one. Mr. Tolman's[1] is at least a more coherent and feasible proposal. Falstaff was created to make the reformed Hal an intelligible and dramatically satisfying figure. He fascinates Hal into evil and us into good humour. He is attractive enough to palliate Hal's roysterings and sufficiently repellent to justify the later Hal's break with him. There is nothing impossible in supposing this to have been Shakespeare's intention. But Mr. Tolman admits that if such was his intention, it went awry. Falstaff outgrew that function.

This brings us to Mr. A. C. Bradley,[2] though, except for the partial agreement in Mr. Tolman's notion that Falstaff's greatness over-reached his author, the writers here named, writing after Bradley, are mainly against him, and some of them, Stoll in particular, entirely and rabidly against him. In his *Rejection of Falstaff*, Mr. Bradley was developing and greatly enriching an apology for Falstaff put forward as long ago as 1777 by Maurice Morgann,[3] and Mr. Bradley's portrait of Sir John impresses one as more like the authentic Falstaff of Shakespeare than any other which the critics have sketched.

Morgann loved Falstaff. He recognised, however, that if Falstaff's character were to be judged by normal moral standards, it would seem hard to find anything worthy of commendation in the man. Yet Morgann loved him. To account for this, he develops a theory that we really estimate the quality of a man, and especially the quality of a man in a play, by two distinct faculties of judgment, by our 'impression,' and by our 'understanding,' faculties more or less corresponding to 'intuitive sympathy' and 'pure reason.' Pure reason, he finds, is

[1]Tolman, A. H., *Falstaff and other Shakespearian Topics*, 1925 (the Falstaff paper had appeared in *P.M.L.A. of A.*, 1919).

[2]Bradley, A. C., *Oxford Lectures on Poetry*, "The Rejection of Falstaff," 1909.

[3]Morgann, Maurice, *An Essay on the Dramatic Character of Sir John Falstaff*, 1777.

frequently in error; it judges on but partially apprehended evidence, for much that is essential to the full assessment can only be perceived by intuitive sympathy. From this, he goes on to argue that Falstaff's seeming delinquencies, cowardice, lying, and so forth, are only apparent, and are, in a way, the instruments wherewith Falstaff shows himself to be possessed of the very virtues which are the direct counterparts of the vices he seems to have. It may be that in his zeal to make a case, Morgann is at times arbitrary in his choice and in his use of this or that detail. But the fundamental basis of his argument is not to be destroyed merely by labelling it 'romantic,' as does Mr. Stoll; it seems indeed to rest on a plain human and æsthetic truth.

Mr. Bradley is in general agreement with Morgann. He gives to Morgann's main proposition a more acute and subtle statement, and strengthens it by developing its bearing on a comprehensive philosophy of art and of life. There is no need to summarise Mr. Bradley's paper. Like the other writings of this, the greatest Shakespearian critic of our time, it is a thing which all who would come nearer to Shakespeare must read for themselves. Its supreme value is its psychological portraiture of Falstaff himself. Here, if anywhere out of Shakespeare, is Shakespeare's Sir John.

But Mr. Bradley was using the portrait of Falstaff for his own specific purpose. Subscription to its authenticity will not preclude our demurring to some of Mr. Bradley's implications when Falstaff is being reviewed from the different angle required by our particular problem.

With diffidence, and with apology, therefore, I remind you that this is the sixth successive year in which I have been honoured by an invitation to talk here on Shakespearian comedy. And, risking being silenced for damnable iteration, I venture to recall to you, what has been for me, though perhaps too obscurely and diffusely for you to have noted it, the persisting and unifying intention throughout my earlier Rylands lectures. My endeavour has been to follow the growth of Shakespeare's idea of comedy.

To talk of an idea of comedy, and to talk about it as one must for such exposition as is now being attempted, may seem to imply a clear consciousness of such things in the mind of the dramatist. But that, it must be insisted, is very wide of the mark. A dramatist's creative power is essentially different from, and largely independent of, his pure reason. The life he imaginatively apprehends may remain, and indeed most frequently does remain, entirely unanalysed and unsystematised by his reason. But when the life he creates by his art displays the completeness of an organic unity, the principles implied in it or presupposed by it may be enquired into, and formulated, though but imperfectly. The formulation of them will be in terms which, more often than not, would appear to the dramatist himself as more or less unintelligible irrelevancies. Shakespeare, it is certain, had no theory of comedy. But his genius created a 'comic' world. To trace the evolution of his idea of comedy is to follow the stages by which his presentation of the 'comic' grew into the creation of a universe which was complete in itself and was held together by its capacity to convince the imagination of man that the fundamental laws of it correspond to man's sense of what he himself is and what, in its essence, is the world in which he lives.

Put so, the search for Shakespeare's idea of comedy has a forbiddingly abstruse appearance. But, however reconditely or left-handedly urged its formulated conclusions may appear, it may well be that in effect they are founded on a very simple proposition about the nature of comedy. A comedy is a play which ends happily. Granted that the author may not arbitrarily interfere with the progress of his protagonist towards his happy ending, then clearly he must find a hero of such sort that, being what he is, he is likely to overcome whatever impediments to his well-being may be presented by the episodes of the play; and these episodes, so the assumption equally requires, must not be devised by the author merely to fit his particular situation; they must be representative of the obstacles which, in experience at large, are presented to man in the dilemmas inherent in more or less normal encounters with the world as the world is. Such a simplified statement is obviously a begging of many questions. What, for instance, is meant by the hero's well-being? Is it his welfare and success in the world as the world seems to be, or is it the state of his immortal soul? Is it his worth as judged at the bar of eternity, or is it his aptitude to meet the thousand and one recurrent rubs which arise through the mere act of living? But the range of comedy suggests the answer. Comedy is concerned with life as a thing to be lived. It has no direct cognisance of thoughts which wander through eternity. It is exclusively concerned with the problems of mortality. Conjectures of immortality are values beyond its competence to assess. "What time of day is it, lad?" That is the immediate concern of comedy. Unless hours were cups of sack, and minutes, capons, or other things no less necessary to the continued existence of man in the world in which he lives, comedy would indeed be superfluous. If time were but a moment of eternity, there would be no more reason to ask for comedy than to demand the time of the day. For tragedy, time is the eternal now; for comedy, it is the condition of present existence. Comedy is immersed in time, in the here and now. Its heroes, to overcome, to end happily and to go on ending happily without end, must be endowed with the temperament and the arts to triumph over the stresses of circumstance. They are not concerned with what man and life might have been. They take it as it is, and seek a way to turn it to their purpose. For them, the world is an oyster. Their primary object is to attain a mastery of circumstance. Endowed with a genius for that, they will go on ending happily as far as this world is concerned, whatever hap they may have in Arthur's bosom.

In our survey of Shakespeare's earlier comedies, we have watched his widening grasp of this situation, followed the stages by which he sought intuitively to embody in his comic heroes more and more of this capacity for conquering the world. In last year's play, *The Merchant of Venice*, there was little progress to report. His natural development as a comic dramatist was interrupted by the strength of his unartistic passion to express his racial prejudices. But even in *The Merchant of Venice*, with its depiction of the temperamental opulence and the easy *savoir-faire* of his young Venetian sparks, there is evidence of his growing sense of the *milieu* of comedy. It is, however, to *A Midsummer Night's Dream* that a return must be made for gauging the progress which Shakespeare's comic genius had attained in his creation of Falstaff.

It was there, and in particular, in the speech of Theseus about lunatics, lovers, and poets towards the end of the play, that an expression of the prevailing idea of comedy was to be found. It was, in effect, an explicit recognition that man depends, not merely for his success in life, but for his survival through life, on his possession of so much 'cool reason' that he may secure for himself immunity from the mortal diseases which, arising from his emotional and imaginative faculties, may render him unable to distinguish between bushes and bears.

That is the 'comic,' the worldly wisdom, of Theseus. But it was the conscious and deliberate conclusion of Theseus himself, and of Shakespeare. It was a comment on the action of the play. It was not an inevitable conviction coming out of the issues presented by the play. And, indeed, stated explicitly as Theseus stated it, it did not completely square with the action of the play itself. Theseus, for instance, bases his case on a temperamental disbelief in antique fables and fairy toys. But his audience had had actual experience of the reality of Oberon and Titania, and seen with its own eyes the effects of a Puckishly administered magic distillation. His plea for the supreme value of 'cool reason' depends entirely on the judgment of our cool reason, and is hardly at all corroborated by an imaginative experience of the operation in life of this same faculty. He rationalises 'cool reason' almost entirely; and is blind to our actual recognition through the play that an intuitive sense, a horse-sense such as Bottom's, may prompt man to similar modes of facing life, and so serve the same end.

But it could hardly be otherwise in a play in which the pro-pounder of its basic attitude to life is no more than a spectator of the action it depicts. Theseus merely watches over the plot of *A Midsummer Night's Dream*. He is not caught up into it. Right or wrong as his doctrine may be, it stands or falls in his case without such relevant evidence as might have come from the imaginative experience of seeing it tried out in the image of life which the play presents.

One waits therefore for a play in which the Theseus-attitude is a prime actor in the situations which make the dramatic plot. That, it would seem, is what Falstaff provides. This joining of Falstaff with Theseus may seem forced; and, of course, if they are considered independently as men and as dramatic characters, it may be that memory will catch at few or no traits to sustain the comparison. But Falstaff is indeed a fuller embodiment of the mentality of Theseus: in mind, Theseus, and in spirit, Faulconbridge are Falstaff's forbears. As with Theseus, his life is governed by the faculty of 'cool reason' in the sense that his valuation of all experience is a wider application of the findings of Theseus's 'cool reason.' It may, of course, well be that in this widening and in this necessarily more extended exploitation, 'cool reason' itself will undergo some change. Probably the common sense, which virtually is Theseus's 'cool reason,' will veer markedly towards a harder material rationalism, the materialism of Faulconbridge; it will disclose implications unsuspected, because not called for, in the simpler proposition of it which was all that his circumstance required Theseus to formulate.

What, then is the 'humour,' the ruling passion, the distinc-tive quiddity of Sir John Falstaff? Fundamentally, it is his infinite capacity for extricating himself from predicaments. Circumstance hems him in at the corner of a room, and, as his opponents stretch out their hands to lay hold of him, this huge mountain of flesh slips through the key-hole. So adept is he in this art of extrication that he revels in creating dilemmas for himself to enjoy the zest of coming triumphantly out of them.

He is insatiably curious to provide situations which test or even strain his genius for overcoming them. Mastery of circumstance is his pride: it is also his supreme qualification to be a hero of comedy.

These are traits which supply the mainspring of the plot. Falstaff has an unslakeable thirst for life. "Give me life,"— he cries—and the cry is in soliloquy, no fetch therefore to delude listeners. Life is his *summum bonum*. "Young men must live"—and he identifies himself with youth—"You that are old consider not the capacities of us that are young." Life is most intoxicating when a jest is forward and spirits are high. Life is indeed itself the greatest of frolics. A fellow whom under no circumstances you can make laugh, knows nothing of life: thin drink has so cooled his blood, and the making of many fish-meals and vegetarian dishes, that he has sunk into a kind of incapacitating green-sickness. High spirits or a good sherris-sack ascends to the brain and "dries me there all the foolish and dull and crude vapours which environ it; makes it apprehensive, quick, forgetive, full of nimble fiery and delectable shapes; which, deliver'd o'er to the voice, the tongue, which is the birth, becomes excellent wit." These, and not merely existing like a weaver singing his psalms, are the conditions which to Falstaff make for life. "He that will caper with me for a thousand marks, let him lend me the money and have at him!" For psalms are a *memento mori*, and Falstaff has no occasion for such things, unless like Bardolph's Death's-Head, he can make good use of them and so spare the cost of links and torches on his exploits as squire of the night's body. Grief, study, and such like perturbations of the brain are diseases to be avoided, an apoplexy, a kind of lethargy, a sleeping in the blood. From time to time, he talks of withdrawing from the heat of life; but that is only because there are few left to revel it at his pace; "virtue is of so little regard in these costermonger times that true valour is turned bear-herd.' "Go thy ways, old Jack; die when thou wilt, if manhood, good manhood, be not forgot upon the face of the earth, then am I a shotten herring: there live not three good men unhanged in England, and one of them is fat and grows old: God help the while! a bad world, I say." But these are moods with which Falstaff amuses himself in the lack of more zestful matter. The remedy is still more life, more bustle, more doing. "Bardolph, am I not fallen away vilely since this last action? Do I not bate? Do I not dwindle? Why, my skin hangs about me like an old lady's loose gown: I am withered like an old apple-john." So long as the liver can be kept hot, all is well. Even old age can be defied by those who can always keep in the vaward of youth: "You that are old . . . measure the heat of youth's livers with the bitterness of your galls." There may come a time for repentance: but it will be "at idle moments," and, rather than in ashes and sackcloth, it can first be in new silk and old sack: and at length, it can surely be suddenly, whilst one is in some liking, and with the last expiring ounce of strength which life retains.

Life's sternest and its ultimate enemy is death: and, as is absolutely inevitable for a hero of comedy whose primary and distinctive duty is to be alive and flourishing at the end of the play, Falstaff has no truck with death. Admittedly, mortal man owes God a death: but "I would be loath to pay him before his day: what need I be so forward with him that calls not on me?" Death is indeed so fatal an enemy to life that even jesting references to it are in bad taste, most unsavoury even in simile. If an ill-bred fellow will persist in talking of the gallows, one must switch over at once and remind him that my hostess of the tavern is a most sweet wench. Your Hotspurs may freely make a hazard of their heads for the mere gratification of easing their hearts. But not Falstaff, whose first duty is to ensure survival. Wherefore food and safety are his main requisites. The latter end of a fray and the beginning of a feast are the most auspicious moments of life. If fighting there must be, well: but he will fight no longer than he sees reason. If danger comes his way, so; but if he do not, then "if *I* come in *his* willingly, let him make a carbonado of me."

The better part of valour is discretion, and discretion compels one to seek safeguards. "Hal, if thou see me down in the battle and bestride me, so; 'tis a point of friendship": and the best moment of a day of battle is the evening of it when all is still well.

Such is Falstaff's sense of the major obligations of life, the groundwork of his philosophy: and he has qualities of mind, of temperament, and of body exquisitely adapted to enable him to make the most of life within his own scheme of it. He has the instinct for self-preservation and for mastery of events. He is a complete pragmatist, weighing everything by its contribution to the one object of his life which is to go on boisterously living. Outside this, there are no sanctions. The difference between truth and falsehood is in an irrelevant order of reckonings. Accepted notions of justice, of duty, of honour. and of valour are built on assumptions which do not apply to his purpose. Nothing is good except in so far as it may be turned to immediate and direct commodity: and he frees himself from every obligation of morality so that he may be alert and unshackled to take advantage of the main chance. All the contortions and the seeming discomfitures in his attempt to make the robbery on Gadshill a tale of his valour are thrown aside as mere retrospect in view of the immediate expectation of further jollity; "but, by the Lord, lads, I am glad you have the money." The moral and even the political implications of rebellion are of no account: "well, God be thanked for these rebels, they offend none but the virtuous; I laud them, I praise them." "A good wit will make use of anything," and Falstaff is the perfect opportunist who will turn even diseases to commodity.

The virtue of Falstaff's wit is its alacrity. His mind is complete master of his body. This sheer mass of gorbellied fat-guts is as a feather when his wit is the lever. As he has more flesh than another man, he has also uncountable frailties of the blood. Yet, intolerable as his deal of sack may be, the man is always above his liquor. Sodden as he always must have been, Falstaff is never fuzzy in mind, never drunk. In the most unexpected situations, however the old Adam may rebel, the flesh, the nerves, the blood and the sinews are always entirely at the command of his mind.

There is the famous occasion of his seeming cowardice at Shrewsbury. He has openly vowed that he does not deliberately seek encounters with fire-eating enemies. But if the encounter comes, he will meet it as he may. "Re-enter Douglas; he fights with Falstaff, who falls down as if he were dead, and exit Douglas." It looks, and indeed is, a travesty of all received notions of heroism. But is it cowardice? When in your nursery stories, the big-game hunter, his last shot fired, feigned death to escape the oncoming lion who will not touch dead flesh, you admired his perfect control of nerves, his amazing heroism. Why not Falstaff's? A heroic Hotspur has no such superb self-command. His nerves get the better of him: over-excited by the plot he is hatching, his manner and appearance are a public advertisement of the conspiracy:—

> Why dost thou bend thine eyes upon the earth,
> And start so often when thou sit'st alone?
> Why hast thou lost the fresh blood in thy cheeks?

Hotspur's body palpably betrays his mind, and unfits itself to serve the mind's decree. He has even lost the capacity to sleep restfully:

> In thy faint slumbers I by thee have watch'd,
> And heard thee murmur tales of iron wars. . . .
> Thy spirit within thee hath been so at war
> And thus hath so bestirr'd thee in thy sleep,
> That beads of sweat have stood upon thy brow,
> Like bubbles in a late-disturbed stream;
> And in thy face strange motions have appear'd,
> Such as we see when men restrain their breath
> On some great sudden hest.

Set Hotspur beside Falstaff again. The sheriff and his officers are at the tavern-door to arrest Falstaff on a capital charge.

There is no quaking, no trembling, no strange motion in his face. On the contrary, a superb nonchalance, a magnificent indifference to such stupid interruptions of gaiety. "Out, ye rogue," he says to Bardolph who is excitedly telling of the Sheriff's arrival, "play out the play." Even when a more importunate notice is given, Falstaff is still too preoccupied with his sport to take heed of it. Then, at his own time, he looks at the situation. He makes no grovelling plea for protection, but almost casually lets it be known that he expects it: "if you will deny the Sheriff, so," he tells Hal; but "if not, let him enter." So completely confident is he that he treats himself to one of his very few vaunts at death—"if I become not a cart as well as another man, a plague on my bringing up! I hope I shall as soon be strangled with a halter as another." The Prince, however, suggests that he should hide behind the arras. The Sheriff enters for a moment and is told on a Prince's word that Falstaff is not within. He retires, having been in the room a matter of a few seconds. The arras is at once withdrawn; and Falstaff is found to be asleep, and so soundly asleep that they can pick his pockets without wakening him. It is a consummate illustration of his mastery of himself and of his magnificent opportunism: he can turn even an occasion like this to his own commodity. There is another character in the play, the King himself, who, as will later appear, earns his success by arts comparable in his sphere of responsibility to Falstaff's in his. Yet even here, Falstaff is the greater master. One of Henry's most human moments is his pathetic lament that sleep no more will weigh his eyelids down and that nature's nurse no longer lulls him into restful repose.

One need not, of course, claim 'courage' for Falstaff. But one cannot indite him of cowardice. Neither are relevant terms. What he has is absolute self-possession and an aptitude to employ all the elements of his being for the furtherance of his own welfare. His counterfeiting of death is policy, just as was the King's scheme for avoiding death in battle by having many others disguised in his clothes. Falstaff's is as successful for his purpose as is the King's for his, and it does not, as does the King's, cost anybody his life. Indeed, in Falstaff's vocabulary, it is not counterfeiting at all. "Counterfeit? I lie, I am no counterfeit: to die is to be a counterfeit; for he is but the counterfeit of a man who hath not the life of a man: but to counterfeit dying, when a man thereby liveth, is to be no counterfeit, but the true and perfect image of life indeed." Almost always, since Falstaff's values are his own and not the conventional ones, he will find it necessary to twist words and things from their normal functions to apparently ludicrous ones. But their ludicrousness is caused by unexpected suddenness, not by inherent absurdity. Going into battle, Falstaff arms himself with a bottle of sack, not with a pistol. One recalls a warrior of our day, Captain Bluntschli, who also relied more on articles of sustenance than on firearms. Being Mr. Shaw's soldier, he preferred Cadbury to Bass, chocolate to beer: but his assessment of the relative value of food and of guns is meant seriously. Was it not at Queen Victoria's suggestion (and Shaw did not amuse her) that chocolate became a regular ration in the Boer war? Is not a tot of rum still served a few moments before zero?

Being what he is, so gifted, so entirely and unswervingly devoted to his single purpose, Falstaff triumphs wherever he goes. Whatever the dilemma, whoever the opponent, Falstaff scores. He sees at a glance the stroke to play, half-sword or his old ward: but he has all strokes at command, and none can anticipate his rapid change from one to another. He never knows when he is beaten. He can wrench any true case the wrong way. He turns defence into attack, and at the end, by audacity and effrontery, he rises above his opponents with superb patronage and in complete victory. With a confident brow and a throng of words, or indeed, with but one word, he can reduce an opponent to abject insignificance, putting him in his proper place in a world of which Falstaff is natural king. "*I* call thee coward! I'll see thee damned ere I call thee coward; but I would give a thousand pound I could run as fast as thou canst." So much for Poins. A moment's notice is too much for Pistol. "Discharge yourself of our company, Pistol"; and when Pistol goes on brawling, Falstaff ignores him until, the noise becoming too uncomfortable, he rebukes him with Olympian brevity: "Pistol, I would be quiet." But Pistol is too far gone to heed. Bardolph is commanded to throw him out, but it soon appears that Falstaff himself will have to dispose of the roysterer. "Give me my rapier, boy," and then, to Pistol, "Get you downstairs." The ease and confidence of it is typical, and the economy. As with his capture of Coleville, there is marvellous thrift in his nice adaptation of means to the desired end: "Do ye yield, sir, or shall I sweat for you?"

A more sustained encounter is his play with the Lord Chief Justice: the pretended deafness; the impressively patriotic reproach to the servant; the strategic friendly concern for the justice's well-being; the deliberate mishearing, and then the bold confession of it; the polite hints that the Lord Chief Justice should ponder whether greater ones than he may not be implicated; then the bid for a sort of moral ascendancy in his own behalf; a patronising reference to the Justice's wisdom and the prince's rudeness; and, a last score, the recognised right of the soldier to round on the stay-at-home. The stupendous effrontery reaches its proper climax—"Will your lordship lend me a thousand pounds?"

Your Shallows, your hostesses, and your Dolls are easier victims. Falstaff merely shifts the responsibility for his debts on to the backs of his creditors; and, with an air of indefeasible righteousness, acts as if the size of his debt to it rendered him proprietor of the inn. "Shall I not take mine ease in mine inn but I shall have my pockets picked?" When Mrs. Quickly is completely exonerated from the charge he has brought against her, he reduces her to absolute subjection by forgiving her for the crime she has not committed. "Hostess, I forgive thee: go, make ready breakfast; love thy husband, look to thy servants, cherish thy guests: thou shalt find me tractable to any honest reason: thou seest I am pacified still." For such benign condescension, she will in the end pawn all she has, plate and gowns, to lend him money, and will commemorate the signal favour he is conferring on her in accepting it, by giving him a supper, and, at her own suggestion, inviting Doll, though she be a rival flame, to add to Sir John's joy at the feast.

Prince Hal, of course, has a hereditary prerogative to deal some smart blows in his bouts with Falstaff. But even in these, Falstaff always wins on points, though the round after Gadshill may seem at first view to have gone heavily against him. Whatever the scrape, and however far Falstaff has put himself at a disadvantage, he can always turn the offence into a claim on the whole nation's gratitude. "No abuse, Ned, i' the world; honest Ned, none. I dispraised him before the wicked, that the wicked might not fall in love with him; in which doing, I have done the part of a careful friend and a true subject, and thy father is to give me thanks for it." The Gadshill episode itself will bear closer scrutiny. To think for a moment that the string of lies about the men in buckram was put out as even nominally credible is to set down Falstaff as a half-wit. They are, and were meant to be, gross, open, palpable lies. But they are finely hit on to serve an unexpected purpose. As soon as the robbers have been robbed, a makeshift excuse has to be concocted: there being no suspicion in their minds that a trick has been played on them, an obvious and, so they believe, an uncontestable tale can easily be rigged up—they were overwhelmed by numbers. As no one, they think, saw the fray, all that is necessary is to hack their own swords and draw blood by tickling their noses—and there will thus be ample corroboration. So Falstaff begins the story in the proper key— "a hundred upon poor four of us"—and continues to throw great glory on his own valour. "I am a rogue, if I were not at half-sword with a dozen of them two hours together. I have scaped by miracle. I am eight times thrust through the doublet, four through the hose; my buckler cut through and through; my sword hacked like a hand-saw—*ecce signum!!* I never dealt better since I was a man: all would not do." But, immediately, he discovers that his confederates are not skilful players at this game of bluff, hard as they may try. Gadshill lets him down as soon as he opens his mouth: "we four set upon some dozen." Falstaff has to jog him discreetly—for the original hundred is rapidly diminishing—"sixteen at least." Then it is Peto's turn to show what a bad hand he plays—"no, no, they were not bound": and Falstaff has to make a hot effort to whip him into the right pace. But he sees that it is hopeless. "I know not what you call all." He must carry it off from his own hand. At first he sticks to the original suit—they were overwhelmed by numbers: "if I fought not with fifty of them I am a bunch of radish"—he even killed two of them—"two rogues in buck-ram suits." But he sees that the original scheme is a failure— "I tell thee what, Hal, if I tell thee a lie, spit in my face, call me horse." He must improvise on it. He has prepared the way for open lying. Abandoning for the moment all thought of plausibility, he can restore his own confidence by running into a riot of lies. But the lie to serve his turn must be one capable of limitless progression: one, four, nine, eleven and so forth. The infinity of such a mathematical series is its real worth. It assures him of a stretch of time long enough to make him confident that within it some other shift will suggest itself. As indeed it does—"upon compulsion?" When the argument has turned from facts to reasons, reasons for Falstaff will be plentiful as blackberries. The opponents know it, and realising that defeat is imminent on the main issue, they fall back on vitu-peration: but that is another game at which Falstaff has the odds. There is nothing now for them to do but to return to a recital of the plain facts. It looks like a trump suit: "we two saw your four set on four and bound them, and were masters of their wealth. Mark now, how a plain tale shall put you down. Then did we two set on your four; and, with a word, outpaced you from your prize, and have it." But they have now for the first time disclosed all their cards: and Falstaff can easily out-bid them by an unexpected lead. "By the Lord, I knew ye as well as he that made ye." Hence the winning trick—"Instinct." He can almost make a grand slam of it, turning it to prove that he himself is a valiant lion, and Hal a true prince—no inconsiderable escape from a predicament in which Hal seemed to have overwhelming odds to prove Falstaff an arrant coward.

That is the way of Falstaff. He can wrest every circumstance to his own advantage. Cast for the moment to play the part of a cold-blooded, water-loving, moralising king, he at once sees in it a chance to begin with a cup of sack: "give me a cup of sack to make my eyes look red, that it may be thought I have wept; for I must speak in passion." That is indeed mastery of circumstance, and such a master has the gift of indestructibility. Irrepressible, he will almost triumph over death itself. At least, he will hear his own epitaph spoken, and rise to confound the speaker: "embowelled! if thou embowel me to-day, I'll give you leave to powder me and eat me too to-morrow."

Yet in the end, Falstaff is rejected. Moreover, as Mr. Bradley has pointed out, though the rejection is devastatingly abrupt, yet, in retrospect, the Falstaff of the second part of *Henry IV* is somehow not the complete victor of the first part. His early frolics are the spontaneous and irrepressible exercise of his nature, scrapes and difficulties often sought for the zest of practising his genius for turning them to advantage. But the later escapades are schemes, deliberate plans forced on him by necessities as mean as any which drive a sharper living on his wits to exploit his sordid trickeries. Robbing the King's exchequer in Falstaff's early way is plainly his vocation; his thefts of later days are merely petty filching. The Gadshill robbery is "for sport's sake, to do the profession some grace." This is recreation. But practising upon the spineless spirit of Mrs. Quickly to make her purse serve his turn, is in another order of exploits. Indeed, after Shrewsbury, Falstaff is perpetually on the watch for gulls whom he can temper between his finger and his thumb and soften into disbursing. There may still be hints of former greatness in the economics of his recruiting scheme, though it is a damnable abuse of the King's press. But the pleasant Cotswold air and the inimitable foolery of Shallow are somewhat spoiled by the known intention to turn them to a thousand pounds loan. And when Falstaff, having cajoled and defrauded Mistress Quickly into abject subjugation, accepts her invitation to supper, his aside to Bardolph as she goes in glee to prepare the feast—" Go, with her; hook on, hook on," is a plot for more loot which is out of all grace.

The wit may be the same, and its agility. But the setting is different. Throughout the second part of *Henry IV*, the Falstaff who hitherto had pitted himself against kings, princes, and gentlemen, is almost circumscribed to brushes with servants, inferior associates, hostesses, and the raggle-taggle who do a bum-bailliff's dirty work. Only once in this second part has he a real bout with the prince; and his sallies against the Lord Chief Justice are but reminders of his former triumphs. He does not so much fool Shallow as permit Shallow to fulfil his own destiny by proving himself naturally a fool. The earlier Falstaff would have despised the Shallows and the Slenders— except as Gadshill victims—as much as he despised the scarecrows he had pressed into his regiment: they would have been good enough to toss, yet not enough seriously to employ his wit. But now that he finds this consumption of the purse to be an uncurable disease, he is at the mercy of the meanest tradesmen. Without their favour, his life can be brought to a standstill: there will be no more satin for a short-cloak. With their talk of security they can withhold all Sir John's requirements, even as did Master Dombledon: "Let him be damned, like the glutton," says Falstaff of this unyielding shopkeeper, "pray God his tongue be hotter! A whoreson Achitophel! a rascally yea-forsooth knave! to bear a gentleman in hand, and then stand on security!" But the tradesman's counter is a barrier Falstaff cannot surmount.

When haberdashery has become an insuperable impediment to Falstaff's existence, his world is no longer what it was. Hitherto, that were all one; there was linen enough on every hedge. But now the low ebb of linen with him is a handicap: he may in a spurt of the old spirit pride himself that he takes but two shirts out with him; but shirts are no longer a super-fluity to him in the perpetual motion of drinking old sack, un-buttoning after supper, sleeping upon benches after noon, and greeting fair hot wenches in flame-coloured taffeta. Yet this is only part, and a smaller part, of a sad change.

Falstaff knows that he is not what he was. "A pox of this gout! or, a gout of this pox! For the one or the other plays the rogue with my great toe." His diseases prove harder to turn to commodity. He had formerly revelled in his vast waist as no slight prompting to his wit. The discomfitures of his heavy going have been an unfailing spur to the quickness of his intellectual sallies. But now he is sensitive to jibes about his bulk. "Men of all sorts take a pride to gird at me." As fodder for their jests, he walks before his page "like a sow that hath overwhelmed all her litter but one," a sad way of causing wit in other men. He, who had once in his humour likened himself to an apple-john, can no longer tolerate the name of it, for the prince set "a dish of applejohns before him, and told him there were five more Sir Johns, and, putting off his hat, said, 'I will now take my leave of these six dry, round, old withered knights.'" Such affronts could only now be borne when, leaving fighting o' days and foining o' nights, though Doll be on his knee, he is beginning to patch up his old body for heaven. His bulk pathetically obstructs him: "an I had but a belly of any indifferency, I were simply the most active fellow in Europe: my womb, my womb, my womb, undoes me." And when Falstaff himself volunteers, as an explanation of comparative ineffectiveness, "I am old, I am old," it is indeed growing late. There may be a merry song or two before the end. But the man who was born about three of the clock in an afternoon, with a white head and a something round belly, and who has lost his voice with halloing and singing of anthems, will scarcely approve his youth much further.

Yet though Sir John's falling away is plain, no less plain is the suspicion of his author's grief at seeing it. Falstaff must still be allowed his supremacy, though it is superiority over meaner mortals than have formerly been his victims. Only comparatively speaking, and when Shallow is the object of comparison, is he still in good liking or does he bear his years very well. He yet may seem to play his old tricks and with the appearance of equal success. He can, for instance, still so far overcome his mountainous flesh to be—for Doll at all events, and though only for her—her "whoreson little valiant villain," a "sweet, little rogue." And shrunk though he be by such association—"You help to make the diseases, Doll; we catch of you, Doll, we catch of you"—it is still occasionally granted to his virtue to be as good a man as was Sir John. His genius can come to yet more proof for the world's ultimate good than can the specious supremacy of its Lord Johns of Lancaster: "I would you had but the wit: 'twere better than your duke-dom." Nor does it need memory to call back the queer pity of his last moments in *Henry V* to feel the moving sadness of his latter end in the second part of *Henry IV*: "A' made a finer end and went away an' it had been any Christom child; a' parted even just between twelve and one, even at the turn-ing of the tide; for after I saw him fumble with the sheets and play with flowers and smile upon his fingers' ends, I knew there was but one way; for his nose was as sharp as a pen, and a' babbled of green fields. 'How now, Sir John!' quoth I: 'what, man! be o' good cheer.' So a' cried out 'God, God, God!' three or four times. Now I, to comfort him, bid him a' should not think of God; I hoped there was no need to trouble himself with any such thoughts yet. So a' bade me lay more clothes on his feet: I put my hand into the bed and felt them, and they were as cold as any stone; then I felt to his knees . . . and all was as cold as any stone."

Though in the second *Henry IV*, the associates left to him now are bottle-ale rascals and wenches as common as the way between St. Albans and London, women related to him as the parish heifers are to the town bull, yet even over such a globe of sinful continents there is spread an air of inexplicable or at least of irrational pathos, in the simple recognition that Sir John, the great Sir John, draws near his end. When he is sent away first to the wars, a man of merit sought after to the last, his departure finds the good wenches so blubbered with tears that their hearts are ready to burst. Between memories of the twenty-nine years come peascod-time that they have known him as the best of honest and true-hearted men, and the fears that he may return no more, there is a weeping which nothing can assuage but such insensibility as comes from sack and still more sack. Doll's kisses may be bought, but her flattering busses for an old decrepit man with an empty purse are the pathetic pledges of a feeling that he is still far worthier than any scurvy boy of them all. The hope is indestructible that, if he have but a care of himself, he may yet fare well enough to give her the riotous joy of dressing herself handsome to celebrate his safe return from the wars. For Doll and such as knew him as she did, he is still "as valorous as Hector of Troy, worth five of Agamemnon and ten times better than the nine Worthies." Men, other men, all men, may die like dogs; but "well, sweet Jack, have a care of thyself." As he departs for the scene of battle, all grievances are forgotten: "Come, I'll be friends with thee, Jack; thou art going to the wars"; but there is the sorrow of happy though reprobate memories in the parting phrase—"and whether I shall ever see thee again or no, there is nobody cares."

This is the Falstaff who lives in the affections of Mistress Doll, of Mistress Quickly, and of the whole world of Shakespeare's readers, the Falstaff who survives in the memory of man. But he was ruthlessly trampled into extinction by Henry V: casting him off, the King killed his heart. Even more cruelly, so too did Shakespeare. It was murder in Hal; in Shakespeare, the crime worse than parricide—the slaughter of one's own offspring.

For Shakespeare, so the story runs, was commanded by his Queen to resuscitate the corpse whose heart had been fracted

and corroborate, and to show him in love. Shakespeare
obeyed: and there can be no clearer evidence of his own
rejection of Falstaff. The boisterous merriment of *The Merry
Wives of Windsor* is a cynical revenge which Shakespeare took
on the hitherto unsuspecting gaiety of his own creative
exuberance. The Falstaff in it bears a name which masks the
bitterness of its author's disillusionment. Any competent
dramatist after Plautus could have followed the conventions of
comedy, and shown a gross, fat, lascivious, old man ludicrously
caught in the toils of his own lust. But for Shakespeare to call
that old fat man Falstaff, that is the measure of his bitterness.
For, as Mr. Bradley has said, the Falstaff of *The Merry Wives*
has nothing in common with our Falstaff except his name, a
trick or two of inspired speech, and—though Mr. Bradley has
not said this—a superficial likeness to Mr. Stoll's pattern of the
'comic' character to be found all the way down the ages of
theatrical history.

The masquerading figure in *The Merry Wives* is an old
fat fellow whom all can gull to make a public sport. He himself
knows how little of the old Sir John survives: it is even time
that little were choked with a piece of toasted cheese. "I have
been transformed, and how my transformation hath been
washed and cudgelled, they [his old associates at court] would
melt me out of my fat drop by drop and liquor fisherman's
boots with me: I warrant they would whip me with their fine
wits till I were as crestfallen as a dried pear." So far is he out at
heels that he can only try to provide for himself by shifts and
cony-catchings which he has no longer the genius to bring
successfully off. He is encumbered with new afflictions. He
carries his wine now only like a Flemish drunkard. Not only
has he quaking fits of sheer fear, but he openly confesses his
intolerable fright. His pride has gone: he himself broadcasts
the story of his ignominy: "I knew not what 'twas to be
beaten till lately." "I suffered the pangs of three several deaths;
first, an intolerable fright, to be detected with a jealous rotten
bell-wether; next, to be compassed, like a good bilbo, in the

circumference of a peck, hilt to point, heel to head; and then, to be stopped in, like a strong distillation, with stinking clothes that fretted in their own grease: think of that,—a man of my kidney,—think of that,—that am as subject to heat as butter; a man of continual dissolution and thaw: it was a miracle to 'scape suffocation. And in the height of this bath, when I was more than half stewed in grease, like a Dutch dish, to be thrown into the Thames, and cooled, glowing hot, in that surge, like a horse-shoe; think of that,—hissing hot,—think of that."

Time and again, in *The Merry Wives*, some situation or another recalls by grotesque contrast the extent of Sir John's transformation. Think, for instance, of his impressive nonchalance in planning his own safety at Shrewsbury: "Hal, if thou see me down in the battle, and bestride me, so": and set by its side his frenzy of fear when news of Ford's return renders him witless to plan anything and makes him appeal in a panic to the women to devise any sort of trick by which he may escape: "good hearts, devise something; any extremity rather than a mischief." His counterfeits, too, are different. His *sang-froid* deceived Douglas into believing that he was dead enough to need no further killing. But now, he counterfeits by a ludicrous disguise as an old woman merely to avoid a jealous husband (think of how Mistress Quickly was recommended to love *her* husband), and, by so doing, after heavy thwackings, a mere stroke of luck prevents his being set in the common stocks by a knave constable. How are the mighty fallen! He cannot indeed fall lower than he does when, to escape, not now a Douglas, but a band of children playing fairies, he lies down ostrich-wise, with eyes pressed close to the ground, oblivious altogether of the receipt of fern-seeds he used to carry with him. "I'll wink and couch."

His wits have lost all their nimbleness. He no longer has the confidence that they will always be quick enough to bring him out of his scrapes. Gone is his old art of creeping into a halfpenny purse, into a pepper box, or slipping through a

key-hole.] fficulties which he would formerly have wel-
comed with zest, no longer excite his exuberance: indeed mere
news of them now distracts him. Worse still, his wit is so
dulled that he does not even see his difficulties. "I do *begin* to
perceive," he ,says—and that, after he has been fooled egre-
giously and often,—"I do *begin* to perceive that I am made an
ass." Truth is, they can fool him even as they wish; once,
twice, three times running, he falls into their toils. Anybody
can fool him: neither Mistress Page nor Mistress Ford ever for a
moment imagines that he will be too clever for her—

> Devise but how you'll use him when he comes,
> And let us two devise to bring him thither.

And these are just citizens' wives of Windsor. Even Pistol
knows Mistress Quickly for a punk who is Cupid's carrier. But,
of all dullards, Mistress Quickly can tell a tale well enough to
gull Falstaff now. When such a go-between is amply adequate
to overreach Sir John, he is indeed gone beyond recovery.
There is scarcely a saving grace. He who had been a prince's
confederate in highway escapades is now a receiver of the petty
loot of pocket-picking and bag-snatching: a fan-handle now,
no longer a king's exchequer: and all for fifteen pence. He
shuffles, hedges, and lurches amongst a sordid gang of uncon-
finable baseness. Mean and low as his associates now are, he is
on no better than an equal footing with them at best, and as
often as not, they round on him and outdo him. With his one-
time familiars, he had been Jack Falstaff, John with his brothers
and sisters, but Sir John with all Europe. Now he is 'bully-
rook' even with a provincial innkeeper. He is on entirely new
terms with rascals like Pistol and Nym: "my honest lads," he
must call them, to ward off their quips. Not only have they
the impudence to jibe at him; they have the audacity to defy
him openly, and flatly refuse to do his bidding. In the end, two
simple bourgeois and their wives, colleagued with a foolish
doctor, a comic Welsh parson, and an innkeeper, can trample
the once mighty Falstaff in Windsor's mud. "Have I laid my

brain in the sun and dried it, that it wants matter to prevent so gross o'erreaching as this? Am I ridden with a Welsh goat too? Shall I have a coxcomb of frize?" "Well, I am your theme: you have the start of me; I am dejected; I am not able to answer the Welsh flannel; ignorance itself is a plummet o'er me: use me as you will." "Use me as you will": that is, in fine, to put a period to the jest.

But why this ruthless exposure, this almost malicious laceration of him who had once rejoiced the hearts of his author and of the rest of the world?

It might be, and has been, claimed that the original Falstaff overgrew his part, and had to be turned out of the cycle at the point when Hal became king. As has been seen, there is matter in the second *Henry IV* to suggest that Shakespeare was leading Falstaff to his dismissal: matter, also, hinting that he did it reluctantly. But if Sir John had necessarily to go, could he not have been allowed a death-bed—a more certain dismissal than a king's rejection—before Hal's coronation? An apoplexy, any affliction to which the body of man is liable might, without stretch of likelihood, have been called in to remove a Falstaff who, on a professional diagnosis, "might have more diseases than he knew for." Moreover, his removal by mere royal edict brought technical troubles with it, the dubieties surrounding the character of Hal. Why then did Shakespeare rest satisfied with Henry's rejection of Falstaff as the expedient by which to get rid of him? Is it indeed Henry, or is it Shakespeare who rejects Falstaff? Throughout the second *Henry IV* Falstaff is falling from Shakespeare's grace; by the end of the play, he has almost forced his author, though reluctantly, to face up to the situation. Falstaff has in fact displayed his inability to be what had seemed to be. He has disqualified himself as a comic hero. He has let Shakespeare down.

The figure which the dramatist's imagination had intuitively compounded, had seemed infinitely better provided than any of his predecessors with the gifts of the comic hero. With such a spirit, such a mind, such intuitions, and such an outlook on life, he appeared to bear within his own nature a complete guarantee of survival and of mastery of circumstance, the pledge of the perfect comic hero. But somehow or other, when the intoxication of creating him is momentarily quieter, hesitancies begin to obtrude and the processes of creation are different. The clogging becomes stronger. Falstaff must be cast off, as he is cast off at the end of the second *Henry IV*. But a pathetic hope persists, and is spoken in the Epilogue: it may still be possible to save Sir John: "our humble author will continue the story with Sir John in it, and make you merry with fair Katherine of France: where, for any thing I know, Falstaff shall die of a sweat, unless already a' be killed with your hard opinions."[1] But before the play with Katherine in it is written, the issue is settled. Falstaff is irrevocably discredited, fit for nothing more but Windsor forest.

This suggestion as to the decline and fall of Falstaff neither requires nor presupposes a conscious purpose in Shakespeare's reason. In the sheer abandon of his imaginative fervour, Falstaff and the circumstances he overcomes are projected by the unthinking zest of the author's imaginative apprehension, and shape themselves into the coherent universe which a play makes for itself. But at moments the world of his creation is threatened by the intrusion of circumstances which will have destroyed its validity if they should prove too much for Falstaff. And by no fetch of his imagination can he endow Falstaff with the aptitude to acquire his customary mastery over these intrusions: nor, springing as did Falstaff himself from his imagination, can they be dismissed more readily than can he. In the way in which, without deliberate judgment, an artist's creation of an image of life is satisfying, Falstaff had satisfied Shakespeare. Within the scope of worldly wisdom, which is the philosophy of comedy, Falstaff had seemed to justify entire trust. In this sense, Shakespeare believed in him; and Falstaff proved to be a god with feet of clay. Hence his bitter disillusionment and his willingness to call the contemptible

[1] *II Henry IV.* Epilogue.

caricature of *The Merry Wives* by the name of Sir John Falstaff.

The argument here set out may seem to rest unduly on a speculative notion of the extent and the nature of Shakespeare's first faith in Falstaff. Since drama depicts man amongst men and against a background of society and of circumstance, a dramatist inevitably fashions a world for his own creatures. A comic dramatist shapes a world semblably like our own, and releases into it from his intuitions a figure equipped to be comfortably at home in it and skilled to adapt himself to its material and human conditions, a figure possessing as by instinct the secret of worldly wisdom and thereby gifted to turn existence to his own security and happiness. No earlier creation of Shakespeare's was so eminently endowed as was Falstaff with these attributes. He appeared to solve the artistic problem of the comic dramatist: one could pledge one's faith to him entirely. From such an artistic faith, it is an easy step to an unquestioning belief that Falstaff has achieved a mastery of life itself, of life, that is, as a thing to be lived, and, within its own conditions, as a thing to be prized above all else.

Conviction in such ranges of value comes to the artist, and to the watcher of the plays, not by argument, but by imaginative demonstration. And it is abundantly clear that the Falstaff of the first *Henry IV* shows himself in very act to be worthier in this respect than the other many sorts of men who confront such problems as he does in the world of which they are all inhabitants.

The situations of *I Henry IV* continually bring the immediate and pertinent worth of Falstaff into comparison with that of Hal, of Hotspur, and of Henry IV. The comparison is usually enriched by dramatic contrasts, and to secure these contrasts, it is generally Falstaff's rôle to be placed at first at a signal disadvantage. But he invariably comes out best. Of Falstaff's relations with Hal, little more need be said: Falstaff's wit is always a sufficiently effective means of his securing even honours. If one doubts this at moments, there is always his final and incontestable appeal to fall back on—"Hal, thou owest me thy love." That is a security so valid and certain that only the unthinkable inhumanity of Hal renders it invalid and worthless in the end.

In contrast with Falstaff, Hotspur has all the gifts which count in the world's admiration:

> I do not think a braver gentleman,
> More active-valiant or more valiant-young,
> More daring or more bold, is now alive
> To grace this latter age with noble deeds.

His beliefs, no less than his temperament, appear to secure him in our affections. He dedicates his vigour and his life to the service of humanity's most inspiring ideal—honour—the very ideal which for Falstaff is a mere scutcheon, a word, thin air.

> By heaven, methinks it were an easy leap,
> To pluck bright honour from the pale-faced moon,
> Or dive into the bottom of the deep,
> Where fathom-line could never touch the ground,
> And pluck up drowned honour by the locks.

Hence, Hotspur revels in danger, whilst Falstaff's unabashed and unhidden code is safety first.

> Send danger from the east unto the west,
> So honour cross it from the north to south,
> And let them grapple.

Danger provides, indeed, a physical thrill for Hotspur which helps to gratify his avid thirst for the excitement of life:

> O, the blood more stirs
> To rouse a lion than to start a hare.

Yet in effect his creed is built on a fundamental contempt for life—his own, and that of others:

> life's time's fool,
> And time, that takes survey of all the world,
> Must have a stop.

But for Falstaff, life is all in all: "give me life: which if I can save, so; if not, honour comes unlooked for, and there's an end."

Yet Hotspur's honour would be scanned. Not only because, pursued as a stimulant to life, it nevertheless leads directly to death. Nor even because, leading him winking to leap into destruction, it also carries his troops with him to their death. But, appearing as a shining example of pure chivalric honour, it yet shows itself contaminated with inglorious elements of sheer selfishness. He will pluck up drowned honour from the deep

> So that he that doth redeem her thence might wear
> Without corrival all her dignities.

Such honour rests largely on a personal pride which measures itself by the prestige gained in the world: and such a personal sense of pride may gratify itself with meaner possessions. Hotspur's honour, for instance, professes itself to be involved in what on the face of it is a merely commercial deal in property: his dissatisfaction with his own share in the material loot of rebellion, he puts forth as an issue of honour:

> But in the way of bargain, mark ye me,
> I'll cavil on the ninth part of a hair.

Honour on such terms is little better at best than a heightened susceptibility to affront, seeing shame where no shame is meant, a sensitiveness to popular reputation which is not always a clear claim on the good thoughts of the world. Sometimes it is not better than an instinct to exact vengeance from those who appear to impugn a reputation: "we'll be revenged on him" is Hotspur's final reason for rebellion. An honour so colourable may be only an envious contempt for others to whom the

world awards its praise, and a contemptible desire to put them
out of competition even though by dastardly measures:

> But that I think his father loves him not
> And would be glad he met with some mischance,
> I would have him poison'd with a pot of ale.

In its ultimate expression, when Hotspur for the last time meets
Hal, his honour is hard to distinguish from a mere brag:

> would to God
> Thy name in arms were now as great as mine!

Dying, Hotspur's regret is not for the loss of brittle life, but for
the loss of those proved titles Hal has won of him, for they
wound his thoughts worse than the sword his flesh.

Such, at least in great part, is what honour is to Hotspur:
and a Falstaff, living in Hotspur's world, is capable of seeing it
for what it is. In any case, whatever be the ultimate moral
basis of Hotspur's honour, the immediate conviction brought
by the action of the play is that honour renders Hotspur a
menace to himself, to his friends, and to the world of his time.
It is an ally of the rashness of his temperament. He is altogether
governed by humours. As his friends tell him,

> Though sometimes it show greatness, courage, blood,—
> And that's the dearest grace it renders you,—
> Yet oftentimes it doth present harsh rage,
> Defect of manners, want of government,
> Pride, haughtiness, opinion and disdain;
> The least of which haunting a nobleman
> Loseth men's hearts and leaves behind a stain
> Upon the beauty of all parts besides,
> Beguiling them of commendation.

Falstaff fights when he cannot help it, and then no longer
than he need. Hotspur rushes into a fight before he is ready
for it, on the specious plea that unpreparedness, shortage of

numbers, and so forth, are in themselves an advantage in the assessment of honour:

> It lends a lustre and more great opinion,
> A larger dare to our great enterprise.

But the end tries all. Falstaff comes with "honours" from Shrewsbury, Hotspur is left there a corpse. And with Hotspur lie also his cause, and the bodies of his adherents. He is indeed utterly incapable of adapting himself to circumstance, or even of remembering to do the obviously necessary thing. He comes to a political conference—and has forgotten to bring the necessary documents and maps. He quarrels with his friends: he antagonises his fellow-conspirators: he brings destruction on everybody and everything he stands to uphold and to protect. In the world of political life, in the world of social man, he himself is a patent failure and a danger to his associates.

Even in the materially smaller society which is marriage he is but fortuitously proficient. His ineptitude in the exercise of domestic sense is flagrant. His wife pressingly and fondly enquires the causes of the distemperature which he cannot hide even in the seclusion of his own room. But he is inattentive, and when spasmodically he starts from his abstraction, it is merely to summon a servant for information about posts and horses. Only at length does he deign to give his wife an off-hand attention—"What say'st thou, my lady?" and before she can reply, his mind is off again. To her further importunity, he has no reply but flippant evasions which culminate in a flat refusal to tell her anything at all on grounds of which the sting is their seeming jollity:

> I know you wise, but yet no farther wise
> Than Harry Percy's wife: constant you are,
> But yet a woman: and for secrecy,
> No lady closer; for I well believe
> Thou wilt not utter what thou dost not know.

Nothing but the mystery of personal affection can explain the permanence of a society conducted on principles like these. Even so, on the score of adherents gained, in the play itself and in the world of readers, by the spell of personality, clearly, though Hotspur has his conquests, Falstaff's are no fewer than his. And in all other things as measured by the play, Falstaff succeeds, Hotspur fails.

In efficiency, indeed, efficiency to live the life to which one is called, there is only one person in the play to set beside Falstaff, namely, the King himself. A comparison of them at length would take us into a consideration of Shakespeare's view of kingship: but this can be deferred for the present purpose.[1] The King's immediate task is to maintain the welfare of the state of England; Falstaff's is to preserve the well-being of the corporation of Sir John. There is a striking similarity in the obligations imposed by each of these purposes, and in the means by which each of the actors secures his ends. The wit of Falstaff and the policy of the King are instruments which rest on similar assumptions. Morality enters into the schemes of neither of them: they remain free from the constraints of all conventions and of all generally accepted principles. Each in his own sphere is the perfect exponent of expediency. "Are these things then necessities? Then let us meet them like necessities." For both of them "nothing can seem foul to those that win." But the political necessities which are the King's sphere require him to purchase success by the complete subjugation of personal affection, human sentiment, and natural instinct. At moments, as a father, he utters the distress of the man; but the politician has already locked the outer world out of doors, when in the privacy of his own room, he unfolds his paternal grief to his wayward son. Falstaff is no less beyond the constraint of general sanctions. But as a social creature for whom life is not, unless it be with his fellows and nowise aloof from them, Falstaff can employ his wit without renouncing the

[1]Something of it, and of the relation of Falstaff to Faulconbridge, will be found in my article "Shakespeare, Politics, and Politicians," *English Association Pamphlet*, No. 72, 1929.

instinctive promptings of his humanity or, at least, of his flesh. At the end, he emerges no less successful than the King, and insuperably superior to this cold-blooded politician in his claims on our regard. Falstaff, without doubt has demonstrated his right to be considered a matchless victor in the world which is the world of affairs and of comedy. But no less certainly, he has been cast out of it.

Why then did Shakespeare reject him? Remembering that doubts as to Falstaff's validity begin to be an under current in *II Henry IV*, it may be well to seek a clue at the latter end of *I Henry IV*. In that place, Falstaff's great display is on the battlefield at Shrewsbury, and it reaches its comic climax in his catechism concerning honour. There is not an article of this catechism which is not a direct consequence of Falstaff's necessary behaviour as the hero of such comedy as that of which he proves himself the most convincing exponent. Formulating his objections to Hal's assertion that he should regard death as a due, he remarks that the only motive to urge him to pay the debt before it is due, is honour. "Well, 'tis no matter; honour pricks me on." And so, his scrutiny of the conditions involved in such a categorical imperative. "How if honour prick me off when I come in?" How, in fact, if I am slain? "How then?" Clearly it is a sacrifice of his essential virtue as a hero of comedy. Further, "can honour set to a leg? No: or an arm? No: or take away the grief of a wound? No. Honour hath no skill in surgery, then? No." And surgery is in the last resort life's protection against death. How far, then, without actually depriving one of the indispensable virtue of comedy, how far does honour tend partly to disqualify one for the rôle of hero of comedy? It is clearly a partial disablement even at best. So in the face of such a reckoning, the direct question must be asked: "what is honour?" and an answer is forced on the questioner. "What is honour? A word. What is in that word honour? What is that honour? Air." It is certainly a trim reckoning. But if corroboration be called for, observation supplies it out of hand. "Who hath honour? He that died o'

Wednesday"; that is, he who last Wednesday resigned all claim to be a comic hero. "Therefore"—and with uncontestable consequence—"therefore, I'll none of it."

It is all as pertinent as could be, and Hotspur's conventionally heroic greeting to death which follows almost at once—"if we die, brave death, when princes die with us"—comes as a patent irrelevance. "I like not such grinning honour as Sir Walter" and other corpses have. Honour, honour as men make it, is palpably not an objective but an accident of life. "Give me life: which if I can save, so; if not, honour comes unlooked for." And there, inevitably, appears to be an end.

But is it an end? The question persists: "wherein is Falstaff good; but to taste sack and drink it? Wherein neat and cleanly, but to carve a capon and eat it? Wherein cunning, but in craft? Wherein crafty, but in villany? Wherein villanous, but in all things? Wherein worthy, but in nothing?" Even in Falstaff's own world, are there no things not to be assessed by the yardstick with which he measures everything? His own instinct, for instance? Or the rationally unaccountable impulse which makes him go counter to his purpose and stick to Poins: "I have foresworn his company hourly any time this two and twenty years, and yet I am bewitched with the rogue's company." It is something unintelligible—witchcraft; "if the rascal have not given me medicines to make me love him, I'll be hanged; it could not be else; I have drunk medicines." These are forces in life which Falstaff's measuring stick cannot measure. Yet he is dependent on their reality. "Instinct" saves him from one mischance; "love" is, in the last resort, his plea to Hal to avoid another; and something which he no doubt would call love is the might by which he secures the indispensable aid of Mistress Quickly. If these elements of life be admitted to such power, then not only is *homo* no longer the common name of all men, it is indeed inadequate to any one sort of man. The meanest band of ragamuffins is something more than food for powder; and that something more is infinitely more humanly valuable than the monies Falstaff got by working on his own premises about them, something which is altogether outside the compass of Falstaff's scales. "Honour," "a good name," not only to Falstaff but also to Hotspur, may appear to be an article of commerce, a commodity to be bought. But in the certified records of human existence, it has been something more, something infinitely more. Honour, faith, love, truth, self-sacrifice—these are things in the light of which men have lived joyously,—the matter for comedy— and at the bidding of which they have happily died—the matter for tragedy, or, may be, for a divine comedy. But for Falstaff they have no existence. "Sirrah, there's no room for faith, truth, nor honesty in this bosom of thine; it is all filled up with guts and midriff."

That is Falstaff's failure. It was in this realisation of Falstaff's incompleteness on the eve before Shrewsbury that Shakespeare felt the wine of life begin to taste like gall and wormwood on his tongue. But, though for a moment, and indeed for a more protracted stretch, the memory of Falstaff as he had seemed to be, excited a sense of disillusionment and even of such scorn as is presupposed by *The Merry Wives*, yet with wider imaginative experience something of Falstaff was finally saved—his common sense, his intuitive apprehension of the facts of existence within the limits which life itself imposes, and his insatiable thirst for such a life amongst the rest of mortals.

But the world in which Falstaff's successors in comedy would have to prove their genius for mastery, would necessarily have to be a larger and a richer world than Falstaff's, one in which room would be found for the things unknown to Falstaff, things proved now to be no less necessary to life, things such as love and faith and truth and honour. Falstaff had indeed acquired a mastery of life. But it was by denying to his universe the very things which give life its supreme values. He had conquered a world, only to reveal that such a world was not worth conquest.

It is a devastating end to such a gigantic effort. It might well appear that Shakespeare had come to a dead end in his progress towards the ideal of comedy. Falstaff had seemed so near it, and Falstaff had failed. To go farther Shakespeare would have to save himself from his own Falstaff. His imagination would have to cast about for a being bigger than Falstaff—*absit omen*—a being in whom the elements of human nature would be richer than in Falstaff, one who would by nature be endowed with a sense for those forces in human life which enrich it immeasurably, and which for Falstaff had been as if they were not. That chapter of Shakespeare's artistic life is to be found in the salvage of those exciting voyages of imaginative discovery which the world has wrongly named his 'dark comedies'; and his final conquest is indubitably recorded in the three great mature comedies. But to follow him through these stages to victory must be the matter of subsequent exposition.

VIII

The Dark Comedies

IN the interpretation of Shakespeare, novelty is its own condemnation. Shakespeare means what, in the long view, the millions of his readers have taken him to mean; and though, in the nearer view, discrepancies and contradictions may seem flagrant, there has grown up through the years an immense community of wise opinion, an implicit sense of Shakespeare's larger significance. Fundamental divergence from this is almost invariably not a revelation of novelties in Shakespeare but merely the display of a critic's idiosyncrasy. Yet assent to the received sense of Shakespeare's ultimate meaning admits and even requires an adjustment, within the faith, of this or that subsidiary article to the individual's angle of approach. Not otherwise will sincerity and truth be attained. Moreover, there are places in the canon where a large licence is inevitable; there are plays of which the trend of underlying idea is confusing not so much through its difficulty as through its obscurity. It is a commonplace of Shakespearian criticism that the so-called "dark comedies," *Measure for Measure*, *All's Well that Ends Well* and *Troilus and Cressida* are a group of plays which confound the critic, baffling his æsthetic interpretation and frustrating his philosophical appraisement of their meaning. The situation itself is not unintelligible. What it means is that, as examples of dramatic art, these plays are much more imperfect than Shakespeare's usually are. That is, Shakespeare's imagination has not been held in intense activity whilst it shaped the destiny of the characters whose progress is the material of these dramas. At best it has burnt intermittently; and so the artist's apprehension of the life behind them, his imaginative grasp of the vital forces which compel the sequence of events to that course which is the plot of the play, is not powerful enough to mould his figures and his predicaments into an organic dramatic form. Indeed, it seems as if his intuitive perceptions are being frequently controlled by his conscious purpose. Intellect rather than imagination is forcing the issue. These three plays are in fact problem-plays.

This is not, of course, a revolutionary proposition. All plays are problem-plays, in so far as in every play one starts with persons of a certain disposition involved in a certain situation, and the play is the dramatist's solution of what the inevitable outcome must be. As an artist's, the dramatist's solution is what his imagination apprehends it to be; but no dramatist is all imagination, and his intellectual comprehension is frequently liable to intervene and seek to play its part in determining the answer. Some characters and some situations—what one might call the more sociological types in character and in predicament—appear to excite this two-fold activity in the author more than do others. Hence "sociological plays" are less frequently shaped into the unity of a work of art than are others. They are moulded according to the dramatist's conceptions, according to his theories of society and of life, rather than by his intuitive sense of living forces or of a world grasped in his imagination as a cosmos. They are part of the dramatist's thought rather than examples of his vision. And few artists, particularly Shakespeare, have either the intellectual equipment or the intellectual habits which fit them for mastery in peculiarly analytic and ratiocinative ways of thinking. Their conscious grappling with situations baffles their imaginative resolution of them. Take *Man and Superman*, a series of scenes written to illustrate the theory that the life-force implanted in woman gives her the irresistible power to seize on the man through whom the life-force will fulfil its function. Has anybody who has seen or read the play ever felt that Tanner must necessarily succumb to Ann? Contrast with that Harold Brighouse's *Hobson's Choice*. There is no theory here, simply the dramatist's presentation of a particular individual, Maggie Hobson; and who has not felt the inevitability with which she captures Willie Mossop? *Man and Superman* is a tract, *Hobson's Choice* is a play; one is a fine piece of sociology, the other is a fine piece of drama.

It is in this more extreme sense that the three dark comedies of Shakespeare are to be called problem-plays. More than most of their kind, they show the intrusion of intellect in frustrating the effort of imagination. But what is the problem which they attempt to handle dramatically?

At this point I feel it necessary to revert to the statement of principle with which I began to-night's lecture—namely, that in the interpretation of Shakespeare novelty is its own condemnation. I have a novel point of view to suggest to you in the interpretation of these three plays; and I wish for the moment to plead exemption in this instance from the general principle— in effect, it is not really exemption I plead for, but I ask you to defer judgment for the time being as to whether my interpretation needs such exemption or not. For myself, I do not think it does. I have called the view I propose to put before you a novel one. It is not novel to me, since it is the view I have been tentatively putting before my students and others for the last twenty years. I should not, however, have ventured to put it into print but for the fact that in the last half-dozen years there is evidence, especially from America, that others are moving to a similar sense of the meaning of these three plays.

The circumstances are these. The epithet "dark" has been almost universally accepted as a right description of these plays. That epithet is generally taken to mean, not only that in these plays the seamier, indeed the nastiest, side of life obtrudes more persistently than elsewhere in Shakespeare, but that their underlying mood is one of bitter cynicism. This diagnosis is then built into a psychological scheme of Shakespeare's spiritual career. It is common ground that up to about 1600 his genius had turned most easily to comedy, and had achieved its supreme comic triumphs before or about 1600 in such plays as *Twelfth Night*, *As You Like It*, and *Much Ado*. But soon after 1600, and for the next half-dozen years, his output is almost entirely tragic, and we have *Hamlet*, *Macbeth*, *Othello* and *King Lear*. It appears to be necessary to explain this desertion of comedy and this triumphant achievement in tragedy by supposing an interval during which Shakespeare the man was harassed by doubts, depressed by sufferings, and driven to a mood of cynical despondency. Here, obviously, so runs the argument, is the period in which Shakespeare wrote the dark comedies, plays superficially or nominally comic, but in fact more than tragic in undertone, plays in which the very semblance of comedy is indeed the bitterest of their cynical implications. *All's Well That Ends Well:* what a title, they say, how devastating, how symbolic of the nihilism which is as ashes in the mouth!

Put abruptly, the views into which I am about to try to argue you are these. These comedies are certainly full of greasy matter, but that in itself is part of their function in Shakespeare's effort to recover the spirit of comedy. It is a greasiness which has only misled critics into seeing it as a banner of cynicism because of their mistaken notions of the relation between a work of art and the artist's psychology. In fact, the spiritual and intellectual temper which is the motive of these plays is in no wise a contempt for life and for its potential worthiness, but on the contrary, an intense impulse to discover the true sources of nobility in man and of joy in life, an intuition so ardent that it frustrates its own artistic fecundity and calls in, as a substitute, the dramaturgical exploration of conscious enquiry and deliberate experiment. These plays are not at all a bridge linking a serene comic mood with the awe-inspiring vision of tragedy. They are the road by which Shakespeare climbed from the misleading comedy of Falstaff to the richer and more satisfying comic air of *Twelfth Night*, *As You Like It*, and *Much*

Ado. In brief, I take these three dark comedies to be mis-leadingly named; I take them to be predecessors and not successors of the three comedies in which Shakespeare's comic triumph is most manifest.

The situation is not, as it might seem, merely a matter of actual chronology. For one thing, Croce has taught us to beware of confusion between the sequences of biographical occurrences, and the ideal chronology of the artist's growth. Moreover, it appears to be generally agreed that no specific date can be allotted to the three dark comedies, since of all of them it is claimed that there is evidence of very considerable revision stretching over a fairly considerable measure of time. But even if it were merely a matter of historical chronology, there is in fact no more solid evidence for placing the dark comedies in the order commonly assigned to them than in that which I suggest. If we knew exactly when Shakespeare first took up and then finished this or that play, all attempts to explain the plays in relation to Shakespeare's artistic development would have to take account of such evidence as primary. But the dating of the dark comedies is, within limits as serviceable to my arguments as to any other, largely a matter of conjecture. Moreover, the trend of that conjecture has been mainly determined by the view that these plays are the expression of a mood of cynical despair.

First, then, let us enquire into this alleged cynicism. Let us glance at the three plays, not, for the moment, to endeavour to assess their comprehensive significance, but merely to see if there be in them anything incompatible with the assumption that at the time of writing them, their author was obsessed with a sense of life's futility. Turn to *Measure for Measure*. At first glance, here is enough of nastiness to justify any view of the author's despair. Its very setting is a hot-bed of immor-ality: Vienna and its suburbs stink. Lucio and Froth, Pompey and Mistress Overdone are its sewage. Their talk is a scurvy bawdry, their jests are mere syphilitic hysteria. And above them is a Duke who lacks the back-bone to govern, and a deputy whose puritanism collapses into sheer bestiality and crime. Its hero frenziedly implores his sister to save his neck by sacrificing her virginity; and the sister, the unsullied heroine, after permitting herself a scornful vituperation of her brother which appears to convict her of inhuman callousness, relapses without a word into circumstances which seem to be making for a conventional ending in the peal of marriage bells. It is no wonder if one's first impression is that the painter of such a repulsive picture of life must have been almost frantic with the thought of life's worthlessness.

Yet there is also matter which seems irreconcilable with this. *Measure for Measure* may be an eye for an eye, a tooth for a tooth, an Angelo for a Claudio. But look at the plot and its outcome. There is an almost intolerable insistence on meting out reward to the virtuous and punishment to the guilty. And even the punishment is determined in the spirit that it is as much a judge's duty to qualify as to enforce the laws. One remembers Isabella's impassioned plea that neither heaven nor man can grieve at mercy:

> No ceremony that to great ones 'longs,
> Not the king's crown, nor the deputed sword,
> The marshal's truncheon, nor the judge's robe,
> Become them with one half so good a grace
> As mercy does.

This sentiment of mortality and mercy humanises, even sentimentalises, the formal organisation of society. Its rulers are enjoined to remember that whilst it is excellent to have a giant's strength, it is tyrannous to use it like a giant. It is no indifferent pessimist, no bitter cynic, who recalls how man, proud man, drest in a little brief authority, is liable to wrench awe from fools and tie the wiser souls to his false seeming. For these are observations implying that grace is grace despite of all controversy; and that of all graces, the exercise of a beneficent mercy is most gracious. It is a sense of the potential richness of humanity rather than despondency at its neglect of those

possibilities. So, too, with life itself. The agonised dread of
Claudio as he contemplates death—

> Ay, but to die, and go we know not where;
> To lie in cold obstruction and to rot;
> This sensible warm motion to become
> A kneaded clod; and the delighted spirit
> To bathe in fiery floods, or to reside
> In thrilling region of thick-ribbed ice;
> To be imprison'd in the viewless winds,
> And blown with restless violence round about
> The pendent world; or to be worse than worst
> Of those that lawless and incertain thought
> Imagine howling: 'tis too horrible!
> The weariest and most loathed worldly life
> That age, ache, penury and imprisonment
> Can lay on nature is a paradise
> To what we fear of death.

—this in itself springs from a sense of the immeasurable possibilities of worth in life, though it be in life the mere living.
There is Pompey, "a poor fellow that would live." And though
the sordid and the horrible and the revolting are part of the
panorama, as it comes full circle, there is evidence of the
benignity even of evil.

> I'll speak all.
> They say, best men are moulded out of faults;
> And, for the most, become much more the better
> For being a little bad.

But it is unsafe to assess an author's mood from the remarks
of his characters. Fortunately, in Measure for Measure there is
less contestable evidence of the temper of its author. As is
well-known, the story he was telling was an old one. Cinthio
told it first in his Hecatommithi (1565), and again in his play
Epitia. An Englishman, George Whetstone, retold it twice—
first of all in his clumsy double-barrelled play Promos and Cas-
sandra (1578) and then as a prose-tale in An Heptameron of Civill
Discourses (1582). But Shakespeare made not a few changes in

the tale. For instance, in Cinthio's story, the counterpart of Claudio is actually executed, and his Isabella is married to an Angelo who is immediately condemned to death, but at Isabella's supplication is respited to a life of happiness with her. In Whetstone, the Claudio escapes and another inmate of the prison is decapitated in his place so that the plot of Angelo's duplicity may run the course which it takes in Cinthio's original. But Shakespeare's alterations of this are striking though small. He does not marry Isabella to Angelo, but to one who was meant to be much nobler and more humane, the Duke himself. He does not allow his Isabella to be defiled by Angelo; by the trick of a substitution in the dark, he arranges for Mariana to take Isabella's place unknown to Angelo. So he finds a bride for Angelo in Mariana of the Moated Grange. In fact, he avoids committing offences against our moral susceptibilities in the matter of Isabella and, at the same time, he gratifies these susceptibilities by inventing a wronged Mariana whose union with Angelo is clearly meant to be an illustration of the fitness of things. This is not to claim that dramatically Shakespeare's solution is better or even as good as Cinthio's: it is only to assert that a desire for the happiness of human beings—in the play and in the audience—was Shakespeare's palpable motive.

But there is even more striking evidence. Cinthio's plot had his Claudio executed; Whetstone saved Claudio by substituting the execution of a condemned criminal. Both of them, that is, wanted a newly cut-off head for their story, as did also Shakespeare: otherwise the extent of Angelo's villainy would not be apparent, for he must send a head (Claudio's or one seeming to be Claudio's) to Isabella as his intimatio. that despite the price paid the contract has not been kept. Cinthio had no problem: Claudio's head was sacrificed. But to save Claudio, Whetstone had to find a head. He employed an obvious and feasible device. He cut the head off another condemned criminal. And Shakespeare clearly meant to do the same. Hence the invention of Barnardine.

Barnardine has been a prisoner for nine years, but now it has been finally decided to execute him. There is no doubt either that Shakespeare intended him to be executed—for Angelo's writ to the Provost specifically names for summary execution not only Claudio but also Barnardine, and the Duke, who is planning to save Claudio, especially enjoins the provost—"Call your executioner, and off with Barnardine's head." Barnardine is a Bohemian born, an utter rascal whose crimes are completely proved. Besides, he is beyond all reasonable sympathy. "A man that apprehends death no more dreadfully but as a drunken sleep; careless, reckless, and fearless of what's past, present, or to come; insensible of mortality, and desperately mortal . . . drunk many times a day, if not many days entirely drunk. We have very oft awaked him, as if to carry him to execution, and showed him a seeming warrant for it: it hath not moved him at all."

It is remarkable that Shakespeare should have displayed such humane scruples in providing the head his plot wanted: and it is certainly incompatible with a mood of cynicism. But that is not the whole story. For after Shakespeare had given himself so much trouble to find a head the cutting off of which would offend no one's humanity, he himself had not the heart to cut the head off. The old reprobate, brought into being to be executed, so used these last few moments of his life that he blustered his way into Shakespeare's sympathy, and was reprieved. To reprieve him, Shakespeare the dramatist did not mind committing the heinous crime of sheer coincidence; he pretended that one Ragozine, a most notorious pirate, had died in prison that night, and so could be used to provide a trunkless head as a necessary property for the plot. The whole episode is a manifest revelation of Shakespeare's sense of human life; his first scruples only to destroy what manifestly deserves destruction, and then his sudden discovery that the apparently worthless human being still has his humanity with which to excite sympathy in a fellow-mortal. "Mortality and mercy" are here palpably the author's sentiments: and they are a complete negation of a mood which could in any sense be called cynical.

In the same summary fashion, turn now to *All's Well That Ends Well*. Once more, the story at first glance yields every excuse for regarding it as the work of a distracted pessimist. There is the nastiness of a dissolute hero, and the heroine's use of a seamy trick of substitution to use his lasciviousness for her purpose. She herself, in this play, is the one who lies between the sheets. There is also the same surfeit of bawdy jokes; not only are they spoken in the presence of the lovable ladies of the piece, but these ladies themselves are not above contributing an innuendo. Lavache is only excelled in filthy obsession by that shapeless lump of cloacine excrement, Parolles. Even worse, the main story tells how a girl, otherwise admirable, seems to throw away all decency in her schemes to secure for herself a man who is not only capable of every kind of dissipa- tion but is so completely devoid of moral sentiment that he prides himself on his vices and lauds them as virtues. Yet *All's Well That Ends Well* is the motto; a nymphomaniac succeeding in her quest and the whole worthless loveless bargain sanctified by the name of marriage.

But once more, there are things in the play incompatible with this seemingly reasonable exposure of its apparent cynicism. There is in the nobler natures of the piece a convic- tion of the essential difference between rank and worth, between appearance and reality.

> If she be
> All that is virtuous, save what thou dislikest,
> A poor physician's daughter, thou dislikest
> Of virtue for the name: but do not so:
> From lowest place when virtuous things proceed,
> The place is dignified by the doer's deed:
> Where great additions swell's, and virtue none,
> It is a dropsied honour. Good alone
> Is good without a name. Vileness is so:
> The property by what it is should go,

Not by the title. She is young, wise, fair;
In these to nature she's immediate heir,
And these breed honour: that is honour's scorn,
Which challenges itself as honour's born
And is not like the sire: honours thrive,
When rather from our acts we them derive
Than our foregoers: the mere word's a slave
Debosh'd on every tomb, on every grave
A lying trophy, and as oft is dumb
Where dust and damn'd oblivion is the tomb
Of honour'd bones indeed.

No less than in *Measure for Measure* does the ending expose the evildoers; no less also, or even more, does mercy mitigate the penalty. For Bertram, there is the reformatory discipline of life with Helena; even Parolles who had demanded mere physical life—

Let me live, sir, in a dungeon, i' the stocks, or anywhere, so I
                                                    may live

—found that amongst good-hearted human beings

There's place and means for every man alive,

and Lafeu assures him

Though you are a fool and a knave, you shall eat.

But here again, as in *Measure for Measure*, there is more significant evidence. It will be found in Shakespeare's alternations of, and in his additions to the Boccaccian story which is his source. Boccaccio's counterpart to Helena is, unlike Helena, a wealthy girl; moreover, her pursuit of her Bertram is undertaken entirely in the spirit of an amorous escapade. It appears unlikely that a mood of cynicism would drive an author to dignify the real, in flagrant distinction from the material, worth of his heroine and to ennoble the enterprise of which she is the agent into an act of dedication rather than of simple conjugal gratification. More important still are the figures

Shakespeare adds to his *dramatis personæ*. Admittedly they include Parolles and the Clown: but these jesters, our argument will plead, are like the nastiness in *Measure for Measure*, a device assisting in the realisation of an entirely uncynical intention. The other additions are of primary importance. The Countess and Lafeu are unknown in Boccaccio's story: and though the King appears in it, it is as a lay figure demanded by the plot. Yet Shakespeare's creations, the Countess and Lafeu, and his re-creation, the King, are amongst the most exquisite figures in the story.

The remarkable qualities they have in common are these: they are all old, they are all benign, and they are all persons in whom the experience of life has strengthened the sense of tolerance, forbearance and love. It is worth while to see their characters more closely.

The Countess has the benign wisdom of experience. She has seen life pass down the years, but it has brought neither bitterness nor indifference. Her summary enunciation of precepts may sound to be limited by a Polonian cautiousness, and "Do wrong to none" strikes a note of merely passive goodness which may not go beyond the political virtue which is Polonius's ideal—the limited virtue of his "To thine own self be true," though the limitations which reduce it to a passively unsocial and unproductive goodness, a fugitive and self-cloistered virtue, appear to have escaped the notice of those who exalt it to the worth of an autograph-album's aphorism. But the very catalogue which the Countess propounds begins with the un-Polonian injunction "Love all." It is her knowledge of life which impels the next article, "trust a few." Yet knowing the fallibility of mortals, she judges with charity. She remembers those unaccountable impulses, which, though thorns, are "thorns which rightly belong to the rose of our youth." Hearing of delinquencies, she attests that "the complaints I have heard of you I do not all believe," even though cold reason assures her that the accused has folly enough to commit the crime and has ability enough to bring off such knaveries: more magnanimously still, she sets down her charity to her own assumed "slowness." Yet she really knows a knave when she meets one.

> A very tainted fellow, and full of wickedness

she knows Parolles to be. But living has strengthened her instinctive knowledge of mortality and endowed her with a genius for taking life as it comes and making the most of it.

> I have felt so many quirks of joy and grief
> That the first face of neither, on the start,
> Can woman me unto 't.

And her unerring sense of human values, strong enough to overcome her natural maternal prejudice, shines out in her championship of Helena against her own son Bertram.

Lafeu, as a man, has necessarily inured himself more regularly to the experience of earth's earthiness. The trick of its less savoury idiom is more frequently on his tongue. Yet even here, the exigencies of the years only strengthen the instincts of tolerance, charity and humanity. His privilege of antiquity enriches his nature; and the flippancy of his lighter deliverances does not obscure the fundamentally humane sanity of his sense of life. He will even excuse his charities as a means of selfish gratification. He knows Parolles, indeed he exposes Parolles before proofs are provided—

> He was first smoked by the old lord Lafeu.

But he will see him fed, and pretend that the charitable office is merely for his own entertainment—

> Wait on me home; I'll make sport with thee.

In the same way, the King's nature, despite his years, despite his affliction, is so generally at all times good, that of necessity it holds up its virtue to the world. Behind his rank, he is a man amongst men, and his intercourse with Lafeu is that of two men in whom life has been enriched by their varied experiences. Their intimacy changes the tone of Court etiquette into the banter of old-time fellowships renewed: and its lightness in no wise diminishes its significance.

> Will you see her—
> For that is her demand, and know her business?
> That done, laugh well at me.

Such, then, are the elders of *All's Well That Ends Well*. They owe their benignity to their years and its discipline in the arts of life. In spite of the mood of the moment, the enrichment through going down the revolving years continues.

> They say miracles are past; and we have our philosophical persons to make modern and familiar things supernatural and causeless.

Old age, indeed, brings its knowledge of the wonderful variety of life, an experience which reason may question or mistrust; but there it is, and it contributes its quantum to the force by which the process goes incessantly on its trend towards a larger happiness for those who are or will be alive. This faith is not merely that of a *laudator temporis acti*. A man holding such a faith might not only be a copy to these younger times: he—or in this case, she—will prove herself to be the efficient remedy for the need of the present. Time, life, experience—these are the ultimate tests: pretentiousness and falsity reveal themselves as time tries them. "Wherein have you played the knave with fortune, that she should scratch you, who of herself is a good lady and would not have knaves thrive long under her?" And the more therefore of time, of experience, and of life, the more of essential wisdom one has secured. Old Lafeu's contempt for the indecision of the young men is a striking instance—

> I'ld give bay Curtal and his furniture,
> My mouth no more were broken than these boys',
> And writ as little beard.

Do they all deny her? An they were sons of mine, I'd have them whipped; or I would send them to the Turk, to make eunuchs of.

This presentation of the benignity of time and of the grace of old age is not only remarkable in a play classed as a "dark comedy." It would be remarkable in any play called a comedy. For, from its beginnings, comedy had realised the technical advantage of old age for the purpose of rudimentary laughter-making. Roman comedy, as we saw in our lecture on *The Comedy of Errors*, rejoices in the recognition that there is no fool like an old fool. We saw also, when we looked at *The Taming of the Shrew*, that somehow the old men seemed too sympathetically conceived to deserve the treatment to which the plot insisted on submitting them. Old age for Roman comedy was folly indurate; for the Romantics it was poetic pathos, as was the intruder Ægeon in *The Comedy of Errors*. But between the two, there is old age which is just what the world makes it, the gathering of so many years of living amongst one's fellows. These indeed are the elders of *All's Well*. They defy the traditions of comedy to be true to the experience of existence. They are living witnesses to the benignity of human life, to the wisdom which mainly comes from the passing of years in the company of fellow-mortals. They are people who could never have existed in the mind of a cynic, and who could only have been created by a dramatist whose faith was fixed in the opportunities of life as a vista of infinite possibilities for the progress of what is human in the human race.

However, there is still *Troilus and Cressida*. Admittedly, that is the most baffling of the three. But, for the time being, one may defer the main significance of its chaotic complexity, to seize on one or two of its elements of which the implication is not obviously cynical or pessimistic. There is no need to insist that, as with the other dark comedies, there is more than enough to persuade the superficial reader that bitter irony is the prevailing note of the play. A Cressida who lightheartedly defiles the ideal of romantic troth; a Pandarus who makes wooing a mere merchandise in flesh; a Helen who, as Nell, converts the Trojan War into a dance-club fracas, and, as herself, turns lechery into the motive of a world war; an Ajax and an Achilles whose impulses and whose actions are a mockery, not merely of heroic ideals, but of even ordinary human decency. Here, clearly, is sufficient to suggest an author out of tune with himself and with life.

But again there are rallying-points, sufficient for the moment. Grant Cressida her deserts, let her become the world's type of falsity—

> Prophet may you be!
> If I be false, or swerve a hair from truth,
> When time is old and hath forgot itself,
> When waterdrops have worn the stones of Troy,
> And blind oblivion swallow'd cities up,
> And mighty states characterless are grated
> To dusty nothing, yet let memory,
> From false to false, among false maids in love,
> Upbraid my falsehood! When they've said "as false
> As air, as water, wind, or sandy earth,
> As fox to lamb, as wolf to heifer's calf,
> Pard to the hind, or stepdame to her son,"
> "Yea," let them say, to stick the heart of falsehood,
> "As false as Cressid."

What, in any ultimate valuation, is the significance of this in the web of circumstance over which presides that old common arbitrator Time, Time with whom is the end which crowns all, and under whose instruction every one is and cannot but be wise? There is of course, in the first place, the extant moment, the blow here and now, in the infliction of which, as from a robber's hand, Time is palpably injurious. Its depredations transform Cressid and seem to destroy Troilus. Troilus finds the world of his faith a ruin—

> The bonds of heaven are slipp'd, dissolv'd and loos'd.

All for which and by which he had lived is annihilated. But,

aloof from the heat of its poetry, and in the calmer contemplation of its visible influences, in what state does the play present
its Troilus? How will the faith in which he has lived bear
scrutiny? How much is Troilus, its victim, worth to the
immediate needs of the world of which he is a part? He is a
Trojan on whom in part depends the existence of Troy. As
Cressid's lover, he is incapacitated from fulfilling his civic and
military obligations—and that is the immediate and pressing
need—to his country. The direct consequence of Cressid's
faithlessness is to enhance his worth as a citizen of his own city.
He becomes for the first time a real asset to his immediate
fellows. The one who had moped sentimentally when the
stress of events threatened destruction to his own group of
society becomes at once an invaluable asset to that society.
He is fired to play his part as never before in the corporate
task of the moment. He will fight with an energy surpassing
all that he has hitherto felt:

> he hath done to-day
> Mad and fantastic execution,
> Engaging and redeeming of himself
> With such a careless force and forceless care
> As if that luck, in very spite of cunning,
> Bade him win all.

Troilus the individual, who as such was a drag on his fellows,
has become an invaluable instrument of their immediate
security and a means by which as a society they may achieve
their aims and their continued existence. Moreover, even as an
individual, he has learnt to know the worth of things he had
misvalued. Pandarus had never been rightly known to him
while he was under Cressida's spell; but now—

> Hence, brother-lackey! ignomy and shame
> Pursue thy life, and live aye with thy name,

—no inconsiderable advance in clear-sightedness for a man who
had hitherto failed to see through Pandarus. Indeed his broken

heart helps him to see Cressida more nearly for what in fact she is, though, as a reaction from what he previously thought her, doubtless he is inclined to blacken the view of what he now thinks she is.

And what, in the summary estimates thrown up by the run of the play, what is Cressida? Leaving, for the moment, our judgment on her own moral nature, though it must be noted that, like Chaucer, Shakespeare is not with the moralists who pursue her to a lazarhouse, the more immediate question is the measurement of her rôle amongst her fellows in the world of which she is a part, the world wherein she will continue to work either good or evil. She has exercised the spell of her nature to the detriment of Troilus and of Troy. She now passes to the camp in which her capacity for similar damage is doubly limited. Her tricks are apparent: simply through his knowledge of men and women, Ulysses can diagnose the condition of Cressid at once—

> There's language in her eye, her cheek, her lip,
> Nay, her foot speaks; her wanton spirits look out
> At every joint and motive of her body.
> O, these encounterers, so glib of tongue,
> That give accosting welcome ere it comes,
> And wide unclasp the tables of their thoughts
> To every ticklish reader! Set them down
> For sluttish spoils of opportunity
> And daughters of the game.

But not only does the wisdom of the Greeks render her charms innocuous, she falls in fact to the particular one of the Greeks, Diomed, who knows her exactly for what she is, and knows how to prevent general ravage in such a circumstance—not because he has special gifts of intuition, but because he is just the average plain Greek who happened to be chosen to transfer her to the Greek camp—

> Good Diomed, furnish you fairly for this interchange.

Diomed knows how the romanticising of the relation of man

and woman is fraught with evil for others. His judgment of Helen—spoken to Paris, too—is an indication of the strength of his horse-sense—

> hear me, Paris;
> For every false drop in her bawdy veins
> A Grecian's life hath sunk; for every scruple
> Of her contaminated carrion weight,
> A Trojan hath been slain: since she could speak,
> She hath not given so many good words breath
> As for her Greeks and Trojans suffer'd death.

When a man like that is appointed to control Cressid, he will doubtless answer to his lust, but, as for her, to her own worth she will be prized; she may try her cajolery on him, but there will be a narrow limit to her paltering—"I'll be your fool no more;" "I do not like this fooling." He will, in fact, render her serviceable to his own desires, good or bad; but, like everybody else except the deluded sentimentalists, he will see her exactly for what she is, and take the proper action to ensure that she remains just what she is and no more.

For the world then, Troilus is a greater asset at the end of the play, and Cressida less of a source of harm. Is this a cynic's solution? But if it be urged that the measurement in terms of worldly values is itself a phase of cynicism, it must be remembered that comedy must grasp life as a thing to be lived, as an immediate problem of achieving happiness in those circumstances which man inherits as the conditions of his life. Moreover, the very play *Troilus and Cressida* shows a larger awareness of the implications of man's necessarily social life than do any preceding ones. For tragedy, life is the relationship of the moment and eternity, of the individual and the absolute, of man and God. For comedy, life is the reality of actual existence, the solving of the problem as to how man may ameliorate his condition in his existence here and now amongst his fellows. Comedy is social rather than metaphysical or theological. It is generally agreed that in no play before *Troilus and Cressida* does Shakespeare give so just a sense of the dependence of the individual on the social conditions in which as an individual he has his existence. The wisdom of Ulysses may have obvious traits of patent diplomacy, but its foundation is a sense of the inescapable interaction of society as such on the individuals who are the elements in its being.

In its most immediate bearing the sense of social organisation is a political one. As we saw in *Henry IV*, and in the group of the English history plays, Shakespeare's imagination has been exercised by the movement of communities as distinct from the progress of individuals. His sense of its basic forces deprives them of moral sanctions and of human compunctions; even in the rhetorically and patriotically glorified *Henry V*, the underlying assumptions, though hidden, are not dissimilar. But in *Troilus and Cressida* Shakespeare's apprehension of the power by which communal life progresses is more humane and more profound. Whilst human ingenuity, mere politics, will still constrain those in authority to trick the individual for the good of the community, as Ulysses tricks Ajax and tries to trick Achilles, nevertheless the governors themselves have a subtler apprehension of their function. Social well-being, the matters of the world at large, are the object of political organisation. The value of individuals is their contribution to the general good; "value dwells not in particular will." There is a specifically Platonic notion in this sense of communal as distinct from individual values—

> "a strange fellow here
> Writes me: "That man, how dearly ever parted,
> How much in having, or without or in,
> Cannot make boast to have that which he hath,
> Nor feels not what he owes, but by reflection;
> As when his virtues, shining upon others,
> Heats them and they retort that heat again
> To the first giver."

Well-being is not a state of isolated individual attainment, but an activity of well-doing:—

> no man is the lord of anything
> Though in and of him there be much consisting
> Till he communicates his parts to others.

Those who serve the general good may or may not have their current fame: an instant's giving way or hedging aside from the direct forthright may throw them as alms to oblivion—

> For time is like a fashionable host
> That slightly shakes his parting guest by the hand,
> And with his arms outstretch'd, as he would fly,
> Grasps in the comer.

But despite inequalities and injustices in the reward of the individuals, there emerges a sort of controlling justice between the endless jar of right and wrong. As by a mysterious law through which

> The heavens themselves, the planets and this centre
> Observe degree, priority and place,
> Insisture, course, proportion, season, form,
> Office and custom, in all line of order,

the progressive good of humanity is demonstrably the law of social life. Those who for their own satisfaction stand out from or oppose this general good are stigmatised as evil-doers whether their offence is deliberate as is that of Achilles here, or whether such emotional upheavals as is the love of Troilus make the sufferer for the time being a social menace.

There is a mystery in the soul of state: and nowhere more than in *Troilus and Cressida* does Shakespeare recognise it. Ulysses, though still a schemer, has a subtler sense of society than any English King of Shakespeare's. His speech on degree is an infinitely profounder political philosophy than is elsewhere to be found in the plays; it is also more realistic and more humane. In the last resort, it relies largely on the half-intelligible processes by which time itself works for good: and against the individual facts of human experience wherein evil

and loss are man's fate, there is the larger view that goodness
comes through evil. Trouble, disappointment, suffering

> are indeed nought else
> But the protractive trials of great Jove
> To find persistive constancy in men;
> The fineness of which metal is not found
> In fortune's love; for then the bold and coward,
> The wise and fool, the artist and unread,
> The hard and soft, seem all affined and kin:
> But, in the wind and tempest of her frown,
> Distinction, with a broad and powerful fan,
> Puffing at all, winnows the light away;
> And what hath mass or matter, by itself
> Lies rich in virtue and unmingled.

Once more, of course, it is necessary to remember that to
find the underlying sentiment of a play in the speeches of its
actors is a method fraught with many dangers. There are,
moreover, passages in the play in which Time is apostrophised
as the enemy of human life; for Time obviously brings to
individual man, if not sufferings in life, yet certainly his final
exit from it. But what one has in mind is not so much that
which is explicitly said about time: it is the conviction that for
those who have seen most of it, take it on the long view, it is a
power making for justice and progress: as indeed, in the mere
action of the play, it does. And surely such a faith in time,
experience, and circumstance is entirely incompatible with the
notion that the author of this play was overwhelmed in
pessimism when he wrote it.

Whether or not the details of the view set out above about
this and the other aspect of the three dark comedies are accepted, it is perhaps safe to say that at least there is sufficient
in them to justify suspension of the opinion that these plays
are the product of a disillusioned dramatist. We must address
ourselves now, not to the negative consideration of what they
are not, but to a positive enquiry into what they signify.

They are problem plays. What is their problem? My own

view is that they are the half-articulate answer to the question which Falstaff left simmering in Shakespeare's mind, to the perturbation of his intellect and the temporary laming of his imagination. I see the plays in this order—*Troilus and Cressida*, then *Measure for Measure*, and then *All's Well;* and I believe that in that order they represent successive stages of a process by which Shakespeare's imagination recaptured its capacity to shape its experience into an organism which satisfied his artistic needs, that is, in this case, his sense of comedy as a form of dramatic art. Let us remind ourselves of the situation in which we left Shakespeare when Henry V cast off Falstaff.

Falstaff had appeared to provide the comic dramatist with a solution to the imaginative problems with which comedy is fraught. For comedy must guarantee its hero a happy ending, an escape from his predicaments and a triumph over circumstance. Falstaff had appeared to possess the recipe for such mastery of life. He had achieved it; but only to reveal to his author that the mastery was achieved, not so much by the possession of such qualities as secure success, as by a blindness to those phases of life which would have made his success appear as a factitious triumph of no fundamental significance. He succeeded in a world not worth conquest: and he succeeded there only through implicit denial of the things in life which by common consent are the things which, suppose indeed they be, are all that make life worth while,—love, truth, faith, honour, religion and such like. In a world deprived of these— and Shakespeare knew them to exist in the real world— Falstaff's seeming triumph was a bitter frustration for the comic dramatist. It was a spiritual and imaginative necessity for him to escape from his own Sir John. He does it in these three plays: he does so by casting about imaginatively for a character who owes his happiness to qualities different from those of Falstaff in that they are qualities which take the ideal phases of living into account, those vast tracts of human experience which had been meaningless to Falstaff.

Falstaff triumphed by his wit, and by the realistic scheme

of values which he adopted as the immediate means to his own welfare. It implied a materialistic and limitedly rationalist sense of reality. Experience was real only in so far as it contributed an immediately measurable gain to the body or to the physical happiness of Sir John. It was in essence a purely intellectual attitude to life, though its objectives were much more physical than intellectual. Falstaff was governed by common-sense alone, and by a common-sense which he hardened into an explicit materialism and a calculating rationalism. As the embodiment of common-sense, he was the product of his predecessors in Shakespearean comedy. He had more of it than had they: but in subduing himself so magnificently to its rule, in revelling in the mastery it gave him, he was sublimely unaware of the limits of its efficiency. Very broadly speaking, he triumphed by asserting intellect and denying emotion, by trusting to the conscious exercise of reason and neglecting the impulses of feeling and the promptings of intuition (although, of course, his wits or his reason always permitted him to use feeling and intuition as pawns in his game).

In the main the three plays with which we are now dealing are representations of men in action so arranged that they exhibit the relative values of reason and of intuition in the search for human happiness. In the sequel (and, of course, only in so far as these plays are concerned) intuitive promptings prove themselves safer guides; they lead to the attainment of a more satisfying happiness in that it is not so much the personal gratification of the searcher but is also the cause of joy in others; and in the upshot, the searchers most apt to this new ideal of life are, not as hitherto in Shakespearean comedy, the men, but, as they are to be in his most consummate comedies, the women. The heroine begins to assert her dominion in two of these plays—in one of the two she is becoming the figure whose will determines the action of the play, and to whose character is due the kind and the degree of happiness which the ending of the story allots to its actors. In Shakespeare's recovery of the comic spirit, Helena of *All's Well* is the most significant figure of the "dark comedies." She is not yet competent to preside over the serene comedy of *Twelfth Night* and *As You Like It*. Her antipathy to all that Falstaff had been is too absolute— and her greater successors, the Rosalinds and Violas and Beatrices, will need in their temperaments those qualities which Helena has abundantly, but also, to balance and enrich them, the temporally rejected realism of Falstaff's intellectual cognition. That, however, Shakespeare was later to perceive. In the meantime, sufficient progress emerges from the three "dark comedies."

Let us remember that even in these specifically called "problem" plays, the author's deliberate questioning of life need be neither continuous nor extensive, and will indeed be evident rather in intermittent failures of imaginative grasp than in positive argumentative speculation. Yet in attempting to diagnose the problem one must use language which will seem to suggest that Shakespeare's attitude was vastly more deliberate and intellectual than it most surely was. The propositions here put forward about the meaning of the three plays are statements about their intellectual implications which Shakespeare most certainly never articulated as conscious articles of his thought. His own problem was indubitably an artistic one—the search for the spirit of comedy: it only became acute in these plays because the material, that is, men and life, from which it had to be distilled, seemed for the time being too obstinate to permit of such alchemy. Our attempt to explain his obstinacy involves a moral and intellectual analysis of the material, in terms which, though proper to an analysis of that kind, are not to be taken as statements of Shakespeare's own sense of the nature of his artistic difficulties.

The order in which the plays are now to be examined is *Troilus and Cressida*, *Measure for Measure*, and *All's Well*. That appears to be the sequence in which they occur in his progress towards the artistic end, the realisation of the idea of comedy. *Troilus and Cressida* has the most stubborn material and the dramatist is more frequently thrown back on deliberate statements of doubts and confusions in the panorama of life which is baffling his imagination. In *Measure for Measure* the imagination is finding itself capable of resolving some of the difficulties. Its exposure of Angelo is, however, much more obviously part of ultimate truth than is its presentation of Isabella's efficiency as a bringer of joy. But in *All's Well* there is virtual triumph. The imagination has apprehended a mode of human character and, projecting it through human predicaments, has demonstrated its efficiency for shaping mortal existence into an assured attainment of happiness. Its solution, as we shall see, is particular rather than general. But it was a particular confusion from which Shakespeare sought escape. Once free, the generalisation of the solution was to follow in the mature comedies.

Troilus and Cressida seethes with questionings of life's value. Throughout, the secrets of nature seem to have a gift of taciturnity and poor man is confounded—

> My mind is troubled like a fountain stirr'd
> And I myself see not the bottom of it.

Existence is such a round of despiteful gentle greetings and noblest hateful loves that there seems to be no means of squaring man's known experience with a belief in the benevolence of the gods and in the way of goodness as the law of life.

> Have the gods envy?
> Aye, aye, aye, aye, 'tis too plain a case.

Living is a series of frustrations—

> There is no help,
> The better disposition of the time will have it so.

Thrown on his own resources and his own pragmatic systems— "What is aught but as 'tis valued?"—man finds himself with nothing of greater sanction than mere opinion. And opinion

a man may wear on both sides. He finds little guidance in
knowledge of the past or in speculation about the future—

> What's past and what's to come is strewed with husks
> And formless ruin of oblivion.

And though there is nothing else to go by, man's own valuation
of circumstance is notoriously distorted. The touch of nature
which makes the whole world kin is a delusive avidity for what
is novel and an indifference to what even on its own standards
has been proved to be good:

> O, let not virtue seek
> Remuneration for the thing it was;
> For beauty, wit,
> High birth, vigour of bone, desert in service,
> Love, friendship, charity, are subjects all
> To envious and calumniating time.

But even frustrate life is not stagnation, and man must act to
live. In such a chaos, to what promptings shall he trust? He
knows himself to be possessed of mighty impulses planted deep
in his unconsciousness—his emotions, his appetites, his intuitions. No less does he know himself to have will and reason.
What is the worth of these frequently contending powers?

> The reasons you allege do more conduce
> To the hot passion of distemper'd blood
> Than to make up a free determination
> 'Twixt right and wrong, for pleasure and revenge
> Have ears more deaf than adders to the voice
> Of any true decision.

In such a conflict, which prevails, and, more important, which
should prevail? The problem is more complex than appears
in such a simplified statement of it. Take for instance a comparatively simple issue, such as that presented in the rivalry
which—for simplication—is called the struggle between love
and duty or love and honour. How do reason and intuition,

thought and feeling muster themselves in this seemingly simple opposition? Is there no reason in love, is duty so obviously a matter of clear reason? Is there this absolute distinction in human motive?

Blind fear, that seeing reason leads, finds safer footing than blind reason stumbling without fear.

How then is man to find a foothold, how to have sufficient security to make life worth while, how to approach the problem

What Cressid is, what Pandar and what me?

The play is the partial answer, partial because but partially subdued to the artist's imagination. But there is a partial answer: and that is not a cynic's contempt. One must not judge too hastily from Cressid's desecration of romantic love and from the caricature of Greek virtue in the warriors. The light-hearted comedy of *A Midsummer Night's Dream* is as complete an exposure of the foundations of romantic love as is *Troilus and Cressida:* Troilus in act exemplifies what Theseus has preached; only, of course, Troilus found himself and lost the lady. Moreover, it has been well demonstrated by research amongst other sixteenth-century writers that Shakespeare was no innovator when he wrote the Greek warriors down to mere unconscionable filibusters. Even the sixteenth century had reached a stage in humane progress sufficient to suggest the questioning of a merely martial heroism: just as it had become humanely conscious enough to question the mediæval assumptions on which the creed of romantic love was reared. Apart from comments by such clearly discredited characters—clearly discredited because discredited in the action of the play—as Pandarus and Thersites, the only heroes who are grossly written down are Paris, Ajax, and Achilles. And it is easy to suggest motives in each case.

At all events, if the dramatist were in the serious frame of

mind which was beating about for some trial of accepted
human values, in *Troilus and Cressida* Shakespeare found a body
of material even more apt to the trial than that usually employed by other practitioners of the problem-play. Mr. Shaw,
seeking to demonstrate the relative value of common sense and
of romantic heroism for the purposes of the military profession, sets a Sergius and a Bluntschli to face military predicaments: and the outcome provides the answer. But Mr. Shaw
factitiously chooses the predicaments, and no less factitiously
embodies his contending qualities in characters of his own
invention. Euripides, at least Euripides as Mr. Gilbert Murray
makes us see him, is more astute. He takes a legendary story—
in his *Orestes*, for instance—in which the deeds and the outcome
of the action were meant to exhibit characters whose motives
had the ennobling sanctions of contemporary religious and
moral beliefs. He retains the story, that is, the deeds and the
outcome.   But he attributes entirely different and entirely
ignoble motives to the characters—and finds that in act they
lead to the same consequences, the same actions, that is, and the
same ultimate outcome.

But if such testing be Shakespeare's purpose then his choice
of the matter of *Troilus and Cressida* is a stroke of genius. It is
a story compounded of ancient and of medieval legend. The
legends of an epoch, defining themselves gradually by the
crystallisation of the public conscience, are far more authentic
embodiments of the epoch's ideals and standards of value than
any individual's invented story can be. A legend is the mirror
of the mind of the race which makes it. Its heroes are types of
what to them is heroic, and its adventures and conclusions are
examples in act of the working of the race's deities in the control of human destiny. Its picture of life is a reflection of contemporary manners, its characters are manifestations of contemporary moral philosophy, and its denouements are witnesses to contemporary theology. Achilles, Hector, Ulysses and
Paris each in his own way is a symbol of ancient notions of the
ideal in manhood. Galahad, Lancelot, Perceval and Tristram

in their turn are symbols of medieval notions of similar human values.

The historic growth of the legend of Troilus and Cressida is the gathering of two vast ages of human experience. That side of it which concerns the war, the camp-scenes, comes down from Greece; what concerns the romance of Troilus and Cressida is the distinctive addition of the Middle Ages. Allowing for a certain degree of fossilisation in deposits, it is nevertheless obvious that here is a tale in which is enshrined all that the ancient world felt to be worth while, and all that the Middle Ages had found to make life worth living. Here then was a marvellous inheritance of standards which had seemed to prove their worth over wide stretches of time. No better touchstone could be devised for the trial of new criteria. A canvas like this would clearly provide matter by which any new system of moral measurement might be tested.

The test in *Troilus and Cressida* is so fair, so unusually objective, that the flagrant absence from it of a bias to come down on the side of traditional virtue is imputed to the author for a mood, not of experimental scepticism, but of rampant infidelity. The voice of Thersites about the warriors, and of Pandarus on the desires of the lovers, is taken as the voice of Shakespeare. But all in the play know, as indeed Homer himself had known, that the opinion of Thersites is of no worth whatever. There is Agamemnon's sarcasm—

> When rank Thersites opes his mastic jaws,
> We shall have music, wit and oracle.

He is a slave whose gall coins slanders like a mint. In the play he is indeed "a privileged man," a fellow allowed to speak the most scurrilous words, for what such scurrility can damage is not worth preservation. "It is a strong composure a fool can disunite." And if the pandaring of Pandar secures for him a temporary allowance, he is duly known in the end. Surely, there is more of Shakespeare in the fate of these figures than in the exploits by which they meet that fate: for it is Shakespeare who is shaping their destiny, and his judgment of them is palpably a condemnation of their ways.

It is not, of course, a denial of all that Thersites says about war and all Pandarus says about love. In the causes of the Trojan war, there was something which, but for politeness, even a modern archbishop might describe as an argument about a cuckold and a whore; he might even admit, in his moral indignation (which, of course, is not what makes Thersites say so), that there is "nothing but lechery! all incontinent varlets!" Admittedly the dramatist's refusal to see the conflict as a strife of noble ideals appears from his depiction of Paris and Helen. A Paris who would fain have armed to-day, but who stayed at home because "My Nell would not have it so" is clearly a dramatist's version of the domestic realism of sexual infatuation and not an epic poet's picture of the bliss of ideal love. Only your Elizabethan romantic Marlowe could dissolve in ecstasy at the contemplation of a face that launched a thousand ships, though it burnt the topless towers of Ilium. Even the Greeks refused to romanticise Helen: to them, indeed, she was the Lamia-like charm which bewitched men into flagrant denials of evident and rudimentary obligations—"*das ewig-Weibliche*" drawing man not to a higher destiny but to a destruction of the self-evident laws of human society; to chaos, not to salvation.

The denigration of Ajax means nothing, except a further chapter in the depredations of *hubris* and a manifestation of the capacity of merely human wisdom to use its imperfections in the furtherance of human welfare, as the political sagacity of Ulysses uses the pride of Ajax to achieve the object of the Greeks. But the blackening of Achilles seems to protrude unpleasantly from Shakespeare's picture. There is the devastating low cunning of his conquest of Hector. Why should Achilles invite such ignominy? On the testimony of the story, his temperamental quarrelsomeness and his pride are mere hearsay, and his homosexuality nothing but the report of a known slanderer. But what is certain is that for personal

reasons—and in the last resort, these are represented as promptings or obligations of romantic love or of sexual gratification—
his hope to achieve the love of the daughter of the enemy
Queen—

> Here is a letter from Queen Hecuba,
> A token from her daughter, my fair love,
> Both taxing me, and gaging me to keep
> An oath that I have sworn

—for reasons such as these he has decided to defy what is
commonly called duty—that is, his service to the well-being of
the society of which he is a part.

> Fall Greeks; fall fame; honour or go or stay;
> My major vow lies here, this I'll obey.

Recalling that the whole gist of the intellectual undertone of
the play is a recognition of the obligations of society, of the
conditions on which alone man can live a rich and ordered life
amongst his fellows, it is clear that an individual who, through
hubris and through an assertion of his claims to a merely personal happiness such as Achilles makes, must cast himself for
the villain's *rôle*. The denigration of Achilles, on the scheme of
the play, is inevitable, and in no wise a cynical speculation. He
is condemned not by the jaundiced outlook of a pessimist, but
by an upholder of Ulysses' code of wisdom in the matter of
corporate well-being.

It is perhaps an accident that in this story the nominal
motive of Achilles' delinquency is his love for Hecuba's
daughter more than his tetchiness at the suspicion of slight. But
it reminds us that not only in these "dark comedies" does
Shakespeare illustrate the ennervating influence love may have
on mortal man. Paris allows his sensuous pleasure to count
more to him than the joy of virtue: but he only appears as an
extreme example because his common-place moral looseness
is the cause of a ten years' war between nations. It may well be
that Shakespeare first thought of dramatising the love-story

of Troilus and Cressida when he was in the mood which saw love's vagaries as they are depicted in *A Midsummer Night's Dream:* contemplating, not now, the lover whose frenzy sees Helen's beauty in a brow of Egypt, but the no less "comic" predicament of the lover who has installed Helen in his kitchen and at his fireside. In the main love-story, however, that of Troilus himself and of Cressida, the irresponsibility of love is apparently making for human dilemmas not obviously to be resolved by laughter and by the liberal-mindedness of common sense. It is easier for the moment to let the comic hero triumph over life by immunising him against love. So Falstaff sweeps to his partial victory: and the finding of a place for a broken-hearted Troilus in a world which is worth while was deferred until value in life began to be seen rather as part of the welfare of the whole than of the pleasure of the particular, until the real measure of man was taken to be his worth to his fellows rather than the achievement of his own desire. When Shakespeare was writing his political plays—*Henry IV, Henry V* (and perhaps *Julius Caesar*) there came to him this realisation of the social implications of human goodness: and the first conscious formulation of it is the chief article in the wisdom of Ulysses in *Troilus and Cressida*, even though in that formulation it is merely the political aspect of the principle which is stressed. It may well be that when Shakespeare's imagination was grappling dramatically with these stories which narrate the destiny, not of this man or of that, but of groups and societies of men, races and nations, he was led to pick up his unfinished love-story of Troilus and Cressida and set it against the background of the wider national scenes in the Greek and Trojan conflict. In these, at least, he finds a worthy place for a broken-hearted Troilus: and more than that, in the trend of their implicit ideas, he is feeling for some sort of a system which makes the fate of Troilus both an intelligible and a tolerable part in a universe which is not hostile to man's effort to secure a larger good.

Throughout the play the situation is perpetually poising the will of the individual against the *volonté generale.* "Value

dwells not in particular will." The achievements of individuals
and their merely personal renown are in a real assessment only
"baby figures of the giant mass of things to come at large."
The real crime of Achilles is that he

> carries on the stream of his dispose
> Without observance or respect of any,
> In will peculiar and in self-admission.

Because he thinks that honour amongst men is the prize of
accident rather than of merit he declines to compete for the
prize.   But again it is Ulysses who formulates the drift of
opinion which the action of the play demonstrates and corro-
borates:

> No man is the lord of anything
> Though in and of him there be much consisting,
> Till he communicates his parts to others;
> Nor doth he of himself know them for aught
> Till he behold them form'd in the applause
> Where they're extended; who, like an arch, reverberates
> The voice again, or, like a gate of steel
> Fronting the sun, receives and renders back
> His figure and his heat.

One must not read this as a code in which philanthropy is
exalted above all other virtues: but it implies a sense of values
from which it is an easy step to the realisation that in the service
of humanity lies the greatest virtue.   And that is an apprehension which is particularly manifest in another of the dark
comedies. In the meantime, it is enough to assert that Shakespeare's picture of the degraded Achilles is no proof of Shakespeare's cynicism: and sufficient evidence of that is provided
by Shakespeare's apprehension of the elements in Achilles'
character through which his degradation came.

The problem which seems to be occupying Shakespeare's
imaginative exploration most is the tracking of those impulses
and motives in man which lead him and the world about him
most securely along paths that prove themselves most worth

while. What does man owe to his deliberately rational endeavour to control his and his world's future? What, on the other hand, does he owe to the non-rational impulses which prompt him to this or that action? How, in fact, does man stand most securely between the dangerous shores of will and judgment? Broadly speaking, the government of public life seems to be most effectively conducted by adopting schemes devised by thought—the wisdom of Ulysses, for example, or the plain common sense of Agamemnon, or the summary principles arrived at by the observation of such long experience as Nestor has enjoyed. On the other hand, in the major moments of individual life, the more decisive and the more irresistible impulses appear to proceed from instinct, intuition and emotion: love, for instance, sexual love, surges up and makes havoc of reason—for, it seems, "to be wise and love exceeds man's might." Troilus knows himself to be torn between irreconcilable postulates, when his eyes see Cressid dallying with Diomed:

> This she? No, this is Diomed's Cressida:
> If beauty have a soul, this is not she;
> If souls guide vows, if vows be sanctimonies,
> If sanctimony be the gods' delight,
> If there be rule in unity itself,
> This is not she. O madness of discourse,
> That cause sets up with and against itself!
> Bi-fold authority! where reason can revolt
> Without perdition, and loss assume all reason
> Without revolt: this is, and is not, Cressid.
> Within my soul there doth conduce a fight
> Of this strange nature that a thing inseparate
> Divides more wider than the sky and earth,
> And yet the spacious breadth of this division
> Admits no orifex for a point as subtle
> As Ariachne's broken woof to enter.

What, then, is man to do? Or at least, on which of these contrary motives does he generally act, and with what effect? The reconciliation of love and wisdom may be for the moment beyond the artist's vision. But a simpler issue is apparent in the artist's finest figure in the play: his Hector stands above the rest of his characters in manhood and in obvious worth. And what are the springs of Hector's nobility? Unlike so many Homeric heroes in the play, he is never written down by Shakespeare. He is not, of course, the idealised pattern of the superman: he is noble, yet still a man:

> Hector, whose patience
> Is, as a virtue, fixed, to-day was moved;
> He chid Andromache and struck his armorer,
> And, like as there were husbandry in war,
> Before the sun rose he was harness'd light,
> And to the field goes he; where every flower
> Did, as a prophet, weep what it foresaw
> In Hector's wrath.

This, so Alexander tells us, was because Ajax "yesterday coped Hector in the battle and struck him down, the disdain and shame whereof hath ever since kept Hector fasting and waking."

As far as the action of the play attests his nobility in act, the motives of his deeds spring from two opposing sources, his deliberate schemes of conduct, and his impulsive intuitive response to an irrational perception of the circumstances of the moment. The situation is clearest in the Trojan conference which discusses whether to seek peace or to continue the war. Hector at the outset is for sending Helen back to Greece and so preventing further bloodshed in guarding a "thing not ours nor worth to us." But the romantic Troilus and the interested Paris are against him. Troilus admits that reason is on Hector's side—but denies that reason has any value in furthering man's attempts to achieve ideal virtue—

> Nay, if we talk of reason,
> Let's shut our gates and sleep: manhood and honour
> Should have hare-hearts, would they but fat their thoughts
> With this cramm'd reason: reason and respect
> Make livers pale and lustihood deject.

Nor will he admit that where honour is engaged, even a common-sense consideration of the probable issue is relevant to the judgment of situation. He refuses to allow what Hector calls the mad heat of his blood to be qualified by even such discourse of reason as the fear of bad success in a bad cause. For his part, Paris, besotted in his sweet delights, covers his own personal concern in the retention of Helen under traditional pleas that the honour of the whole race is now mortgaged. But Hector knows that both Paris and Troilus have but glozed superficially on the cause and question in hand. He gives his own view of the manner in which the situation must be faced. The fundamental problem is to make up a free determination 'twixt right and wrong. Hot passion proceeding from dis- tempered blood does not help; it frustrates a sound solution, for pleasure and revenge (a striking diagnosis of the motives, pleasure, of Paris, and revenge, of Troilus—that is, pleasure is Hector's word for love, and revenge, his description of honour) for pleasure and revenge have ears more deaf than adders to the voice of any true decision. He then proceeds with his own examination of the situation. He sees it in the light of the moral laws of nature and of nations:

> Nature craves
> All dues be render'd to their owners: now,
> What nearer debt in all humanity
> Than wife is to the husband? If this law
> Of nature be corrupted through affection,
> And that great minds, of partial indulgence
> To their benumbed wills, resist the same,
> There is a law in each well-order'd nation
> To curb those raging appetites that are
> Most disobedient and refractory.
> If Helen then be wife to Sparta's king,
> As it is known she is, these moral laws
> Of nature and of nations speak aloud
> To have her back return'd.

The conclusion is absolute in the way of truth—

> thus to persist
> In doing wrong extenuates not wrong,
> But makes it much more heavy.

There is no resisting the reasonableness of Hector's analysis. He has done all he could to persuade his people into reason. But even as he concludes his unanswerable plea for justice and for right, he enlists himself on the other side:

> Yet ne'ertheless,
> My spritely brethren, I propend to you
> In resolution to keep Helen still.

Dramatically the situation is a mere confusion in that the play presents no psychological clue to this sudden and complete change of front. We are thrown back on speculation. Does Hector decline from a wider to a narrower vision, and, for the voice of humanity's need, substitute that of personal opportunity? Is it a rejection of the common good, to secure as much as he can of his family's joint and several dignities? Is it that he perceives that the nicely calculated less or more is a mean intrusion where the theme is one of honour and renown? Is it that the rich advantage of a promised personal glory drives him into obliviousness of the wide world's revenue? Who knows? Who can hope to know from this play? It is a problem-play; it presents the problem. It does not provide the answer.

Yet the hint of a way to an answer emerges from the play. Is not demonstrable reason, because by its nature it is demonstrable, too liable to be over-estimated? Is there not a sort of irrational reason in instinct? Are not the obligations of our blood sanctions as valid as the findings of our conscious deliberations? In the last resort, is not the acquired experience of mankind somehow incorporated in his instincts even as certainly as in the momentary decision of his conscious judgments? Again, another problem. But the mere statement of it implies a willingness to allot a large validity to instinct as against reason: and a mood which is even so far willing to find time and experience a guide to humanity is certainly no cynic's mood.

Perhaps the most striking of the many complex threads of *Troilus and Cressida* is its persistent exposure of the limitations of what may be called the Falstaffian approach to life. There is a growing suspicion that a man like Falstaff wears his wits in his belly and his guts on his head. The assumptions on which he builds his realistic pragmatism are inadequate, for *homo* is palpably not a common name for man, when a Thersites and a Hector both are men. Grant Falstaff his assumption, and Achilles' horse makes many Thetis' sons—in other words, Swiftian Yahooism is a true picture of life: but the work of those that with the fineness of their souls by reason guide the execution of human effort is a plain refutation of this consequence.

In many ways the criteria by which Falstaff measures worldly worth are in the same kind as those of Thersites. The determination to cling to life, to mere existence, at all costs is a Falstaffian ideal which is only set in another angle when Thersites puts it in his own idiom: "To be a dog, a mule, a cat, a fitchew, a toad, a lizard, an owl, a puttock, or a herring without a roe, I would not care. . . . Ask me not what I would be, if I were not Thersites." Remember of course that when he says "I would not care," he means "it would nothing perturb me." Though he is here expressing scorn in a mode of humour entirely his own, his acts fit into a plan of life not markedly dissimilar from this conception of it as mere animal existence. To preserve it, he will assume any indignity—

I am a rascal; a scurvy railing knave and very filthy rogue,

he pleads with Hector, and so saves his skin. Again he claims the ignominy of bastardy to get out of a conflict with Margareton—

I am a bastard too; I love bastards: I am a bastard begot,

bastard instructed, bastard in mind, bastard in valour, in every thing illegitimate. One bear will not bite another, and wherefore should one bastard? Take heed, the quarrel's most ominous to us: if the son of a whore fight for a whore, he tempts judgment.

It is almost as if there was a deliberate writing down of the trickery by which Falstaff avoided combat with Douglas. Falstaff's mimicry of Henry IV lamenting the evil ways of Hal is all for our laughter. Patroclus's slanderous pageantry, imitating the Greek leaders with ridiculous and awkward action, is, in the eyes of Ulysses, a mere scurril jest. It is wit misused, it distorts real and proved values—"our abilities, gifts, natures, shapes, severals and generals of grace exact" are unscrupulously made to serve as stuff to make paradoxes. The wit by which Falstaff achieves his mastery has become a dubious instrument: and the realistic rationalism, the cold reason, which it assumed in measuring the worth of things is directly challenged:

> Here are your reasons:
> You know an enemy intends you harm;
> You know a sword employ'd is perilous,
> And reason flies the object of all harm:
> Who marvels then, when Helenus beholds
> A Grecian and his sword, if he do set
> The very wings of reason to his heels
> And fly like chidden Mercury from Jove
> Or like a star disorb'd?

And though the challenger has in his own way no more reason on his side than has the challenged, he secures the plaudits of human sympathy. It is hardly an overstatement to assert that, if there is anything positive and constructive in the seeming desolation of *Troilus and Cressida*, it is this drift away from Falstaffianism and the exposure of its contemptible though specious triumphs.

But much more constructive notions are revealed in the other two dark comedies, more positive hints of the ways in which life becomes worth while. *Troilus and Cressida* is mainly a presentation of the problem at its worst: there are fellows like Thersites; how far can even such as he write down life within the limits of a specious plausibility? It is, of course, a depressing picture—but not the cynical picture it would be if Shakespeare were Thersites. *Measure for Measure* and *All's Well* are more than presentations of the problem. They are attempts to solve it—exhibitions of the way in which grace in one sort or another may successfully counter whatever ills the flesh is heir to, and re-establish human kindness as the means by which humanity can and will attain to its richest happiness.

Measure for Measure exhibits the conditions under which an ideal is effective in attaining the good it proposes to itself. But in the course of its achievement, the ideal itself is in danger of failing when it lacks the tolerance of sympathy with human beings as such and the good-will to enhance their welfare. *Measure for Measure* is dramatically more successful in exposing the limitations of the ideal of the Puritan than in establishing the effectiveness of the ideal of formal purity: Angelo's fall is a clearer instance of the beneficence of mere human nature than is Isabella's nominal success. But between them, they suggest imaginative conjecture concerning the capacity of simple human kindness as an instrument for multiplying the happiness of humanity. *All's Well* is a positive assertion of the illimitable capacity of human instincts to serve the noblest purposes of human nature.

Hence, *Measure for Measure* at this point. It is, more explicitly than *Troilus and Cressida*, a problem play. The nature of the problem is sufficiently established by *Troilus and Cressida;* and, taken over into *Measure for Measure*, the situation is that in this world of ours—

> there is so great a fever on goodness, that the dissolution of it must cure it: novelty is only in request; and it is as dangerous to be aged in any kind of course, as it is virtuous to be constant in any undertaking. There is scarce truth enough alive to make societies secure; but security enough to make fellowships accursed.

Hence the riddle which confronts the wisdom of the world.
What is goodness? How can real goodness be distinguished
from seeming goodness? A well-disposed contemplative man
such as the Duke needs confirmation of his trust that things
are not as bad as they appear. He devises circumstances with
the declared object of discovering what our seemers really are.
He rigs the plot; it is a leaven'd and a prepared choice. Explicitly, it is a trial of Angelo's virtue, a deliberate test of his
metal. But when this is woven into the dilemmas which constitute a dramatic story, it becomes an experiment in measuring
the effective goodness of all the characters involved in the
course of the story. The incidents run on and each in succession
is the outcome of energies contributed by the will or the
judgment of the various people involved in it. In so far as this
outcome is palpably for good or for evil, to what energies, and
to energies exerted on what sorts of impulse, is it to be set
down? The issue of the action is artistically the visible or
dramatic answer. And every episode which is part of the plot
of *Measure for Measure* appears to be even more plainly than in
most of Shakespeare's plays an experimental demonstration of
the results proceeding from the operation of given forces. The
play is literally an assay of virtue, to practise the author's and
the audience's judgment in the matter of the disposition of
natures, of the effective worth, that is, of its chosen types of
human beings. Each person in the play is seen in the light of his
contribution to the sum-total of human welfare: and though
many of the people involved add but little, they are nevertheless accessories in a comprehensive judgment which, of course,
bases itself primarily on the attainments in this particular of
such major characters in the story as Angelo, Isabella, and the
Duke.

Angelo plays the villain's part. But he is not primarily
shaped for evil-doing. He does not seek villainy; it overtakes
and conquers him. He has earned amongst those who know
him a high repute for a specific kind of virtue. The Duke
chooses him as deputy: he never hints even a suspicion that

Angelo has not in fact the sort of virtue which is attributed to him; what the Duke is uncertain of is how far a virtue of that kind is a real virtue. One must remember this, because the issue is later confused by Shakespeare's divergence from the original story. The invention of Mariana, for motives already mentioned (and those quite incompatible with Shakespeare's alleged cynicism), involves a retrospective blackening of Angelo's character. His perfidy to Mariana is necessary to the new plot, and is therefore brought in as an episode remembered by the Duke. But it had no place in the Duke's mind when he nominated Angelo for Deputy, nor would it have had any existence in fact if the new form of the denouement had not required it.

Angelo is a man who has governed his life on a rigorous system. He is a man of stricture and firm abstinence. He has not disciplined his human nature to confidence in its active exercise; he has rigidly suppressed it. So completely has he secured control of his instincts, impulses, and emotions, that without boasting he confidently asserts

> What I will not, that I cannot do.

He has so far conquered impulses of the blood that he seems to have attained passionlessness. He is precise,

> Stands at a ground with envy; scarce confesses
> That his blood flows or that his appetite
> Is more to bread than stone.

He is a man whose blood

> Is very snow-broth; one who never feels
> The wanton stings and motions of the sense,
> But doth rebate and blunt his natural edge
> With profits of the mind, study and fast.

No one doubts that Angelo has reached this sort of control of himself. His integrity in that kind is common knowledge:

and even men about town like Lucio know it for a certainty, though their way of expressing it is more remarkable for its smart smuttiness than for its propriety. "They say this Angelo was not made by man and woman after this downright way of creation. . . . Some report a sea-maid spawned him; some, that he was begot between two stock-fishes. But it is certain that when he makes water his urine is congealed ice; that I know to be true: and he is a motion generative; that's infallible."

For most of the situations of life, Angelo's is a kind of virtue which seems to serve. But it is fundamentally insecure: blood may at any time assert itself, and the more violently because it has been so rigorously restrained. The way of Angelo's fall, however, almost seems a conspiracy of nature against his calculated probity. He does not lightly step into temptation. Isabella s pleading has a kind of malicious suggestiveness. When she comes to beg her brother's life, Angelo is eager to dismiss her as soon as he can—"Pray you, be gone." Her plea that Angelo should knock at his own bosom and ask his heart whether it knows anything in himself like the natural guiltiness of her brother is a telling blow: it recalls to Angelo the temptations of the blood which he has so far overcome. But it recalls them in circumstances which make him fear his mastery. He will prevent danger by dismissing the pleader. "Fare you well." She will not go—but to get rid of her disturbing presence, he promises to see her again tomorrow. The phrase by which she meets this is fatal to Angelo. "Hark how I'll bribe you." The wicked plan is formulating itself in Angelo's mind. He knows it and he prays to be saved from it. To Isabella's formal "Heaven keep your honour safe," he replies devoutly

> Amen: for I am that way given to temptation
> Where prayers cross.

On her departure, Angelo realises how frail are the foundations of his virtue. His monologue is at least an honest diagnosis of his case. He has succumbed: "This virtuous maid subdues me quite." "Never could the strumpet, with all her double vigour, art and nature, once stir my temper." But now his appetite overcomes him. From that point onwards—

> I have begun
> And now I give my sensual race the rein.

Once the system on which he has built up his life has collapsed, there is no limit to the evil of which he is capable. His worst crime is his intent to sacrifice Claudio after the price of his safety has been paid. And that is his worst crime because it displays an absolute callousness towards a human life. It is a clue to his undoing. His virtue has been built on purely formal or intellectual motives of probity: it has discounted all sentiments of human kindness. It has been a virtue in and for itself, the attempt to set up a state of individual well-being, regardless of obligations towards the well-being of others. It has been erected on a denial of the human nature which is the bond of humanity. It has reduced blood to snow-broth.

Yet even Angelo, sunk in sin, comes to truer notions of life. His penitence is absolute, and the sense of his own unfitness to go on living is a mark of his redemption.

> Then, good prince,
> No longer session hold upon my shame,
> But let my trial be mine own confession;
> Immediate sentence then and sequent death
> Is all the grace I beg.

In the plea of Isabella for his life there is a saving of something in him worth the saving.

> I partly think
> A due sincerity govern'd his deeds,
> Till he did look on me: since it is so,
> Let him not die.

The action of the play has put him on trial. It has found in him a false virtue, a virtue erected on a nicely-calculated scheme of rigid principles. It has also found the source of his weakness, a disregard of, even a contempt for, the sub-conscious and non-rational impulses which for good and evil are amongst the most potent forces in man's heritage. But a dramatist who finds an attempt at calculated virtue frustrated through the starving of mere human instinct, is surely not a dramatist writing under a sense of life's futility. Like Falstaff, Angelo has a narrow and formal scheme of values, the value to oneself here and now. His pragmatical realism is even more obviously delusive than is Falstaff's: for Falstaff at least had veins through which the blood ran hot. The exposure of Angelo is a stage in the reintegration of belief in the essential goodness of human nature.

The more positive exposition of its goodness in the person of Isabella is dramatically far less satisfying. The action of the play requires her as an active contributor to the happy ending. Her character and her acts are meant to be visibly convincing forces in the overthrow of evil and the triumph of good.

> For in her youth
> There is a prone and speechless dialect
> Such as move men: besides, she hath prosperous art
> When she will play with reason and discourse,
> And well can she persuade.

Somehow or another, the audience is unpersuaded. Her goodness is, so to speak, traditional. She is to be vowed to chastity: she is to dedicate her life to a mode of living which in the experience of mankind has been the manifestation of a high degree of spiritual well-being. If, in a sense, it is a notion of formal goodness, a fugitive and cloistered virtue, it has nevertheless a wider and a larger sanction than the selfish and individual notion of goodness which is Angelo's puritanism, because it has the approbation of many centuries of human experience. Yet somehow, as if its implicit denial of natural law confused Shakespeare's apprehension of its living reality, the dramatist's embodiment of it does not come to convincing life. Isabella in act does not dramatically compel the results which theoretically her character is cast by the story to achieve. Too frequently she makes the ideal for which she lives seem more like a formal code of verbal presumption than an intense spiritual dedication. When she hears of Claudio's crime, her first recommendation is of no higher order than any other suggestion for making an honest woman of the victim: "O, let him marry her"—and all apparently will be well. Moreover, she utters not a single word of doubt when the substitution trick is suggested. Too frequently, she seems to regard the letter as the fundamental thing in the law. She protests in general principles at large: her first words in her plea to Angelo are in that manner:

> There is a vice that most I do abhor,
> And most desire should meet the blow of justice.

An air of self-righteousness attaches itself to her; she professes herself, when she is not called upon to make it, to be capable of extreme sacrifice:

> O, were it but my life,
> I'ld throw it down for your deliverance
> As frankly as a pin.

Her final threat to Angelo when he has revealed his iniquity is sheer blackmail:

> I will proclaim thee, Angelo; look for't:
> Sign me a present pardon for my brother,
> Or with an outstretch'd throat, I'll tell the world aloud
> What man thou art.

Somehow she makes herself unattractive: "I have no superfluous leisure": that is the sort of self-possessed hussy she

sometimes seems. Her own affairs and her own sense of their
righteousness are of paramount importance. Her belief begins
to look like a narrow formal dogmatism, and her turning on
her desperate brother appears as a mere cheap triumph in verbal
theatricality. The violence of her denunciation of his cowardice
utters itself in language more like that of cruel badinage than
of shocked virginal purity—

> O you beast!
> O faithless coward! O dishonest wretch!
> Wilt thou be made a man out of my vice?
> Is't not a kind of incest, to take life
> From thine own sister's shame? What should I think?
> Heaven shield my mother play'd my father fair!
> For such a warped slip of wilderness
> Ne'er issued from his blood.

Nor is there a spark of humanity in the pose of utter contempt
she assumes when she declares herself unwilling to do the
slightest thing to save her brother:

> Take my defiance!
> Die, perish! Might but my bending down
> Reprieve thee from thy fate, it should proceed:
> I'll pray a thousand prayers for thy death,
> No word to save thee.

But this only means that dramatically she is a failure.
Shakespeare has conceived of a sort of goodness efficient to
overcome such evil as there is in the play. Nominally, Isabella's
virtue does so triumph. But it is a forced triumph: one, that
is, which as it proceeds through the story, carries no conviction
of its necessity to the minds of the audience. Still, even if
Shakespeare's imagination has failed to apprehend a traditional
form of goodness as a power demonstrably and compellingly
making for a better world, the fact that he chose a story in
which goodness is cast for that rôle, is surely no pessimist's view
of life. Even the failure is reassuring—for what obstructs his

imaginative grasp of Isabella is her lack of the simpler and commoner traits of mere humanity. In a way, her goodness has this in common with Angelo's: it is a condition of the individual soul within the narrow sphere of its own identity. But even in this play, there are other characters who are becoming aware of the imperfection of this limited kind of personal goodness. The Duke has been generally censured. He seems to run away from unpleasant duties: and perhaps he is unfitted for the kind of government which a hard-hearted Henry IV can bring off so well. His humaneness is in fact a hindrance to his practical efficiency. But his instincts are benevolent. He is one who rather rejoices to see another merry than prone to be himself merry at anything which professes to make him rejoice. It is this active benevolence which prompts him to the questionable schemes and the verbal lying of his plot. His code of goodness is a larger one than any which has hitherto ruled in Shakespeare's comedy. Falstaff's virtue was his aptitude for securing his own welfare. But the Duke's standard is not self, it is service:

> Thyself and thy belongings
> Are not thine own so proper as to waste
> Thyself upon thy virtues, they on thee.
> Heaven doth with us as we with torches do,
> Not light them for ourselves; for if our virtues
> Did not go forth of us, 'twere all alike
> As if we had them not. Spirits are not finely touch'd
> But to fine issues, nor Nature never lends
> The smallest scruple of her excellence
> But, like a thrifty goddess, she determines
> Herself the glory of a creditor,
> Both thanks and use.

This is a point of view which not only hopes for a larger nobility in life, but seeks to promote it. There is charity, a tolerance grown of experience, in Escalus; it is particularly evident in his appeal to Angelo:

> Ay, but yet
> Let us be keen, and rather cut a little,
> Than fall, and bruise to death. Alas, this gentleman,
> Whom I would save, had a most noble father!
> Let but your honour know,
> Whom I believe to be most strait in virtue,
> That, in the working of your own affections,
> Had time cohered with place or place with wishing,
> Or that the resolute acting of your blood
> Could have attain'd the effect of your own purpose,
> Whether you had not sometime in your life
> Err'd in this point which now you censure him,
> And pull'd the law upon you.

Charity and humour go together in his instructions to Elbow:

> Truly, officer, because he hath some offences in him that thou wouldst discover if thou couldst, let him continue in his courses till thou knowest what they are.

Is it not therefore palpably an error to take *Measure for Measure* as a cynic's play? The most loathsome creature in it is Abhorson, the man whose profession it is to cut life off. Even its most fallible mortals, like Lucio, and Pompey, and Mistress Overdone, somehow creep into our sympathy if not into our affection. And in those whose lot brings them into closest touch with the erring there grows a benevolent sense of human kindness: the governor of the prison, the Provost as he is called, is one of the most humane figures in the play. The mere bulk of evil which is spread across the scene of *Measure for Measure* is in itself no indication of the mood of the author. The greater the evil, the greater the author's faith in the goodness which can overcome it. And the evil in the play is nominally vanquished by the forces of virtue which the Duke and Isabella bring against it. That their conquest is more nominal than real simply means that Shakespeare's dramatic art has not welded his matter into an imaginative organism. But the intention seems patent. There is virtue in man to make life well worth the living.

It is with *All's Well*, however, that Shakespeare most positively emerges from his doubt. Evil is rampant here too: but All's Well that Ends Well—and it does indubitably end well. Perhaps in no other of Shakespeare's plays does the issue of the action depend so exclusively on the action of its heroine. The plot is in fact what Helena wills it to be: and the upshot of the plot is to her the happy dissolution of her sufferings. What, then, is it in Helena's nature which makes her the discoverer and the purveyor, or, indeed, the maker of happiness?

Falstaff's effectiveness in life was built on his unswerving devotion to a realistically calculated scheme of his own advantages, and a refusal to be diverted by imponderable ideals. Isabella triumphed through a more conventional goodness which incorporated spiritual ideals, but which formalised them by their abstraction from instinctive human sentiments and common human feelings. Helena defies all the schemes of human reason, all the injunctions of systematised common sense. She relies entirely on the "prompture of the heart."

She achieves her happiness in the first place by her cure of the King. Her project is an impossibility in common sense. The King recognises it as a gross piece of unreason:

> We thank you, maiden;
> But may not be so credulous of cure,
> When our most learned doctors leave us and
> The congregated college have concluded
> That labouring art can never ransom nature
> From her inaidible estate; I say we must not
> So stain our judgment, or corrupt our hope,
> To prostitute our past-cure malady
> To empirics, or to dissever so
> Our great self and our credit, to esteem
> A senseless help when help past sense we deem.

Nor does Helena pretend that her hope is reasonable: it is simply a blind faith—

> There's something in't
> More than my father's skill, which was the greatest
> Of his profession, that his good receipt
> Shall for my legacy be sanctified
> By the luckiest stars in heaven.

But the event proves the truth of her faith. Similarly, in the
eyes of plain reason, her pursuit of Bertram is folly, and the
prospect of her fulfilling his conditions well nigh impossible.
But once more, she succeeds.

To what does she owe her operant power?

> Impossible be strange attempts to those
> That weigh their pains in sense.

Like the Countess, aware of her love both for her son and for
Helena, she has no skill in sense to make such distinctions. She
trusts implicitly to her instinctive feelings and refuses to square
her guess by apparent reason. The promptings of her blood are
for her the show and seal of nature's truth. With this as her
guide, she achieves her goodness. But in achieving her own
good, she is the instrument by which the good of others is
attained. She cures the King, she inspires joy in the hearts of
the Countess and of Lafeu, her most questionable trickery does
good to the Florentine girl, and in the end she will surely work
out Bertram's salvation. The search for happiness, prompted
by love and sympathy, has in the event become service
dedicated to the happiness of others. Even her love for Bertram
is the dedication of herself to his service:

> I give
> Me and my service, ever whilst I live,
> Into your guiding power.

When Bertram turns scornfully from her, she requests the
King to withdraw the promised reward:

> That you are well restored, my lord, I'm glad:
> Let the rest go.

When Bertram imposes his impossible conditions, she hears them in selfless humility:

> What's his will else? What more commands he? In every way
> I wait upon his will.

And when his resolution to leave France for the Italian wars is conveyed to her, her comment on his cruel letter is merely self-recrimination:

> Poor lord! Is't I
> That chase thee from thy country and expose
> Those tender limbs of thine to the event
> Of the non-sparing war? And is it I
> That drive thee from the sportive court, where thou
> Wast shot at with fair eyes, to be the mark
> Of smoky muskets? O you leaden messengers,
> That ride upon the violent speed of fire,
> Fly with false aim; move the still-piecing air,
> That sings with piercing; do not touch my lord.
> Whoever shoots at him, I set him there;
> Whoever charges on his forward breast,
> I am the caitiff that do hold him to't;
> And, though I kill him not, I am the cause
> His death was so effected; better 'twere . . .
> That all the miseries which nature owes
> Were mine at once. No, come thou home, Rousillon,
> Whence honour but of danger wins a scar,
> As oft it loses all: I will be gone;
> My being here it is that holds thee hence:
> Shall I stay here to do't? no, no, although
> The air of paradise did fan the house
> And angels officed all.

Here, then, is Helena, the embodiment of sheer natural goodness, and her career is a demonstration of the effectiveness of mere natural goodness in dispensing happiness to mankind. Helena's happiness is contingent on the happiness of others: her success is not the mere consummation of her own desires, but the amelioration of human lot by her pervasive benevolence. That the world, and man, should be at woman's command, and no hurt done; on the contrary, that everything should be so radiantly the better for it: all *is* well that ends well.

Admittedly, the play leaves Bertram's regeneration as a mortgage on the future. And until Helena's miraculous power has been realised, it may seem as if Bertram is beyond salvation. There is for instance the sublime impertinence of his final acceptance of Helena

> If she, my liege, can make me know this clearly,
> I'll love her dearly, ever, ever dearly.

—that, too, from a man who has just been exposed as an unconscionable twister and an arrant liar. But Bertram is still young; he has fallen into bad company: and the real cause of his wickedness is that he lacks the intuition by which the worth of men is measured. He is completely wrong in his judgment of Helena, of Lafeu and of Parolles. His very poltroonery is a negative tribute to the value of instinct and intuition in guiding man through life.

At an earlier point, attention was drawn to the presence in *All's Well* of a group of elders in whom the passing of years and the growing experience of life had instilled a rich benignity of temper, a group whom time had endowed with grace and benevolence. Of other motifs in the affairs of *All's Well*, the most striking is one which seems to be a coherent refutation of Falstaffianism. In many ways, Parolles is Falstaff viewed with other eyes. Parolles has prattled himself into peril: to save himself from the foolhardiness of his tongue, the plausive invention with which he tries to carry it off is a replica in detail of one of Falstaff's major coups: "I must give myself some hurts, and say I got them in exploit: yet slight ones will not carry it; they will say, 'Came you off with so little?' and great ones I dare not give." And although for a week a man like Parolles may escape a great deal of discoveries, although a knowing man like Lafeu may think him for two ordinaries a pretty wise fellow, his tricks are soon apparent to all. He will return with an invention, as did Falstaff, and clap upon you two or three probable lies. But he is soon known for what he is, found a very sprat, and when you once find him out, you know him ever after: never will you find it in your heart to repent.

When Helen describes Parolles—

> I know him a notorious liar,
> Think him a great way fool, solely a coward;
> Yet these fixed evils sit so fit in him,
> That they take place, when virtue's steely bones
> Look bleak i' the cold wind: withal, full oft we see
> Cold wisdom waiting on superfluous folly—

the description seems applicable, not only to Parolles, but to Sir John, once the appraiser has become aware that "where an unclean mind carries virtuous qualities, there commendations go with pity; they are virtues and traitors too." Is not the final discomfiture of Parolles, his ignominious acceptance of mere existence, a veritable re-assessment of Falstaff's ideal that the preservation of the body and the appetitive organism is the major end of life?—

> if my heart were great,
> 'Twould burst at this. Captain I'll be no more;
> But I will eat and drink, and sleep as soft
> As captain shall: simply the thing I am
> Shall make me live . . .
> Rust, sword! cool, blushes! and, Parolles, live
> Safest in shame! being fool'd, by foolery thrive!
> There's place and means for every man alive.

Helena, too, has her own comments on the Falstaffian principle that discretion is the better part of valour. "You go so much backward when you fight," she tells Parolles; and to his plea that "That's for advantage" she caustically rejoins "So is running away, when fear proposes the safety: but the composition that your valour and fear makes in you is a virtue of a good wing, and I like the wear well." The King in his turn assesses the worth of wit in life, and remarks on its hostility to honour. Bertram's father, he says, in his youth

> had the wit which I can well observe
> To-day in our young lords; but they may jest
> Till their own scorn return to them unnoted
> Ere they can hide their levity in honour.

Similarly, the King's exposition of honour is almost a counterblast to Falstaff's catechism of it:

> She [Helena] is young, wise, fair;
> In these to nature she's immediate heir,
> And these breed honour: that is honour's scorn,
> Which challenges itself as honour's born
> And is not like the sire: honours thrive
> When rather from our acts we them derive
> Than our foregoers: the mere word's a slave
> Deboshed on every tomb, on every grave
> A lying trophy, and as oft is dumb
> Where dust and damn'd oblivion is the tomb
> Of honour'd bones indeed.

It is odd that a play in which so many of those values which have proved themselves in the real experience of men down the centuries are reasserted and confirmed should be accounted the work of a cynical dramatist, whilst the very propositions concerning human conduct which they confute are those embodied in a play which is taken to be the outcome of his hilarious delight in the richness of life.

All's Well is Shakespeare's escape from the tyranny of Falstaff and from his infectious and rapturous denial of the spiritual life. "Instinct," apart from the appetite for food and drink, was for Falstaff a mere counter which his wit, his calculating reason, could use for the good of his own belly. "Instinct" for Helena is an incalculable inspiration, something embedded in the consciousness of man by the pressure of circumstance in every successive epoch of human existence, a force which surges in her heart and guides her towards endeavours which are for ever extending the resources and revealing the opportunities in man's existence.

It is, of course, easy to find that Helena's trust in her intuitions is arbitrarily arranged to lead to a successful achievement. Dramatically, the play hardly generates the imaginative conviction that the good she secures must necessarily come out of the circumstances presented. But the wresting of the tale to a nominally happy ending is surely a mark of Shakespeare's deliberate opinion that love and human charity are what makes living worth while. The view imposes itself too strongly on his artistic impulse, which is constrained to shape the play to a given pattern, and is forbidden to let the imagination carry the persons to a destiny such as might have been perceived only by its own unimpeded insight into the ways of man.

In fact instinct and intuition are deliberately written up, because neglect of them had brought about the collapse of Falstaff. But in the reaction too much is claimed for them. Doubtless

> holy writ in babes hath judgment shown,
> When judges have been babes; great floods have flown
> From simple sources, and great seas have dried
> When miracles have by the greatest been denied,

but experience hardly justifies certainty and confidence in every claimant to inspiration. "As we are ourselves, what things are we!" Experience, knowledge of life and of men, the wisdom which comes from traffic with the world, the *savoir faire* which a Lafeu has learnt from living: this is the temper which helps to discriminate between right and wrong impulse. It is a temper, a sense of worldly wisdom, which, one suddenly recollects, is one of the gifts of John Falstaff.

Can Shakespeare's imagination shape a human figure in whose nature sensibility to intuitive promptings will be joined with respect for plain reason? One, that is, in whom heart and mind will work in unison? One who will be the embodiment of a common sense all the richer and the more widely common because it is not the common sense of mere reason, but the common sense which is the product of all man's susceptibilities? The discovery of so rich a personality was Shakespeare's last step in the consummation of comedy. Rosalind, Viola and Beatrice are the final answer. They are the spirit of comedy incarnate.

IX

The Consummation

THIS is the eighth successive year in which I have ventured to make Shakespearian comedy the subject of a Rylands' lecture. So, on this occasion, I will omit all apology, and will merely give you an assurance that if in the future I continue to be honoured by an invitation to lecture to you, the subject will be something other than Shakespeare.

My object to-night is first of all to pull certain loose ends in the series together, and then to try to assess Shakespeare's comic achievement in the group of plays consisting of *Much Ado about Nothing, Twelfth Night*, and *As You Like It*, which, with most of those who have written about Shakespeare, I regard as his greatest triumphs in comedy. They are the consummation of a process of growth in the art of comedy the main stages of which it has been our endeavour to indicate to you in the earlier lectures of this series. With them, Shakespearian comedy realises its most perfect form, and therefore in them Shakespeare's comic idea, his vision of the reach of human happiness in this world of men and women, is richer, deeper, more sustained, and more satisfying than in any other of his plays. They embody his surest clue to the secret of man's common and abiding welfare. Being that, they are also, technically speaking, his happiest examples of the characteristically Elizabethan kind of romantic comedy, the plays in which he most fully satisfies the curiously Elizabethan æsthetic demand for a drama which would gratify both the romantic and the comic instincts of its audience.

In claiming so much for this group of plays, I do not forget that towards the end of his days, in the benevolence of his older age, Shakespeare averted his eyes from the abyss of universal tragedy they had pierced, and, fixing them once more on the springs of human joy, he—or rather the poet in him—saw those benign idylls of human charity, the so-called romances, which we know as his *Cymbeline*, his *Winter's Tale* and his *Tempest*. These romances have obvious affinities with Shakespeare's earlier comedies; they are comedies even more than tragi-comedies. Nor could one wish any other valediction to Shakespeare's life's work than is uttered in these. But their benignity must not sentimentalise our judgment into a false appraisement of their dramatic worth. Poetically, they are of great price. As glimpses, too, of the ingrained charitableness, the temperamental gentleness, the serene and benevolent tolerance of Shakespeare the mortal, they are even beyond all æsthetic price. It is easy then to value them wrongly; and Dowden, having grouped the preceding tragedies under the rubric "In the Depths," allures one to the delusive slope by labelling these "On the Heights." But in no sense are they an answer nor even a substantial make-weight to the great tragedies. Shakespeare's vision of the depths of man's suffering, of the essential tragedy of his lot, remains as his deepest insight into human destiny. Yet, though the tragedies abide as Shakespeare's firmest grasp of ultimate truth, unaltered and un-answered by these last plays, there is nevertheless a pleasant recompense, if but a very partial mitigation, in these romances. They are an old man's consolation for the inescapable harshness of man's portion, a compensation which pleases the more because with the coming of age, something of the terror of the things the dramatist in his strength has hitherto seen has been blunted by the weakening in him of his power of imaginative vision. It is touching to the rest of mankind, and even to its philosophers, to find that Shakespeare, having peered more deeply than any other man into the depths of human misery, can yet find some sure promise of joy in the freshness, the innocence, the simplicity of girlhood's unspoilt nature. Miranda, however, and Perdita, and even Imogen are but an old man's consolation. They are a touching hope for the world rather than a certain pledge of its welfare to be. One remembers how another great dramatist, perhaps the one who alone is comparable with Shakespeare in grasp of mortal misery, Euripides, also found that when all else failed, when mankind in its power and its maturity seemed but to frustrate its own happiness and to will its own woe, there were still children, untainted by custom and experience, who at the mere prompting of native innocence would offer themselves as did Iphigenia to be saviours of their world and so give promise of a not impossible happiness for humanity. It is much that two such seers of mortal tragedy should utter their final faith in the native goodness of mere human nature. But it is literally true that, as its presentation in the motive of the plays runs without complete dramatic conviction, this belief is nothing more than a faith; it is a faith, too, which seems to imply a heavy bias towards evil in the world of men. Its trust is especially in those who are apart from it rather than in those who by the extent and the variety of their living have inured themselves to human weakness and have thereby become more representative of human life.

To this extent, even the benignity of these last plays is diminished. But the essential truth is that their view of life is less profound and less compelling than the view of it presented either in the tragedies or in the earlier and mature comedies. Though the romances are Shakespeare the man's last words on humanity and on destiny, they are not therefore his profoundest words. The finding of Shakespeare in Prospero, true as it may be, has deluded criticism. There can scarcely be a shadow of doubt that, in the romances, Shakespeare the dramatist is declining in dramatic power. The hand still retains its cunning, the stage-carpenter is still master of his craft, and the poet is still the consummate magician of words. But the dramatist is losing his intuitive sense of the essential stuff of drama, of the impact of man on men and on the things which in the mass make that experience which we call life. *The Winter's Tale*, and most of all in its Leontes, plays with figures who are markedly lacking in the positive identity of personality which would stamp them as recognisably and consistently human. *The Tempest* and *Cymbeline* rely too often on the depiction of a mood or on the use of a convention as a substitute for the fundamental art of characterisation. These plays have, of course, their own virtue. But there could be no clearer evidence of the weakening of Shakespeare's dramatic genius. For our own particular argument, its most manifest symptom is seen by comparing the heroines of the romances with those of the mature comedies. To set a Perdita or a Miranda by the side of a Rosalind or a Viola is to put a slip of girlhood by the side of women who have grown into the world, become a part of its fabric and enriched their personality by traffic with affairs and with other men and women. For the purposes of comedy, which by its nature seeks to envisage the way to happiness in a material world, the experience of a Viola or of a Rosalind is worth infinitely more than the charming innocence and ignorance of the world which are the peculiar virtue of a Perdita and a Miranda. Let there be no mistake. Shakespeare's last plays, the romances, are rich in such pleasure as none but Shakespeare could provide. But, as comedies, they are of little account. They can and will be omitted from our survey of Shakespearian comedy. For our enquiry, the peak is reached by *Much Ado*, *Twelfth Night*, and *As You Like It*.

Though these lectures have been separated from each other by a year's interval, they have been planned as steps in a consecutive argument. In the course of that argument, all Shakespeare's comedies have been the subject of more or less lengthy treatment, except *Love's Labour's Lost*, which we take to be Shakespeare's first trial of comedy. The omission was deliberate. Not that *Love's Labour's Lost* can be neglected by the student of Shakespearian comedy. But if our sense of comic values, and of the conditions under which those values came artistically to be revealed and realised, is not very wide of the mark, *Love's Labour's Lost* has small importance in establishing the line along which Shakespeare's comic genius grew. Its value is rather biographical. It lies mainly in what is revealed of Shakespeare's gifts, of his interests and of his aptitudes when he first thrust himself onto the London stage.

But as a last prelude to the assessment of Shakespeare's comedies at their best, it may not be inappropriate—and it will certainly make for the completeness of our survey—to set down in some detail the qualities and the shortcomings of *Love's Labour's Lost*. Its demonstrable imperfections of form and the measurement of their effect on the dramatic and philosophic worth of the play will illustrate the underlying principles on which our appraisement of the excellence of the mature comedies is based.

Love's Labour's Lost is more like a modern revue, or a musical comedy without music, than a play. It is deficient in plot and in characterisation. There is little story in it. Its situations do not present successive incidents in an ordered plot. Holofernes and Nathaniel could drop out, and yet leave intact the story of the aristocratic lovers. So, too, Armado, although he is allowed to purchase a specious entry at the price of his moral character: his liaison with Jaquenetta brings him into the plot. Even Costard could disappear, for his employment as a bungling postman is a convenient rather than a necessary way of exposing Biron's misdemeanours; equally easily, a supernumerary with a staff could replace Constable Dull. There remain as essential persons for the conduct of the story only the king and his associates and the princess and her ladies. Four men take an oath to segregate themselves from the society of woman for a term of years: circumstance at once compels them to a formal interview with four women: they break their oath. That is the whole story. Complications are avoided. For instance, the tale of four pairs of lovers runs its course without the slightest hint of possible rivalries and jealousies: a theme of such sort would have added intrigue to the story, but would have detracted from the interest in manners. Instead of the variety which the introduction of rivalry would have brought, there is a minor complication arising out of mistakes in identifying the disguised ladies. Clearly a story as simple as is this permits of little elaboration in the dramatic plotting of it. The oath is patently absurd. Even private individuals, retiring to a temporary hermitage, make some provision for such emergencies as may befall in their absence: but here is a king who runs away from public life on a hare-brain scheme without even so much foresight as to appoint a deputy who might inform enquirers that his present address is unknown. The taking of such an oath as the king propounds is refractory dramatic material. In the play, it is managed with as much skill as is possible. Biron is allowed to make fun of its absurdity, and to be first moved to bind himself by it only as a joke, whilst, more seriously, he assures himself of a safe means to come out of it by a verbal quibble. But the vow promises little compensation in the way of dramatic suspense. Clearly it must be broken, and the only interest aroused is in the manner of the breach. All four men might foreswear themselves in chorus, and have done with it: but by letting each lover try to hide his lapse from his fellows, a way is made for progressive revelations in the one scene of the play which is really diverting as a dramatic situation. It is the only scene strictly belonging to the story which is really dramatic, that is, a scene in which what the actors are doing is as engrossing as what they are saying, and where the situation in which they act and speak gives definite point to the whole. There are other scenes in which the actions and the words contribute equally to the theatrical interest; for example, that in which the men are led to a wrong identification of the masqued ladies; but they are accidental to the working out of the story, not really different in kind from the pageants, the masques, and the dances which make the padding of the play.

But the worst consequences of the poverty of the story appear in the persons who perform it. The four courtiers could not but resemble each other in a wooden conformity; for they have all to do the same sort of thing, and have all to be guilty of an act of almost incredible stupidity. To have attempted human differentiations would have been to explore a world of the spirit where deep-rooted passions, conflicting instincts, and complex promptings mould distinctive personalities: and thereby to have made the oath-taking humanly impossible. Hence the courtiers in the play lack personality, and are equally without typical character of the human sort. They have manners, and beyond that, nothing but wit. So, when an older Shakespeare, revising the play of his youth, came again to its end, he despatched his Biron to a suffering world that thereby he might attain a tincture of humanity. Whilst, in the earlier version, the King is relegated for a twelvemonth to a hermitage, and Biron to a hospital merely as a penance, the later sentence converts the penance to an act of social service, from day to day visiting the speechless sick, conversing with groaning wretches for the specific object of forcing the pained impotent to smile. Only so may wit acquire sympathy and count itself human.

To the eye, at all events, the ladies of *Love's Labour's Lost* are a little more individualised than are the men; for, being ladies, the colour of the hair and the texture of the skin are indispensable items in the inventory. A whitely wanton with a velvet skin will not be confused with another of a dark complexion, nor with one so auburn-haired that she stands apart like the red dominical letter on a calendar. Yet under the skin, these ladies are as empty and as uniform as are their wooers. So when Katharine says that she had a sister who died of love, she is accused by all the commentators of speaking out of her part, for no one in this play was ever related so closely as that to the world of real grief. Biron and Rosaline are frequently said to have something of essential individuality. But in effect, it is only that more of them is seen than of their associates. Biron has indeed more wit and perspicuity than have his fellows. But it is a possession which is dramatically more of an encumbrance than an asset. To save his reputation for wit, he is allowed to expound the absurdity of the oath before it is sworn; thus his subscription to it is doubly fantastic; it is entirely without reasonable motive. Moreover, his scoffs at love and his rhapsodies on its virtues are apparently at haphazard, and he passes from the one condition to the other without a trace of conflict in his nature. Rosaline, dramatically, is in equal plight. To justify her supremacy in wit, she has no time to be anything but witty. There is apparently neither sentiment nor passion in her nature, and without these she will scarcely be taken as a human creature. Like the rest of the courtiers, she is a figure sporting in a world of fantasy where words are meat and drink, and where wit alone is law and conscience.

Of course, in dress and gait and feature, these lords and ladies are as much like man or woman as is any he or she who passes in the street. Armado, on the other hand, will never be encountered in the walks of daily life. Yet there is in him more truth to human nature than in all the court society. He has no more claim to personality than have they, but he has more dramatic substance. He belongs to a race long established in the tradition of comedy. He is at first a type of all vainglorious claimants to gentility, whose title-deeds are but excessive adoration of the tricks of fashion's choicest etiquette. No single member of his species was ever so extravagant as he: but he is a caricature and not a portrait. His features are strained to comprehend the limits of his type. Unfortunately, however, the singularity of fashion he affects tends to obscure the family traits he exhibits. He dwindles eventually from the stock-type of the pretender to gentility into a sheer oddity whose idiosyncrasy is merely that of minting fire-new words. In a play like *Love's Labour's Lost*, fashion's own knight has little chance of showing his chivalry and his new-devised courtesies except in lexicographical exploits.

Holofernes, Nathaniel, and Dull are smaller figures and are less involved in the stream of the play, and hence there is nothing to distort their features from the type. They give the play its footing on the earth, for here at last are men as War-wickshire has known them. Dull is twice-sod simplicity to the life. Holofernes has all the attributes of his profession. He seizes each mellowing occasion to patronise his fellows by a display of learning, disgorging from the ventricle of memory ill-digested grammatical scraps of his diet of ink and paper. He has a genius for making his little learning go a long way: a Latin phrase and a professionally dogmatic manner have made him in his own locality the undisputed arbiter of poetry, wit, and invention.

Nathaniel is a masterpiece in miniature. Every line expresses both his native quality and his professional habit. He improves every occasion by a thanksgiving in which the voice of the curate appropriately phrases his pennyworth of gratitude for a full stomach and a void mind. He has the art of accepting benefits of patronage from his superiors in status or in learning in such a way that the patron is gratified and the recipient suffers no loss of prestige. He snaps up a fine phrase for next week's sermon. The man, and his calling, and his place both in his congregation and amongst his associates, are all revealed in his praise for Holofernes' "reasons at dinner". He is grateful to Holofernes for the dinner; he is impressed by the schoolmaster's superior intellect, and he pays his tribute in terms which have just enough of admiring deference to please Holofernes, but not so much as to deprive them of authoritative impressiveness to the vulgar, and which yet have nothing at all in them more substantial than platitudinous common-place.

But the most considerable character of them all is Costard, the unlettered, small-knowing, blundering hind. By sheer lack of every rational gift, he is immune from diseases which are epidemic in the play. Wit and words are not for him, un-less, like spades and poles, they make for his immediate and material welfare. If "remuneration" is three farthings, it is well to have it, and its worth is just elevenpence farthing less than that of "guerdon." The wit which knocks a rival down is a ponderable possession equivalent at least to a pennyworth of gingerbread, but for the rest, it may be cast to the alms-basket. Horse-sense and mother-wit are sufficient for Costard. His horse-sense smells out his advantage, and his mother-wit secures it. When he fasts it is on a full stomach. No occasion overcomes his imperturbability. His stupidity is proof against all shocks. Neither king nor courtier daunts him, and, airily misunderstanding, he dismisses himself with credit from the court. More consummate is his complacent patronage of Nathaniel when the curate fails in the show of the Worthies:

> a conqueror, and afeard to speak! run away for shame, Alisaunder. There, an't shall please you; a foolish mild man; an honest man, look you, and soon dashed. He is a marvellous good neighbour, faith, and a very good bowler: but, for Alisaunder,—alas, you see how 'tis,—a little o'erparted.

This is not mere brag, for Costard justifies his superiority by proving the best Worthy of them all. He will decline to be pushed aside when the intellectual substance of the play is being sought.

No profound apprehension of life will be expected from *Love's Labour's Lost*. That a flagrantly absurd vow will be broken is a proposition too self-evident to call for substantiation. Its reason is as patent as is Moth's deduction that when a man grows melancholy it is a sign that he will look sad. The story of the making and the breaking of the vow needs but to be shown to the eye. For anything deeper than mere observation of the surface of life, there is neither room nor need. The imagination is not called upon to reveal powers working in the deeps, silently controlling the currents on the face of the waters. Moreover, the surface here displayed is that of so remote a backwater that to reveal in it the operation of the great ocean-tides of life would be well-nigh impossible. Of apprehension of life in the dramatic way, therefore, there can be very little; but of opinion prompted by the dramatists' observation of living men there may be much. The course of an action which shows that foolish men are guilty of folly, that the best way to the back-gate is not over the house-top, that we cannot cross the cause why we were born, will hardly excite its author's passions to flashes of inspired insight.

So much and so little was Shakespeare when he began. Superficially, there are resemblances between *Love's Labour's Lost* and the three plays to which we now finally turn. The interest in all of them is in lovers, and especially in their wooing. The main characters are aristocrats, young, witty, and often either poetic or sentimental. There is also in all of these plays another stratum of *dramatis personæ*, lower in the social scale, and cast mainly to play the part of 'low' comedians. But whilst *Love's Labour's Lost* is merely a verbal display and a stage spectacle, the later comedies have been forged into a vital organism which embodies a distinctive and coherent apprehension of life. They are dramatic representations of the comic idea. They are an artist's creation, original and distinctive. Formally, they are the full realisation of a novel dramatic kind; substantially, they are the projection of an artist's ripest wisdom.

It is easy to make this claim; but far less easy to substantiate it. When an artist reaches the consummation of his achievement, there is left for most of us, who have seen and heard, little but to consider and bow the head. Especially does a mere scholar find his critical acumen inadequate to the task of expressing precisely what is the supreme virtue of these comic masterpieces. At most, he can hope that the tracing, as in our previous lectures, of the course along which Shakespeare was heading for his triumph, may have prompted a manner of thinking which listeners can complete in their own way. Yet, though he knows the impossibility of the task, he must make some attempt to put his sense of Shakespeare's final comic achievement into words.

On a purely and superficially formal consideration, it is remarkable that these mature plays seem to exhibit little pro-

gress in such external things as plotcraft and dramatic illusive-
ness when set beside Shakespeare's earlier experiments in
comedy. *Much Ado* is so informal that it makes its sub-plot
much more significant than its nominally main plot. *Twelfth
Night* builds itself formally on circumstances like those of *A
Comedy of Errors*, and even increases the theatrical improbability
of all plays of mistaken identity by adding sex-disguise to make
stage-illusion still more difficult. *As You Like It* gratuitously
imports lions into the forest of Arden; it trades as extensively
as *Twelfth Night* in sex-disguise, and it rounds off its action
with a hastier and even less suitable marriage than is that of
Olivia and Sebastian. But the appearance of casualness in plotcraft is delusory. These plays are held together, not by the
nexus of external circumstance, but by the coherence of their
spiritual substance. Their apparent diversity is moulded into
unity by what Coleridge would have called an esemplastic
power. They are the unified shape of an embodied idea, the
representation of a created world which has become an
organic universe because its every operation manifests the
universality of its own proper laws.

To see these plays as a form of comedy, it is perhaps easiest
to begin by realising that in kind they are essentially and obviously different from traditional classical comedy. Their main
characters arouse admiration; they excite neither scorn nor
contempt. They inspire us to be happy with them; they do
not merely cajole us into laughing at them. Therein lies the
fundamental difference between classical and Shakespearian
comedy. Classical comedy is conservative. It implies a world
which has reached stability sufficient for itself. Its members
are assumed to be fully aware of the habits and the morals
which preserve an already attained state of general well-being.
The main interest is the exposure of offenders against common
practice and against unquestioned propriety in the established
fitness of things. Hence, its manner is satire, and its standpoint
is public common sense. But Shakespearian comedy is a more
venturesome and a more imaginative undertaking. It does not

assume that the conditions and the requisites of man's welfare have been certainly established, and are therefore a sanctity only to be safeguarded. It speculates imaginatively on modes, not of preserving a good already reached, but of enlarging and extending the possibilities of this and other kinds of good. Its heroes (or heroines, to give them the dues of their sex) are voyagers in pursuit of a happiness not yet attained, a brave new world wherein man's life may be fuller, his sensations more exquisite and his joys more widespread, more lasting, and so more humane. But as the discoverer reaches this higher bliss, he (or rather she) is making his conquests in these realms of the spirit accessible not only to himself but to all others in whom he has inspired the same way of apprehending existence. He has not merely preserved the good which was; he has refined, varied, and widely extended it. Hence Shakespearian comedy is not finally satiric; it is poetic. It is not conservative; it is creative. The way of it is that of the imagination rather than that of pure reason. It is an artist's vision, not a critic's exposition.

But though the ultimate world of Shakespeare's comedy is romantic, poetic, and imaginative, it is by no means unsubstantial and fantastic. The forest of Arden is no conventional Arcadia. Its inhabitants are not exempt from the penalty of Adam. Winter, rough weather, the season's differences, the icy fang and churlish chiding of the winter's wind invade Arden as often as they invade this hemisphere of ours. Nor does manna fall to it from heaven. One may come by a sufficient sustenance of flesh, if one has the weapons and the impulse to make a breach in the conventionality of idyllic Nature by killing its own creatures, the deer, to whom the forest is the assigned and native dwelling-place. Arden, too, is not ignorant of the earthly landlordism which cramps the labourers' life with harshness:

> My master is of churlish disposition
> And little recks to find the way to heaven
> By doing deeds of hospitality.

And, after all, pastoral life in Arden is merely episodic in the round of man's fuller existence: "when I was at home, I was in a better place." Rosalind and Orlando will return to live their adult life in the society of man and in a civilisation which will impose on them the duties of extended social responsibilities. Only by hearsay is life in Arden reputed to be a fleeting the time carelessly as they did in the golden age; even young Orlando knows that it may be a losing and a neglecting of the creeping hours. Arden, indeed, may properly excite the witticisms of Touchstone by its rusticities; it may arouse the twisted sentimentalism of Jaques by its Darwinian illustrations of the cruel struggle for survival.

But Arden survives. It survives as an immeasurable enlargement of the universe of comedy. No longer is the comic spirit confined to the city and to the market-place. And not only is there Arden. There is Illyria. There are the vast expanses of a less known world; romantic countries on whose coasts all the strange and stirring episodes that man has dreamed may come true: shipwreck, piracy, warfare, marvellous escapes from imminent death, hazards boldly and even recklessly encountered. Or, may be, lands of *dolce far niente*, where music is the food of love, where corporeal and material exigencies offer no impediment to man's grasp at the opulence of a merely sentimental existence. In such a climate, a duke may wallow orientally in the luxuriance of sheer sensuous excitement: but, in the same air, the witchcraft of adventure will strike from a simple ship's captain a nobility of benevolence which will sacrifice all for another's good.

"This is the air, this is the glorious sun." But it is not only in its geographical atmosphere that the world of these comedies is so vastly larger than that of classical comedy, so much more radiant than that of Shakespeare's earlier romantic comedies, and so much more rich than that of Falstaff's Eastcheap. In its own turn, the world of the spirit has been equally extended. As one obvious sign of it, man has become more exquisitely conscious of music. Of course, there has always been a human impulse for caterwauling; and, in their cups, men have commonly felt themselves to be such dogs at a catch that they could rouse the night-owl and make the welkin dance. But it is in these great plays that men are suddenly brought up against the stupendous and apparently incredibly foolish circumstance that sheep's guts are potent to hale the souls out of their bodies.

There had, of course, always been music in Elizabethan plays. It was hallowed by their earliest tradition. In daily life, too, an Elizabethan, whether nobleman or peasant, had found music as much an habitual part of his occupation as was eating or drinking or working.

> O, fellow, come, the song we had last night.
> Mark it, Cesario, it is old and plain;
> The spinsters and the knitters in the sun
> And the free maids that weave their thread with bones
> Do use to chant it.

It is not only that song and music irradiate these plays—the very clown of one of them has almost lost his clownage to qualify as a singer—the important point is that the men and women of the play, and Shakespeare and his audience, are becoming conscious of what the spell of music implies. 'That strain again'; these old and antique songs were apt to arouse amorousness in Orsino and yet "to relieve him of his passion much". To recognise the palpable effect of music was the first step: to become aware of its implications was another. In men's secular lives, music ministered most powerfully to their passion of love. "If music be the food of love, play on." And so they found themselves at the very heart of the mystery, the recognition that, however strange, sheep's guts did in fact hale their souls out of their bodies. They were feelingly aware that the soul is susceptible to strange and unaccountable impulses, and that, responding to them, it enters a rich and novel spiritual kingdom.

What this means for the purposes of Shakespearian comedy

is this. Man had discovered that he was a much less rational and a much more complex creature than he had taken himself to be. His instincts and his intuitions, his emotions and his moods were as real and as distinctive a part of him as his reason and his plain common sense. They were, in fact, a much more incalculable yet often a much more exciting and satisfying part of his nature than was his sober intellect. Man was rediscovering the validity of his intuitions and of his emotions; he was, in particular, and for the express purposes of comedy, becoming intellectually aware that the tumultuous condition of his being which followed his falling in love and urged him on to woo, was in fact no mean and mainly physical manifestation of his personality; it was, in fact, the awakening in him of the fuller capacities of his spirit.

So, amongst the themes of Elizabethan comedy, love had now justified its primacy. It had willy nilly always been the major interest. But, as the earlier comedies have shown, its usurpations had been hazardous for the spirit of comedy. It had hitherto forced itself into a Pyrrhic triumph as an alien invader backed only by the forces of popular preference. It could now rightly take its place in Elizabethan comedy as the recognised presiding genius. It was the touchstone by which fine spirits were struck to their finest issues. It was also, of course, a test by which weaker mortals revealed their weakness, grosser ones their grossness, and foolish ones their folly. It is noteworthy, however, that though these three great comedies are even more exclusively the plays of lovers and their wooing than are the earlier ones, seldom does Shakespeare allow their wooing to express itself through the full gamut of its lyric modulations. Its utterance is adapted to a dramatic, and, indeed, to a comic scene: depth of affection is displayed rather by hints and by deeds than by the conventional phrase of the love poet. The homily of love from its gentle pulpiters is felt to be tedious, and is seldom allowed to weary its hearers. Often, indeed, when the wooing itself is an extended episode of the story, it is camouflaged in circumstances shaped by the wooers to cover their real passion. Beatrice and Benedick deliberately adopt a kind of inverted technique of love-making; and for them, the normal idiom of lovers is feigned by others so as to be overheard by the two who are to be the victims of the device. Rosalind, disguised as Ganymede, pretends to be herself in order to teach Orlando to woo. Viola expresses her own love only by innuendo, and finds a sort of outlet for her inhibition, as well as a gratification for her own sense of restraint, in unfolding to Olivia the passion of the Duke's love, as if hallooing her name to the reverberate hills to make the babbling gossip of the air cry out "Olivia". But having done this, Viola will find it easier to be her natural self. "I took great pains to study it, and 'tis poetical." In the throes of her own love, she will revert to sanity.

Indeed, deeply as these heroines fall in love, no person in the plays is more aware of the follies into which love may delude its victims. It is Rosalind who reproves the foolish shepherd Silvius for following Phebe like foggy south puffing with wind and rain:

> 'tis such fools as you
> That make the world full of ill-favoured children.

But she will advise silly giddy-brained Phebe to go down on her knees and thank heaven fasting for a good man's love. Lunacy and love are yet not entirely different diseases. "Love is merely a madness, and, I tell you, deserves as well a dark house and a whip as madmen do: and the reason why they are not so punished and cured is, that the lunacy is so ordinary that the whippers are in love too." Madness, but inevitable madness: and a madness in which the visions are a mingling of revelation and of hallucination. Who shall know which is which? Who better than the one who knows most of the frequency of hallucination? Rosalind is well aware of what may be falsely claimed for love, so well aware that she can make mock of the possibilities: "the poor world is almost six thousand years old, and in all this time there was not any man died in his own person, videlicet, in a love cause. Troilus had his brains dashed out with a Grecian club; yet he did what he could to die before, and he is one of the patterns of love. Leander, he would have lived many a fair year, though Hero had turned nun, if it had not been for a hot midsummer night; for, good youth, he went but forth to wash him in the Hellespont and being taken with the cramp was drowned: and the foolish chroniclers of that age found it was 'Hero of Sestos'. But these are all lies: men have died from time to time and worms have eaten them, but not for love." Yet there is no wrestling with Rosalind's affections, when they take the part of the man with whom she has fallen desperately and suddenly in love.

Rosalind, Viola, and, to a less extent, Beatrice, are Shakespeare's images of the best way of love. They, and the men in whom they inspire love, are Shakespeare's representation of the office of love to lift mankind to a richer life. So, by the entry into it of love, not only has the world of these comedies become a bigger world: the men and women who inhabit it have become finer and richer representatives of human nature. They have entered into the possession of spiritual endowments which, if hitherto suspected to exist at all, had either been distrusted as dangerous or had become moribund through desuetude. They have claimed the intuitive, the sub-conscious, and the emotional as instruments by which personality may bring itself into a fuller consciousness of and a completer harmony with the realities of existence. They have left Theseus far behind; they have also outgrown Falstaff.

But if the new world of these mature comedies is one of which Falstaff could never have attained the mastery, there is yet room in it for much even of the corporeal and for all of the immortal parts of him. He is relegated, however, to his proper place therein. Perhaps Sir Toby is as much of him as will survive a final approbation. To both Toby and Falstaff, care is the chief enemy of life; its main sustenance is capons and canary. Their values are much the same: Falstaff's deepest contempt is for a brewer's horse; Sir Toby's symbol of a world without life is an unfilled can. Both live by their wits, deluding the gullible into disbursing. "Let's to bed, knight; thou hadst need send for money." But if Toby never attains the plenitude of Falstaff's dominion, at least he escapes rejection, and achieves ultimately a more settled survival. He lives on under the leading or misleading strings of Maria: and, characteristically, this is a kindly fate into which he was inveigled by his admiration for the devilry of Maria's wit. It is Toby, too, who puts into words the most pertinent principle which can be propounded in defence of the Falstaffian life, a principle which goes beyond the mere assertion of high spirits and acclaims the cordial law of tolerance: "because thou art virtuous, shall there be no more cakes and ale?"

But the acceptance of Toby as an integral part of the ideal world of romantic comedy does not fully indicate how much of the essential virtue of Falstaff Shakespeare, after the antipathy of his dark comedies, endeavoured to find permanently serviceable to humanity. For Toby has not the full measure of Falstaff's wit. Perhaps Beatrice of *Much Ado* is Shakespeare's completest picture of the way in which sheer wit may serve the cause of human sanity in human society and thereby extend the scope of its possible happiness. But whereas it is only Falstaff's wit which prompts him sportingly to plead instinct as a final protection, it is the complete surrender of wit and the actual resort to instinct which makes Beatrice the instrument of happiness in the crucial moment of the plot of *Much Ado*. Still, it may well be that in the make-up of Beatrice, allying the exercise of wit with the innate geniality of a disposition born under a star which laughed, Shakespeare was giving such intellectual agility as was Falstaff's its opportunity to display how much of real human good it was capable of effecting. But even Beatrice—and we take her to have been grafted by Shakespeare on to an earlier play of his own which thus became *Much Ado*—even Beatrice has not grown into the full liberality of Rosalind's and Viola's humanity, close as her birth must have been to theirs. She is the direct counterpart of

Helena, and perhaps her next successor: and she in turn was followed almost at once by Rosalind and Viola.

Technically, the most remarkable achievement of Beatrice is that, with hardly anything at all to do in what is nominally the main plot, she nevertheless becomes the chief figure of the piece, and the primary instigator of the sentiment which leads to the happy solution of the story. She is a lively symbol of the new state of affairs in the domain of comedy. The hero has been dethroned, losing not only his rank but something also of personality; he has been replaced by the heroine. It is a commonplace that the main men of these comedies are but pygmies compared in stature with the heroines. Moreover, these ladies are not only the heroines in the material and formal sense that they have most of the scenes of the play. They are heroines in the sense that they provide the efficient force which resolves the dilemma of the play into happiness. That happiness is palpably a state of affairs which, in so far as it springs from human effort, is specifically an outcome of their making.

Nor is it difficult to see the virtue by which they are the bringers of so much joy. Shakespeare's enthronement of woman as queen of comedy is no mere accident, and no mere gesture of conventional gallantry. Because they are women, these heroines have attributes of personality fitting them more certainly than men to shape the world towards happiness. His menfolk, a Hamlet or a Macbeth or an Othello, may have a subtler intellect, a more penetrating imagination, or a more irresistible passion. But what they have more largely in one kind of personal endowment, they own only at the expense of other properties no less essential to the encountering of such varied circumstances as are presented by the act of living. These heroes, in effect, are out of harmony with themselves, and so are fraught with the certainty of tragic doom. Their personality is a mass of mighty forces out of equipoise: they lack the balance of a durable spiritual organism. It was in women that Shakespeare found this equipoise, this balance which makes personality in action a sort of ordered interplay of the major components of human nature. In his women, hand and heart and brain are fused in a vital and practicable union, each contributing to the other, no one of them permanently pressing demands to the detriment of the other, yet each asserting itself periodically to exercise its vitality, even if the immediate effect be a temporary disturbance of equilibrium, for not otherwise will they be potent to exercise their proper function when the whole of their owner's spiritual nature is struck into activity. Perhaps it was primarily because Shakespeare found women more sensitive to intuition and more responsive to emotion that he first promoted them to dominion in the realm of comedy. He found, moreover, in their instincts a kind of finely developed mother-wit, a variety of humanised common sense which, because it was impregnated with humane feeling, was more apt to lay hold of the essential realities of existence than was the more rarified and isolated intellect of man. But, though it was what to this extent may be called their essential femininity which gave his heroines their first claims to ruler-ship in comedy, Shakespeare insisted in his maturest comedies that all the qualities which his heroines owed to the promptings of intuition and instinct were only certainly beneficent in human affairs when instinct and intuition were guided by a mind in which a sublimated common sense had established it-self as the habitual director of action and behaviour.

It is unnecessary here to attempt to describe these heroines one by one, or even to name in detail all their generic traits. It will be enough to indicate one or two of their characteristic virtues. They have all the gift of inspiring and of returning affection. They have the good will of all who know them. They are simply human and patently natural in their response to emotional crises like that of falling in love. Rosalind's excitement when she first meets Orlando is as palpable as are her transparent endeavours to hide it. Their own passion still further sharpens the affection through which they seek the good of others. Once they are conscious of their own desire they are

master-hands in reaching it. Rosalind is the main plotter of
the flight to Arden; it is she who devises the means of ensuring
Orlando's frequent company. Viola resolves at once to remedy
her lot by taking service with the Duke; and immediately
becomes his confidant and his private minister. She overcomes
all the ceremonial obstacles which bar access to Olivia, using,
when need be, the bluster and the rudeness which she learns
from her opponents. She seizes a situation on the instant; and
even when the outcome is not clearly to be foreseen, she acts
in a manner which will save unnecessary suffering to others:
"she took the ring of me," is her lie to Malvolio, guessing at
once how the distraught Olivia had tried to hide her device from
her steward and messenger. In crises, all of them, Rosalind,
Viola, and Beatrice, are guided by intuitive insight. Beatrice
acclaims Hero's innocence in the face of damning evidence.
Viola judges her ship's captain by the same inner vision, and she
confides in him implicitly. Yet the instinct and the intuition
are always open-eyed and cautiously safeguarded against mere
casual vagary or whimsical sentimentality. When Viola judges
the captain's worth by his fair and outward character, she remembers that nature with a beauteous wall doth oft close in
pollution. Rosalind and Celia are equally immune from this
wide-spread romantic fallacy. They know that there is no
certain and predictable relation between beauty and honesty
in mankind: they would have laughingly recommended all
the Tennysonian moralists of their day, who thought beauty
to be either truth or virtue, to stroll through the equivalent of
their West End after the theatres were shut and when the
restaurants were coming to the end of their cabarets. Yet, with
all the efficiency and savoir faire of which these heroines prove
themselves to be possessed, they are amazingly modest. It is
this modesty which prevents them from endeavouring to compass what is beyond mortal reach. Fortune, they know, is but
a blind worker; and she doth most mistake in her gifts to
woman. Viola undoubtedly is confident, but not over-
confident: she will do what she can, but

O time! thou must untangle this, not I;
It is too hard a knot for me to untie.

And Rosalind never forgets how full of briers is this work-a-
day world. But in the end, they triumph; and they triumph
because they are just what they are, the peculiar embodiment
in personality of those traits of human nature which render
human beings most loveable, most loving, and most serviceable to the general good.

But these ladies are not only doers and inspirers of action.
Merely by their presence in the play, they serve as standards
whereby degrees of worth and worthlessness in other characters are made manifest. Hence the rich variety of theme,
of episode, and of person in these plays is knit together and
holds as a coherent structure. The beneficence of emotion and
of intuition is no wise belittled by the revelation of the follies
which spring from feeling in less stable creatures than are the
heroines. So, *Twelfth Night* is largely occupied with the dis-
closure of unbalanced sentiment. There is the enervating
sentimentality of Orsino, there is the unrestrained emotionalism
of Olivia. *As You Like It* handles an allied theme by its exposure of merely conventional pastoralism. Indeed, once the positive construction of their larger world has been effected by the
heroines, there is now place, not only for their own safeguards
for it, such as this perpetual alertness to expose the dangers of
unbalanced sentiment, there is also place for the sort of direct
satire and the forthright comicality which were the manner of
the older classical tradition. Just as Sir Toby finds his station
in *Twelfth Night*, so do Andrew and even Malvolio; there,
in Andrew's case, simply to display his own foolish inanity as
do the witless in all sorts of comedy; and in Malvolio's, to
enter almost as Jonson gave his characters entry, for a more
subtle but still classical kind of discomfiture. As Malvolio in
Twelfth Night, so Jaques in *As You Like It*, another of the few
attempts of Shakespeare to project malcontentism for comic
purposes. Besides these, traditional clowns may now also

play their part, whether the English Shakespearian ones of the tribe of Bottom, such as Dogberry and Verges, or the more technical ones, Feste and Touchstone, grown now by contact with natural Costards into something more substantial and more homely than the mere traditional corrupters of words, and therefore playing not the part of an added funny interlude, but an essential rôle in the orientation of the idea of comedy. "Since the little wit that fools have was silenced, the little foolery that wise men have makes a great show." The true fool's return is restorative. A fool of his sort will use his folly like a stalking-horse, and under the presentation of that, will shoot his wit. Yet his range will necessarily be limited now. Only the crassest folly falls to such arrows, for those who have become expert in human traffickings can assume an easy indifference to simple and direct hits:

> He that a fool doth very wisely hit
> Doth very foolishly, although he smart,
> Not to seem senseless of the bob; if not,
> The wise man's folly is anatomized
> Even by the squandering glances of the fool.

Thus the motley of romantic comedies is subtler than the slap-dash skittle-knocking of the satire in classical comedy. Their reformatory way, too, is fundamentally different from the simple exposure of ludicrous abnormality which had been the approved manner of older comedy. They entice to a richer wisdom by alluring the imagination into desire for larger delights. They are not mainly concerned to whip offenders into conventional propriety by scorn and by mockery. They persuade one to the better state by presenting it in all its attractiveness: they depict a land of heart's desire, and, doing that, reveal the way of human and natural magic by which it is to be attained.

Hence, in the last resort, the greatness of these greatest of Shakespeare's comedies will be measured by the profundity and the persuasiveness of the apprehension of life which they embody, by the worth, that is, of their underlying worldly wisdom. What then is this comic idea of which these plays are the dramatic revelation?

Something of the answer has already been given in estimating the characteristics of the heroines. But the conclusions may be made more general: in the first place, however, it must be noted that though these romantic comedies break through the traditional scope of classical comedy, their sphere is still rigorously confined within the proper orbit of comedy. They limit themselves to acquaintance with life here and now; the world, and not eternity, is their stage. It is, of course, a world presenting many more woeful pageants than comedy is capable of transmuting to happiness: and comedy must confine itself to those threats of fate and those rubs of circumstance which can be reconciled with man's reach for assured joy in living. In these ripest of Shakespeare's comedies, comedy is seeking in its own artistic way to elucidate the moral art of securing happiness by translating the stubbornness of fortune into a quiet and a sweet existence.

It finds that this art comes most easily to those who by nature are generous, guiltless, and of a free disposition, just, indeed, as are Shakespeare's heroines. It finds the art crippled, if not destroyed, in those who lack the genial sense of fellowship with mankind. A Malvolio, sick of self-love, thanking God that he is not of the element of his associates, sees the rest of men merely as specimens of the genus 'homo,'—"why, of mankind". The springs of sympathy are dried up within him. He becomes merely a time-server, planning only for his own selfish gain. The aptitude to do this successfully had been a positive asset to the earlier, even to the Falstaffian, kind of comic hero. But now, in the radiance of these maturer plays, it is seen in truer light. Malvolio has lost the art of life; his very genius is infected.

The corruption of man by the coldness of his blood and the stifling of his sense of brotherhood is seen even more clearly in Oliver and in Don John: it is the source of their villainy.

Don John lives only to gratify his own antipathies. Not only is he without desire to do good to others; he prefers the delight of increasing their woes. "I wonder that thou, being, as thou sayest thou art, born under Saturn, goest about to apply a moral medicine to a mortifying mischief." His spirit toils in nothing but in frame of villainies. Even Jaques has been corrupted into superciliousness by cultivating superiority and habituating himself to contemplative mockery and polite persiflage. He patronises humanity; but there is no love. He thinks he knows himself and the world; but, perhaps because he fled from both to purge himself of his earlier sensuality and his libertinage, his knowledge is superficial, impressive no doubt to the hearers by its philosophic seeming, but inadequate in its findings and distorted in its values. His psycho-analytic formula of his own melancholy is nothing but the covering up of moral deficiency by a pseudo-scientific explanation of it, an excellent prototype of a habit which has increased vastly in popularity. His compendious summary of the seven ages of man is seen to be grossly inaccurate when its heartlessness is immediately followed by the breaking into the scene of Orlando and Adam: for there is no place for either of these in Jaques's catalogue. Charity and gratitude are beyond his comprehension: "well then, if ever I thank any man, I'll thank you; but that they call compliment is like the encounter of two dog-apes, and when a man thanks me heartily, methinks I have given him a penny and he renders me the beggarly thanks." Here, indeed, is the deepest root of human evil: the most outstanding feature of the moral valuation of human worth in these comedies is its departure from almost all accredited codes of conduct in its relative lenience towards crime and even vice in comparison with its condemnation of ingratitude:

> I hate ingratitude more in a man
> Than lying, vainness, babbling, drunkenness,
> Or any taint of vice whose strong corruption
> Inhabits our frail blood.

This, indeed, is the very heart of Shakespeare's humanism. So, with all his vaunt of wisdom, Jaques is less aware of the things which really are than is the simple-minded Corin. Corin is, in fact, a profounder philosopher than is Jaques: "hast any philosophy in thee, shepherd?" "No more but that I know the more one sickens the worse at ease he is; and that he that wants money, means and content, is without three good friends; that the property of rain is to wet and fire to burn; that good pasture makes fat sheep, and that a great cause of the night is lack of the sun; that he that hath learned no wit by nature nor art may complain of good breeding or comes of a very dull kindred."

Such a natural philosophy is adequate to more than the forest of Arden. A Touchstone may be only partly pleased with what he gets there, even with Audrey. A native born in its woods may find that trouble enters not so much with the encounter of winter and rough weather and other such natural enemies, but rather with the complications of its human relationships: yet perhaps even Silvius is no more a real denizen of Arden than is Phebe. Living is, indeed, not a colloquising with oneself on the top of Helvellyn, nor an exploring of the ultimate nature of matter in a laboratory. It is the setting up of harmonious and beneficent relationships with human beings. It is an active membership in the society of man. That, at all events, is what life is taken to be in Shakespeare's comedies. Of all virtues, that which best promotes its well-being is the passion for serving the world, the instinct for sacrifice in the cause of the general good, or, rather, for the good of Tom and Dick and Harry, of Maud, Bridget, Marian, Cicely, Gillian and Ginn. Shakespeare's heroines seek what they want for themselves, but, securing it, they give joy to others. They are not deliberate philanthropists; they are only being their spontaneous selves when they instinctively proffer kindness to others. Paper-policies of virtue, theories of right and wrong, play no part in the active goodness of Shakespeare's nobler figures. Abstract propositions formulated in mere words are a false moral coinage: their currency is not even valid in their own home country. "Every one can master grief but he that has it." Purely intellectual convictions do not avail even their professors: men

> Can counsel and speak comfort to that grief
> Which they themselves not feel; but, tasting it,
> Their counsel turns to passion, which before
> Would give preceptial medicine to rage.
> Fetter strong madness in a silken thread,
> Charm ache with air and agony with words:
> No, no; 'tis all men's office to speak patience
> To those that wring under the load of sorrow,
> But no man's virtue nor sufficiency
> To be so moral when he shall endure
> The like himself.

For there was never yet philosopher

> That could endure the toothache patiently,
> However they have writ the style of gods
> And made a push at chance and sufferance.

For men are flesh and blood: we are all mortal; and man is a giddy thing. Yet he is much more the matter through which our happiness is to be earned than are the natural or the material objects in our environment. Hence the foundation of all lasting pleasure is the gift of intuitive sympathy, and the habit of forbearance and of tolerance. In the finest spirits, those who create more happiness than they receive, these instincts will be consecrated to the constant service of the world, where service sweats for duty, not for meed, or where the meed is but the unsought spontaneous joy of well-doing.

But a caveat must here be entered. Shakespeare's heroes and heroines are not sworn crusaders for universal regeneration. They are not idealists swept along in a surge of philanthropic sentiment. They are, in the last resort, as unswervingly conscious of the obligations of common sense as ever hero of comedy was. But in them it is a faculty which is nourished

by so much more of their personality than was Falstaff's.
It still requires them, as it required him, and as it requires
all comic heroes, to know exactly what the world is and what
man is, rather than what one might dream they ought to be.
These heroines know the world as unerringly as did Falstaff.
The fundamental sanity of Beatrice is that she can see a church
by daylight. All of them recognise the immutable conditions
of human existence: an hour after nine o'clock, it is ten o'clock.
and after one hour more 'twill be eleven.

But knowing the world no less securely than did Falstaff,
they know the more important phases of its experience so much
better. They have discovered the mystery of man. Their
knowledge gives them a truer estimate of the extent to which
there is fixity in the conditions of existence; they discover a
freedom within its limits hitherto undreamed of. An hour
after nine o'clock it undubitably is ten o'clock, and sixty
minutes are an unalterable and unvarying measure of time.
But "time travels in divers paces with divers persons". One
man's hour is another man's minute. There are even moments,
sure though seldom, worth the whole course of a lifetime.

To recognise this is not to defy the authority of common
sense. It is to account its findings more comprehensively and
more truly. Time is measured by the clock; it is valued by
man. Both assessments are part of truth; but it is a larger
sanity which comprehends both of them. This is the sanity of
Shakespeare's heroines. It endows them with the advantages
of a truly realistic apprehension and it safeguards them against
the narrowness of exclusive rationalism. It releases them from
the bondage of wit and convention, freeing them to grasp the
undreamed-of promises of each new moment. "I did never
think to marry . . . I may chance to have some odd quirks
and remnants of wit broken on me, because I have railed so
long against marriage: but doth not the appetite alter? When
I said I would die a bachelor, I did not think I should live till
I were married." Here, surely, is a higher and a more effective
notion of reason. Man has learnt life more deeply. He knows

what prudence and general preference want in a wife: "rich she shall be, that's certain; wise, or I'll none; virtuous, or I'll never cheapen her; fair, or I'll never look on her; mild, or come not near me; noble, or not I for an angel; of good discourse, an excellent musician." It is, of course, a catalogue which commands general assent: and granted its requirements are fulfilled, "her hair shall be of what colour it please God". It is all so satisfactory. Indeed, all it leaves out is the most vital factor of all. Loving goes by haps. It is a thousand to one that fancy will first be caught in the frail net of golden, or auburn, or brown, or black, or any other colour of hair for precisely the reason that it is of that colour. That is what life is. The circumstances with which it confronts humanity are incalculable, and especially so are those through which men and women shape their highest happiness. To achieve this, an aptitude for mastery, an unerring eye for the major chance, a gift for seizing opportunity are even more necessary than they were in Falstaff's world. And Shakespeare's heroines have these endowments. But they have something more. They have the genius not only for seizing opportunity, but, having seized it, for making its worth of widest human service. They have that because they are the choicest patterns which mere human nature can bring forth. They *are* human nature; and first by temperament, then by habit, and then by will, they make joy, and service, and love the guiding motives of their life. They have grown to a trust in nature and a confidence in man. This earth has become their heaven, a heaven unknown to classical comedians, undreamed of by theologians, a heaven to be realised by the natural goodness of human nature before it or heaven is contaminated by theorist or politician, by sentimentalist or puritan, by precisian or visionary. "But now abideth faith, hope, love, these three; and the greatest of these is love."

That, in a phrase, appears to be the summary conclusion of Shakespeare's worldly wisdom. Our attempt to track it through the plays and then to set it out in words will doubtless seem to have been a characteristically academic mishandling of comedy. Comedy, it will be felt, is a thing of joy, all for our delight, and not an original document for a moral treatise. The radiance of it is sullied by such insensitive analysis, and the broad laughter of it is stifled in a sigh. Moreover, what has emerged from such tedious mishandling? "The greatest of these is love": nothing but a moral commonplace, something which sounds like a mere truism. It may well be that our long course in reaching this conclusion has been like climbing the house-top to unlock the little gate, or like any other instance of love's labour's lost. Besides, what is new in this alleged discovery of Shakespeare's? It is a proposition which was set forth once for all well nigh two thousand years ago, and worthy men have been echoing it ever since. Moreover, is it not flagrantly retrograde at this late day to degrade Shakespeare, the world's artist, into a merely trite moralist, a very tedious pulpiter?

If the hearer of these lectures feels like that, then they have failed in their main object, and their underlying principles are false. It is surely not a dramatist's business to preach. Still less is it his office to propound a systematic body of moral doctrine. It is his primary business to see, to see the world and man and life. Then, as a poet, he projects his vision. He puts what he has seen into the shape which presents it in the precisely proportionate modulations which display the elements of it performing what it is in life their nature to perform. His presentation fails or succeeds by the power of it to impress us with its actuality, its comprehensiveness, its truth. And it impresses not only one faculty of our perceptual and cognitive organism. To secure artistic conviction, it must impress all at once. Shakespeare in these comedies is not in fact telling us that he thinks that charity ought to be man's way of dealing with his fellows: he is not persuading us on ethical and religious grounds that we should cultivate sympathy and nourish love. On the contrary, he is exercising a purely artistic gift. He is revealing to us that, whether we like it or not, whether we ought or ought not to do it, it is clear to the eye of the seer that love is the one way to supreme happiness on this earth. He saw this as a fact by the sensitiveness of his poetic apprehension. And his creative genius so translated it as the guiding principle of the world it bodied forth that we weaker mortals are permitted to see it too. And seeing is believing.

INDEX